URBAN SUSTAINABILITY

Reconnecting Space and Place

Edited by Ann Dale, William T. Dushenko, and Pamela Robinson

Given ongoing concerns about global climate change and its environmental and economic impacts, the need for urban sustainability has never been greater. This book explores concrete ways to make cities more sustainable through integrated planning, policy development, and decision-making.

Urban Sustainability is the first book to provide an applied interdisciplinary perspective on the challenges and opportunities that lay ahead in this area. Bringing together researchers and practitioners to explore leading on-the-ground innovations, this volume sheds light on the theoretical underpinnings of urban sustainability through narrative case studies. The contributors also provide fresh perspectives on how initiatives related to sustainable urban planning and development can be promoted through collaborative partnerships and community engagement.

ANN DALE is a professor in the School of Environment and Sustainability and Canada Research Chair in Sustainable Community Development at Royal Roads University.

WILLIAM T. DUSHENKO is Vice-President Academics at Yukon College and former Dean of the School of Sustainable Building and Environmental Management at the Northern Alberta Institute of Technology.

PAMELA ROBINSON is an associate professor in the School of Urban and Regional Planning at Ryerson University and a regular contributor to *Spacing* magazine.

Urban Sustainability

Reconnecting Space and Place

EDITED BY ANN DALE, WILLIAM T.
DUSHENKO, AND PAMELA ROBINSON

UNIVERSITY OF TORONTO PRESS
Toronto Buffalo London

© University of Toronto Press 2012
Toronto   Buffalo   London
www.utppublishing.com
Printed in Canada

ISBN 978-1-4426-4481-6 (cloth)
ISBN 978-1-4426-1288-4 (paper)

Library and Archives Canada Cataloguing in Publication

Urban sustainability : reconnecting space and place / edited by Ann Dale,
William T. Dushenko, and Pamela Robinson.

Includes bibliographical references.
ISBN 978-1-4426-4481-6 (bound).   ISBN 978-1-4426-1288-4 (pbk.)

1. City planning – Case Studies.   2. City planning – Environmental
aspects – Case studies.   3. Sustainable development – Case studies.
4. Public spaces – Case studies.   5. Rural-urban divide – Case studies.
I. Dale, Ann, 1948 –   II. Dushenko, William Terrance, 1960–
III. Robinson, Pamela J., 1968–

HT166.U73 2012   307.1'216   C2012-903687-0

University of Toronto Press acknowledges the financial assistance to its
publishing program of the Canada Council for the Arts and the
Ontario Arts Council.

 Canada Council   Conseil des Arts
for the Arts   du Canada
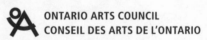 ONTARIO ARTS COUNCIL
CONSEIL DES ARTS DE L'ONTARIO

University of Toronto Press acknowledges the financial support for its
publishing activities of the Government of Canada through the
Canada Book Fund.

*This book is dedicated to Dr. Paz Buttedahl (1942–2007),
former academic head of the Human Security and
Peace-building Program, Royal Roads University, who never
failed to speak out when others were afraid.*

It is true that, inside every Chilean, there is indeed a general.

Contents

Part III: Reconnecting Place and Space in the Rural-Urban Divide

URBAN SUSTAINABILITY

Reconnecting Space and Place

Introduction

ANN DALE

We felt compelled to compile this book to delineate the evolution of and lessons learned from the Canadian challenge to implement sustainable development (we use sustainable development and sustainability interchangeably; see Robinson 2004) since the publication of the work of the Brundtland Commission (WCED 1987). We were also very concerned about a conceptual creeping away from the more integrative thinking generated from the popularization of the term 'sustainable development' in 1987 and towards reintroducing more siloed qualifiers of the concept – namely, economic, environmental, and social sustainability. In this volume, we attempt to determine why these qualifiers have crept back into the Canadian discourse. We also felt it was important and informative to share with practitioners and students leading-edge, applied case studies with a particular focus on urban sustainability in the twenty-first century. The focus on urban sustainability is timely, considering that Canada's major population growth has occurred in four major urban areas – Montreal, Toronto and its surrounding area, the Edmonton-Calgary corridor, and British Columbia's Lower Mainland – where half of all Canadians now live. Soon, 90 per cent of Canadians will live in urban areas (Canada 2006).

In discussing the Canadian experience with sustainable development, we differentiate three general time periods – first-, second-, and third-generation sustainable development responses – each with distinct characteristics, although the distinctions are not strictly bounded. The three stages can be characterized as a discourse on definitional debates about sustainable development that has moved from shallow to deeper conceptualizations, from singular to more systemic changes, and evolving from an emphasis on defining sustainable development to a recognition of the critical need for fundamental institutional reform, which many identify as a key barrier to its implementation (see, for example, Young and von Moltke 1993; Pierce and Dale 1999; Roseland 1999; Dale 2001, 2009; Sabel 2001; Kemp, Parto, and Gibson 2005; Robinson 2006). In this book, we bring together case studies that exemplify the need for equal emphasis on both process and product and reconciliation of place and space in third-generation responses. The case studies highlight the differences between, and implications for, what we describe as the third-generation responses of the most recent decade and a half and the first- and second-generation responses of past years.

The Brundtland Commission report, *Our Common Future*, popularized the definition of sustainable development as 'development that meets the needs of the present without compromising the needs of future generations to meet our own needs' (WCED 1987, 23).

Two key concepts, however, that formed an integral part of the Commission's definition – namely, the concept of 'needs,' particularly the essential needs of the world's poor, to which the overriding priority should be given, and the idea of limitations imposed by the state of technology and social organization on the environment's ability to meet present and future needs (WCED 1987, 43) – never received the extensive promotion that the more general definition offered. Accordingly, in this volume, we adopt the definition of sustainable development as a process of reconciliation of three imperatives: the ecological imperative to ensure global biophysical carrying capacity for the future, the social imperative to ensure the development of culturally sustainable systems of governance, and the economic imperative to ensure a viable standard of living for all. And equitable access to these three imperatives – ecological, social, and economic – is fundamental to sustainable development implementation (Robinson and Tinker 1997; Dale 2001). In the specific urban context, Camagni (1998, 9) defines sustainability as 'a process of synergetic integration and co-evolution among the great subsystems making up a city (economic, social, physical and environmental), which guarantees the local population a non-decreasing level of well-being in the long term, without compromising the possibilities of development of surrounding areas and contributing by this towards reducing the harmful effects of development on the biosphere.'

First-generation responses to sustainable development (1987 to 1995) can be characterized as intense debates over the definition of the term, sparked by the Brundtland Commission and leading to the analogy of the three-legged stool of the economy, the environment, and society. Canadian deliberations involved exhaustive debates about whether or not 'sustainable development' should be qualified as either sustainable *economic* development or sustainable *environmental* development (see National Task Force on Environment and Economy 1987). The Canadian government subsequently chose to focus on the promotion of sustainable development widely across the county with the creation, in 1989, of the National Round Table on the Environment and the Economy.

While criticisms of ambiguity and the lack of a precise definition of sustainable development persisted during the first period (see, for example, Jickling 1994), others maintained that continuing controversy over the definition created a unique space for constructive dialogue (Dale 2001; Robinson 2004). Prior to this period, however, the two 'silos' of the economy and the environment never, or rarely, met in civil society, and little discourse occurred between these two sectors. Experience – such as the creation of the Economic Council of Canada in 1963, which brought together labour and business – shows how difficult it is to begin a constructive dialogue between sectors that traditionally view each other as adversaries. Thus, many believed that the constructive ambiguity of the concept of sustainable develpment during this time bridged these traditional economic and environmental adversarial silos and was instrumental in bringing the economic and environmental communities together with the development community.

Arguments about precise definitions can be one means of delaying action on the part of competing interests, and there was bound to be conflict during definitional debates as the two silos tried to develop a common understanding and a common language, and to build the trust necessary for meaningful collaboration. Second-generation responses (1995 to 2005), therefore, lent deeper meaning to the early-stage definitions of sustainable development, and led to the reconciliation of the 'three imperatives' definition mentioned earlier.[1] This second-generation definition was also adopted by other entities such as the Canadian Consortium of Sustainable Development Research (CCSDR).[2] Each imperative was seen as fundamental and interconnected; integrating all three imperatives was regarded as necessary and sufficient to sustain human societies. Implicit in this definition is that sustainable development is dynamic and evolving (Jokinen, Malaska, and Kaivo-Oja 1998; Rammel and van den Bergh 2003) and that it is an unending process (Hjorth and Bagheri 2006).

Integral to third-generation responses (2005 to the present) is an understanding of the pervasive institutional and societal barriers to the implementation of sustainable development, the need for institutional transformation, and the prerequisite for reconnecting place and space. Third-generation responses are about form and function, product and process, and both are necessary conditions for the implementation of sustainable development: unless the 'rules of the game' (Robinson 2006) and our systems of governance fundamentally change, implementation will not happen.

Sustainable development is clearly not about 'big is better' or 'small is beautiful,' which are arguments characteristic of second-generation responses; rather, it is about sustainable development for all, not just some (Dale and Newman 2009). In addition to the ecological, social, and economic imperatives associated with earlier generational understandings, third-generation responses illuminate the emerging realization of how important place-based policy-making is to meaningful implementation in Canadian communities.

Part I of the volume, 'Bridging Solitudes, Silos, and Stovepipes,' explores the breaking down of institutional barriers and knowledge systems leading to third-generation responses. The three chapters in this section describe different case studies drawn from diverse sectors that illuminate nascent third-generation responses. Each case study represents a different stage in the emergent third-generation responses, and potential and concrete achievements yet to be determined. What each case study shows, however, is how the ultimate success of each is based on breaking down societal and institutional barriers, including fundamental changes in governance. In Chapter 1, Pamela Robinson and I outline the history and evolution of the responses to the concept of sustainable development, define first- and second-generation responses, and provide an analysis of the challenges that urban communities still face in on-the-ground implementation. In Chapter 2, Kevin Hanna and D. Scott Slocombe, drawing upon the experiences of British Columbia's Fraser Estuary and Ontario's Oak Ridges Moraine, illustrate the need for current local government institutions to move to deliberatively designed collaborative processes leading to integrated regional planning approaches. In Chapter 3, Nina-Marie Lister examines the importance of map-making as a critical first step for evidence-based decision-making and engagement to integrate socio-ecological mapping techniques into place-based mapping as part of social capital.

Part II, 'Social Capital and the Built Environment,' explores the nature of the social imperative in the built environment and its importance in making communities and cities more sustainable. In Chapter 4, Pamela Robinson describes the regeneration of the Toronto waterfront and the important lessons to be learned for third-generation sustainability responses, including governance. In Chapter 5, Lenore Newman and Levi Waldron explore a particular reconnection of people and place: walkability and the contribution that more pedestrian-friendly opportunities and greater access to diverse transportation modalities make to enhanced urban sustainable development. In Chapter 6, I examine a social enterprise in Vancouver's Downtown Eastside organized exclusively around the needs of the homeless, including critical lessons for local governments in recognizing the locality of social capital and agency.

Part III, 'Reconnecting Place and Space in the Rural-Urban Divide,' examines diverse features of urban and rural life and the different ways people live in and connect with their communities. In Chapter 7, Nick Weigeldt discusses how individuals can contribute to enhancing urban food security through local food production, and the institutional barriers and societal conditions required to support this. In Chapter 8, Nik Luka talks about the duality of the lives of urban dwellers with summer cottages, and explores how cottage country settings can help people to think about living more sustainably in urban areas, thus reconciling and reconnecting nature and culture. In Chapter 9, William T. Dushenko focuses on how the threat of annexation often exposes and heightens community identity and the connection to place of its members, and he explores possible alternative governance models for reconnecting place and space in supporting local community sustainability and identity. In Chapter 10, Rodney C. McDonald explores the evolution of sustainable building design, demonstrating how buildings can contribute to the environmental, economic, and community imperatives of sustainable development.

Finally, in the Conclusion, William T. Dushenko and I address the question, where do we go from here? We focus on defining and clarifying third-generation responses to sustainable development drawn from the case study chapters, and explore the dynamic relationship between the reconciliation of the ecological, social, and economic imperatives and the meaning of place. We describe seven critical tenets to bridging the implementation gaps identified throughout the book to realize fully the third-generation responses of this decade and the next.

The cases and ideas presented in this volume signal a resurgent imperative: the need for place-based policy-making by all three levels of government to drive urban sustainability efforts effectively. This will require new and more highly integrated governance models to address these needs as part of third-generation responses. There have been recurrent critiques of first- and second-generation sustainable development efforts – for example, that the concept is too vague to offer meaningful direction and that goals are inadequately defined. Some have used this as a rationale to reintroduce the qualifiers and previous silos of those favouring environmentally sustainable development versus those arguing for economically sustainable development and some socially sustainable development. This is a reaction to the failure in previous responses to implement effectively the more integrated reconciliation definition in large urban centres.

Despite this, real people have taken concrete action in real places to respond to the challenges of moving to more integrative models of development. The cases and the ideas presented here range from those that serve as tangible examples of the evolution Canadian communities have taken towards sustainable development to others in which the 'evidence' is still forthcoming because the processes are still very much under way. The breadth of place-based responses in this book reminds us that there are many pathways to desired future states. The actions we take will require new ways of thinking and doing by processes that are community-based and that involve a wide diversity of actors and decision-makers from a diversity of sectors and with expertise across disciplines, as shown by the contributors to this volume. Given the wide perspective of this book, we trust this compilation will be of considerable value to urban planners, government decision-makers, community leaders, civil society leaders, academics, and students alike.

NOTES

1 In 1992, a team of fifty researchers led by Professor John Robinson of the University of British Columbia developed consensus around this definition in a series of three workshops.
2 The CCSDR is a consortium, established in 1989, of thirty heads of post-secondary Canadian research institutes and major teaching programs across the country.

REFERENCES

Camagni, R. 1998. 'Sustainable Urban Development: Definition and Reasons for a Research Programme.' *International Journal of Environment and Pollution* 10, no. 1: 6–27.

Canada. 2006. External Advisory Committee on Cities and Communities. *From Restless Communities to Resilient Places: Building a Stronger Future for All Canadians*. Final Report. Ottawa: Infrastructure Canada.

Dale, A. 2001. *At the Edge: Sustainable Development in the 21st Century*. Vancouver: UBC Press.

–. 2009. 'Post-Brundtland 2007: Governance for Sustainable Development as if It Mattered.' In *Innovation, Science, Environment*, Special Edition, *Charting Sustainable Development in Canada 1987–2027*, ed. G. Toner and J. Meadowcroft. Montreal; Kingston, ON: McGill-Queen's University Press.

Dale, A., and L. Newman. 2009. 'Sustainable Development for Some: "Green" Urban Development and Affordability.' *Local Environment* 14, no. 7: 669–83.

Hjorth, P., and A. Bagheri. 2006. 'Navigating towards Sustainable Development: A Systems Dynamics Approach.' *Futures* 38, no. 1: 74–92.

Jickling, R. 1994. 'Studying Sustainable Development: Problems and Possibilities.' *Journal of Education* 19, no. 3: 231–40.

Jokinen, P., P. Malaska, and J. Kaivo-Oja. 1998. 'The Environment in an Information Society: A Transition Stage towards More Sustainable Development.' *Futures* 30, no. 4: 485–98.

Kemp, R., S. Parto, and R.B. Gibson. 2005. 'Governance for Sustainable Development: Moving from Theory to Practice.' *International Journal of Sustainable Development* 8, nos. 1–2: 12–30.

National Task Force on Environment and Economy. 1987. *Report,* submitted to the Canadian Council of Resource and Environment Ministers. Ottawa. 24 September.

Pierce, J., and A. Dale, eds. 1999. *Communities, Development and Sustainability across Canada*. Vancouver: UBC Press.

Rammel, C., and J. van den Bergh. 2003. 'Evolutionary Policies for Sustainable Development: Adaptive Flexibility and Risk Minimising.' *Ecological Economics* 47, nos. 2–3: 121–33.

Robinson, J. 2004. 'Squaring the Circle? Some Thoughts on the Idea of Sustainable Development.' *Ecological Economics* 48, no. 4: 369–94.

–. 2006. 'Climate Change and Sustainable Development: Realizing the Opportunity.' *Ambio* 35, no. 1: 2–8.

Robinson, J., and J. Tinker. 1997. 'Reconciling Ecological, Economic and Social Imperatives: A New Conceptual Framework.' In *Surviving Globalism: Social and Environmental Dimensions*, ed. T. Schrecker. London: Macmillan.

Roseland, M. 1999. 'Natural Capital and Social Capital: Implications for Sustainable Community Development.' In *Communities, Development and Sustainability across Canada*, ed. J. Pierce and A. Dale. Vancouver: UBC Press.

Sabel, C. 2001. 'A Quiet Revolution of Democratic Governance: Towards Democratic Experimentalism.' In *Governance in the 21st Century*. Paris: Organisation for Economic Co-operation and Development.

WCED (World Commission on Environment and Development). 1987. *Our Common Future: Report of the World Commission on Environment and Development*, chaired by Gro Harlem Brundtland. Oxford: Oxford University Press.

Young, O., and K. von Moltke. 1993. 'To Avoid Gridlock: Governance without Government.' *Working Progress* 14, no. 2: 4.

PART I

Bridging Solitudes, Silos, and Stovepipes

1 Generational Responses: Why a Third?

PAMELA ROBINSON AND ANN DALE

Our Common Future serves notice that the time has come for a marriage of economy and ecology, so governments and their people can take responsibility not just for the environmental damage, but for the policies that cause the damage. Some of these policies threaten the survival of the human race. They can be changed. But we must act now.

– Report of the World Commission on Environment and Development (1987)

Thomas Homer-Dixon (2000) argues that, as the world becomes more complex, the problems that arise are more complicated, interdependent, and thus harder to solve. Urban sustainability is certainly one of these problems given the dominance of cities in the twenty-first century. Cities and communities consume some 75 per cent of the world's energy and produce 80 per cent of its greenhouse gases, and yet the enormous potential for change by reconciling the dynamic relationship between the built and non-built environment within communities is not being realized adequately. The remedy to bridge the gap between modern problems and their solutions, Homer-Dixon says, is ingenuity. Yet, after twenty-odd years of struggling with sustainable development at the local scale, we as practitioners, scholars, and educators find ourselves with an implementation deficit. That is to say, much ingenuity has been invested in sustainability thinking, and planning, so that we now know enough about what to do, but the pressing challenge we face is how to respond in a timely way, particularly as the issues become more synergistic and dynamically interconnected. This implementation gap is exacerbated by the fact that efforts to operationalize integrated planning and decision-making, so critical to their realization, are too often 'champion based,' representing the efforts of well-meaning people despite the weak support of those more senior in the organization of more senior governments (Dale and Hamilton 2007).

The implementation deficit does not arise from inaction or sidelined hand wringing. For two decades, communities have been trying to respond to the causes and effects of unsustainable urban development. But as these efforts continue to fall short, the important question is why? The implementation gap appears to be underpinned by a fundamental gridlock of overlapping and often conflicting government jurisdictions, path dependence, technological lock-in, and institutional rigidities. One unsustainable infrastructure investment, for example, is intrinsically tied to another investment. This sort of lock-in applies to non-technical matters as well; a good example of this occurs in much current municipal planning, where the introduction of more integrated decision-making processes might not be able to overcome the momentum of older established processes that militate against the implementation of sustainable development. In effect, economics and politics are less a game of survival of the fittest and more that of survival of the first or more established. There are always energy and investment costs associated with changing to a new path (Arthur 1994), and often these costs appears too high to bear, especially when planning is shorter term (Dale and Hamilton 2007). As there is no real market mechanism to facilitate such transformative changes, they must be conducted by strong government leadership, and will, at all levels.

We begin this chapter with a description and assessment of first- and second-generation responses to sustainable development. Through evaluation of the gap between where we find ourselves and the ultimate goal of urban sustainability, the nascent and third-generation responses revealed in the case studies of urban sustainability from practice on the ground are the raison-d'être behind the genesis of this book.

First- and Second-Generation Responses

A historical analysis of the evolution of sustainable development in Canada allows us to characterize two generations of approaches falling into, roughly, two time frames: from 1985 to 1995, and from 1995 to 2005. The period from 2005 to 2009 is a transition phase in which we continue to see second-generation approaches deployed, but we also witness the emergence, on a case-by-case and community-by-community basis, of new experiments with third-generation responses. This new generational approach is emerging and ongoing. Although this temporal framing is somewhat arbitrary, it is helpful in trying to delineate the evolution of the concept of third-generation responses and the failure of its widespread adoption and diffusion.

First-generation approaches can be characterized mainly by defini-tional debates (see Newman and Dale 2005) that framed sustainable development as a future state or a desired outcome – in essence, an 'outcome-driven' approach (see, for example, WCED 1987; World Bank 1992) – as well as by normative discussion about the nature of growth in the economy. Early efforts to respond resulted in the development of more than one hundred and fifty definitions (Dale 2001) during this pe-riod. Common to the majority was the conceptualization of sustainable development as the sum of economic, environmental, and community considerations, which often led to its being depicted as the intersection of three circles on a Venn diagram or as a 'three-legged stool.' Original thinking, especially in the private sector, very much revolved around the idea of trade-offs among the three; however, this private sector tra-dition of determining 'winners and losers' was not conducive to wide-spread acceptance by established groups and vested interests (Dale 2001). With respect to growth and the economy, ecological economics was achieving higher visibility, as evidenced by the publication in 1989 of *For the Common Good: Redirecting the Economy Toward Community, the Environment, and a Sustainable Future*, by Herman Daly and John Cobb, which built on Daly's earlier work on steady-state economics, and by the introduction by Paul Hawken in 1992 of *The Ecology of Commerce*. At the same time, notions of systems uncertainties (Funtowicz and Ravetz 1991, 1993) and ecological system dynamics (Regier and Baskerville 1986) were rapidly advancing.

During this period, the emphasis was on efficiency (especially of en-ergy), dematerialization, substitution, natural resource use, and popu-lation growth, on the premise that we knew enough to act now – that is, that we had enough science and enough information (Dale and Rob-inson 1995). An interesting evolution of the theoretical and conceptual development of this view can be seen in the work of C.S. Holling (1986, 1993, 1994, 2001; Holling and Sanderson 1996). During this time, Hol-ling's research focused on ecosystem function and processes, describ-ing how an ecosystem evolves – from exploitation to conservation to release and renewal – as typified by his extensively referenced ecosys-tem function diagram (Holling 1986). Holling maintained that system of human activity also followed a similar process of exploitation to con-servation, but with little release and renewal due to institutional rigidi-ties. Flowing from Holling's research, there was considerable debate and significant work on the question of measurement and indicators for sustainable development (Mitchell 1996), as well as discussion of principles – such as the precautionary principle and subsidiarity (Cordonier Segger 2004) – strategies, and tools. The latter included environmental management systems, International Organization for Standardization 9000 and 14001 life cycle assessment, sustainable technologies, full-cost accounting, and the 3 'R's (reduce, reuse, recycle), among others. An important conceptual framework developed during this time was the Natural Step and its four system conditions (Robert et al. 1992). A nascent understanding also emerged that human systems were now so dominant that human and natural systems were now co-evolving (Norgaard 1994).

This period could also be characterized as one of government leadership and top-down organizational models. As Dale mentions in the Introduction to this volume, by the end of 1995 quasi-government organizations – such as the National Round Table on the Environment and the Economy (NRTEE, created in 1988) and the International Institute for Sustainable Development (created in 1990) – provincial roundtables, and more than a thousand municipal roundtables were flourishing. Additionally, a number of post-secondary research institutes were created, the largest being the Sustainable Development Research Institute (SDRI, established in 1992), at the University of British Columbia. In 1993, the Consortium for Sustainable Development Research – a network of post-secondary research institutes and teaching programs encompassing the areas of sustainable development, environmental policy, and sustainable development technology in Canada – was also established. Internationally, there was the seminal 1992 United Nations Conference on Environment and Development, in which two Canadians – Maurice Strong and Jim MacNeill – figured prominently and many industrial participants touted the strategy of 'eco-efficiency.' During this period, MacNeill also identified the need to reduce and ultimately to eliminate what he called ecologically damaging and economically perverse government incentives.

Resultant activities included a focus on measurable and often technologically driven activities such as energy efficiency projects and green buildings, and end-of-pipe solutions such as naturalized open-spaced and efficient stormwater retention ponds. Yet these projects were neither fundamentally transformative in their positioning nor did they effectively consider elements of intra- and intergenerational equity, despite the clear directive of the Brundtland Commission (WCED 1987) to do so. It could reasonably be said that there was a growing understanding of the need to integrate environmental and economic considerations, with very little consideration or understanding of the social imperative. As well, different conceptions of the meaning of sustainable development and sustainability began to appear, which were more a reflection of the political and philosophical positions of those proposing the definitions than any unambiguous scientific view (Robinson 2004).

It is interesting to note that, as of 1992, despite the government leadership that characterized the beginning of the first-generation responses, federal government cabinet ministers no longer attended the meetings of the NRTEE, which prompted the resignations of several of its high-level members. An analysis of the creation of novel ad hoc advisory and new organizations by the federal government reveals a similar trajectory: initially, high-level appointments at the chief executive officer and senior decision-making levels and a subsequent slippage in the level of appointments and ultimately to dissolution (Dale 2009).

By 1995, second-generation approaches were much influenced by the Intergovernmental Panel on Climate Change, which stated that climate change was now primarily being influenced by human-induced effects. Awareness began to grow, therefore, about the necessity for systems thinking, and greater understanding emerged of the dynamics of coupled socio-ecological systems (Berkes and Folke 1998), greater system uncertainties (Grunwald 2007), and threshold effects and biosphere limits (Regier 1995). At the same time, consensus emerged in the academic community around a common definition of sustainable development, largely through the work of John Robinson at SDRI. Sustainable development was seen as a reconciling process of the three imperatives – ecological, social, and economic – and this next phase of the response emphasized the need to develop new processes for engaging in sustainability, including, to name just three, public engagement, collaboration, and deliberation (see, for example, Beatley and Manning 1997; Hempel 1999; Bell, Halucha, and Hopkins 2000; Dale 2001).

Discussion by researchers and some government policy-makers then began to focus on the failure both to operationalize and to implement sustainable development, with government gridlock identified as a major barrier to its realization (Young 1989; Dale 2001, 2009; Agyeman and Angus 2003; Kemp, Parto, and Gibson 2005). At the beginning of the 1990s, the concept of natural, social, and cultural capital (Berkes and Folke 1994; Daily 1997; Hawken, Lovins, and Lovins 1999; Roseland 1999) began to emerge and developed throughout the decade.

From 1995 to 2005, as understanding of the nature of the barriers grew, many scholars identified sustainable development as a broad, horizontal concept, in which vertically organized government structures made it impossible to develop a coherent policy development framework. Government departments still organized around nineteenth- and twentieth-century issues such as national defence, transportation, natural resources, security, the environment, and so forth were unable to respond to horizontal issues such as climate change, biodiversity, and conservation. The twenty-first century, however, demands something quite different in terms of successful governance (see Dale and Hamilton 1997; Smith and Stirling 2010). Moreover, the disciplinary structure of our knowledge systems and the traditional separation of the natural and social sciences increasingly were identified as other major impediments.

As research moved towards an augmented understanding of the complex and dynamic interconnectivity of human and natural systems, threshold effects, and a focus on ecosystem processes and functions, the term 'panarchy' was conceived. Gunderson and Holling (2001) define panarchy as a theoretical framework for understanding complex systems. In brief,

> [h]ierarchies and adaptive cycles comprise the basis of ecosystems and social-ecological systems across scales. Together they form a panarchy. The panarchy describes how a healthy system can invent and experiment, benefiting from inventions that create opportunity while being kept safe from those that destabilize because of their nature or excessive exuberance. Each level is allowed to operate at its own pace, protected from above by slower, larger levels but invigorated from below by faster, smaller cycles of innovation. The whole panarchy is therefore both creative and conserving. The interactions between cycles in a panarchy combine learning with continuity. An analysis of this process helps to clarify the meaning of 'sustainable development.' Sustainability is the capacity to create, test, and maintain adaptive capability. Development is the process of creating, testing, and maintaining opportunity. The phrase that combines the two, 'sustainable development,' thus refers to the goal of fostering adaptive capabilities and creating opportunities. It is therefore not an oxymoron but a term that describes a logical partnership. (Holling 2001, 390)

The focus on efficiency and socio-technical solutions enlarged to demonstrations of industrial ecology (Cote, Tansey, and Dale 1995), design for the environment, and biomimicry (Allenby and Richards 1994; Benyus 1997; Hawken, Lovins, and Lovins 1999), while energy-efficient buildings led to green buildings (see McDonald, in this volume) and, later, to integrated design and sustainable buildings. Official planning moved from community planning (see Dushenko, in this volume) to integrated community sustainability planning, although more integration needs to occur (Ling, Hanna, and Dale 2009). And at the global scale, the seventh of the United Nations' Millennium Development Goals – 'to ensure environmental sustainability' – served as a reminder of the global to local positioning of second-generation responses (United Nations 2010).

Paradoxically, during this phase, many top-down organizations disbanded – in Canada, for example, all of the provincial round tables – and many interdisciplinary post-secondary research institutes were quietly absorbed into the traditional disciplinary silos. However, a plethora of civil society organizations emerged, many building on innovative public-private strategic partnerships, alliances, and coalitions. The scale of focus also shifted from national to community-based programs, such as the Green Municipalities program and others at the level of the Federation of Canadian Municipalities. Business-oriented organizations for sustainable development also began to emerge, such as, in Germany, the *Bundesdeutscher Arbeitskreis für Umweltbewusstes Management* (German Environmental Management Association) (Winter 1988), the World Business Council for Sustainable Development (in 1992), and the World Green Building Council (in 1998). Also springing up were research collaborations such as the Resilience Alliance (1999), a multidisciplinary research group, including universities and government and non-governmental agencies, that explores the dynamics of complex adaptive systems. Finally, the social imperative began to be seriously considered in terms of integration. The concept of natural capital began to be quantified (Daily 1997; Hawken, Lovins, and Lovins 1997), and linkages between social capital and sustainable development (Dale and Onyx 1995; Onyx and Bullen 2000) were explored and conceptualized (Dale and Newman 2005, 2008; Newman and Dale 2007; Dale and Sparkes 2010). Corporate social responsibility manifested itself in many private sector firms through the use of the triple bottom-line approach to accounting (Freeman 1984; Willard 2002).

In summary, this period can be described as one of a deepening understanding of the magnitude of the changes required, of a growing appreciation of the need for new governance models – to change the 'rules of the game' – and of seeing institutional transformation, the complexities of implementation, and the process of sustainable development as a moving target whose boundaries evolve as the dynamics of the three imperatives shift. As local governments began to frame their responses to urban sustainability, the challenges of translating this second-generation idea into practice began to emerge. As McDonough explains regarding eco-efficiency, doing more with less 'is an outwardly admirable . . . concept, but, unfortunately, it is not a strategy for success over the long term, because it does not reach deep enough. It works within the same system that caused the problem in the first place . . . It presents little more than an illusion of change' (1998, 85). Sustainable development would require not merely institutional reform, but transformation of the economy, industrial systems, and governance. Awareness was rapidly disseminating among the practitioner and research communities and some enlightened business leaders that the issue was not about trade-offs, that it was deeper than reconciliation; fundamentally, it was about integration.

In 2004, John Robinson elaborated on the meaning of integration:

> If sustainability is to mean anything, it must act as an integrating concept. In particular, it is clear that the social dimensions of sustainability must be integrated with the biophysical dimensions. This is the central message of the Brundtland report and it is no less compelling now than in 1987. Developments over the intervening period have made it clear just how difficult this will be. But it is also increasingly obvious that solutions that address only environmental, only social or only economic concerns are radically insufficient. What is needed is a form of transdisciplinary thinking that focuses on the connections among fields as much as on the contents of those fields; that involves the development of new concepts, methods and tools that are integrative and synthetic, not disciplinary and analytic; and that actively create synergy, not just summation. (378)

Previous responses clearly illuminated that it was beyond any one sector, community, or level of government to solve (Dale 2004). Clearly, as long as the institutional and societal structures of significance stay in place, the whole system will not transform, but rather will return to a previous equilibrium (Frankl 1985). It is ironic that, although strong, top-down government leadership characterized first-generation responses, implementation of second-generation responses was slowed by lukewarm political will and government retreat as the solitudes, stovepipes and silos retrenched.

Referring specifically to urban sustainability, Katie Williams notes that choosing the actions needed to achieve it have always suffered from an inability to conceive what 'sustainability' means: 'the range of actions focussed on achieving sustainable urban development is often characterized as being split between "technical" and "social"' (2009, 130). Because there is no hierarchy between the two, and because technical and social actions as well as processes are needed to achieve sustainable outcomes, cities are confronted with having to determine the strategies, plans, and programs that will bring the technical and the social together. The challenge of reconciling the imperatives of urban sustainability remains persistent, despite efforts to overcome it by addressing public engagement processes and governance structures. As Bulkeley and Betsill (2005) note, the 'propensity for analyses of urban sustainability to focus on technocratic models and wish lists of measures which should be introduced has meant that critical questions concerning the political struggles, which take place in defining what urban sustainability might entail have been neglected' (cited in Williams 2009).

As a result, municipalities have tended to focus on the more attainable and tangible notions of sustainability as represented by environmental actions (Parkinson and Roseland 2002), forgoing economic and, especially, social equity concerns (Saha and Peterson 2008; Saha 2009). Local government preoccupation with the 'low-hanging fruit' of implementation is significant on two levels. It suggests that staff and politicians feel pressure – perhaps from the ever-growing consensus around the social and ecological peril in which we find ourselves – to deliver on sustainability outcomes through easy victories. The emphasis on the short-term return, however, may also be evidence of a gap between the complexity of urban sustainability as a problem and our collective, citizen-based understanding of the time, resources, and institutional experimentation required to transcend our limited governance structures (Dale 2001). But the pressure local governments feel is also undermining the very process of reconciliation of the three imperatives that is need to achieve the goal of sustainability.

An obvious remedy for 'haste leads to underdeveloped sustainability' is to recommend that local governments be more strategic and purposeful in their emphasis on integrating sustainability priorities into their governance structures and civic engagement efforts. Yet assessments of local practices reveals that, despite mobilized sustainability efforts, local governments have not fully realized these strategic, second-generation approaches. A recent evaluation of sustainability efforts in all medium- to large-sized American cities found that, rather than taking a strategic approach to developing a sustainability framework, local governments were taking 'piecemeal and ad-hoc approaches to their sustainability efforts' (Saha and Paterson 2008, 21). The use of indicators and benchmarks was uncommon. This absence of a strategic approach is also noted by Parkinson and Roseland; their analysis of the Federation of Canadian Municipality's first annual Sustainable Community Competition finds that many entrants, whom we might consider 'leaders of the pack,' lacked a 'clear, holistic vision' (2002, 411) or benchmarks to track success. These findings signal areas in need of further attention with regard to implementing sustainability. Berke and Conroy (2000), in their review of thirty comprehensive community development plans (also referred to as official plans or official community plans) from US communities find that, for sustainable development goals and principles to be fully operationalized, staff need to possess a deep understanding of the concept and its implementation, while Parkinson and Roseland (2002) emphasize the importance of stakeholder participation to the success of local government projects.

In short, pressure to yield results has had procedural or governance implications, as well as substantive outcomes. Research across North America consistently reveals that the social, economic, and environmental imperatives are not being reconciled effectively. Sustainability plans tend to be made with built-form elements, and issues of equity and place-based elements are not addressed (Berke and Conroy 2000) – indeed, there is a persistent disconnect between sustainability efforts and equity issues (Saha and Paterson 2008). In a study of the sustainability efforts of six large Canadian cities, Robinson (2008) reports mixed results in the ability of local governments to differentiate between environmental and sustainable development initiatives and that, in responding to sustainability, they shared the challenges of higher orders of government in attempting to break down the 'silos, stovepipes, and solitudes' (Dale 2001) erected by traditional government units. The absence of effective collaborative governance structures also resulted in a lack of integrated decision-making. The collective urban sustainability track records of North American local governments serve as a reminder that simply stating sustainability as a goal is insufficient. Meaningful and effective reconciliation requires that 'the commitment to giving equal importance to equity issues alongside environmental and economic development issues has to be made first in research evaluating local sustainability efforts' (ibid., 28).

Third-Generation Approaches

As Canadian communities struggle with how to implement sustainable development at the local scale, efforts by local governments in North America thus far confirm that we have moved beyond an ingenuity gap. Through experimentation with, and implementation of, first- and second-generation efforts, a collective evaluation of local government efforts reveals the following insights:

- sustainability will not look after itself; integrated and holistic efforts require early, persistent, and deliberate design efforts to reconcile the social, economic, and ecological imperatives coupled with long-term integrated planning;
- the pressure to deliver outcomes in the short term leads to technical and environmental actions that do not respond meaningfully to equity issues;
- the discourse has failed to address systematically issues of power and conflict, and class, race, gender, and poverty issues;
- meaningful diverse stakeholder inclusion and widespread community engagement are key to delivering an integrated sustainability effort;
- despite our growing awareness of the limits of our current forms of governing for urban sustainability, we have yet to develop effective administrative, governance, and political structures to support that effort; and
- policy congruence and policy alignment are critical to the implementation of urban sustainability (Dale and Hamilton 2007).

Suffice it to say that the first- and second-generation approaches deployed thus far are emblematic of the dynamic nature of sustainability work. The emphasis on processes of reconciliation (Dale 2001) reminds us that the process of achieving sustainability is as important as the outcomes (Robinson 2004). From early on, it was recognized that progress on sustainable development should be seen as a continuous journey towards a constantly moving target whose end cannot be attained (Salwasser 1993). Since sustainable development concerns both human and natural systems – complex systems that are co-evolving (Norgaard 1994) and dynamically interconnected – systems thinking is integral to its realization. As Kenneth Bush notes, '[w]hile the scope for possible action may grow with technological developments, it is very clear that the obstacles to sustainability are not technical or even economic: they are social, institutional and political' (1990, 1).

It is clear that working at macro scales alone has not resulted in significant on-the-ground implementation, despite the breadth of ingenuity from which immediate actions could emerge (Dale and Robinson 1995). One single framework for sustainable development is no longer sufficient. The moving target of sustainability requires a diversity of responses, on multiple levels, at multiple scales, and among many actors. Thus, in local institutions and communities, sustainable development requires us to consider the intricacies and uniqueness of place. Accordingly, the case studies presented in this volume represent the nascent emergence of third-generation sustainability approaches characterized by a knowledge of the dynamic interaction of place and space. It is the intersection at which generic policy and goals developed in pursuit of sustainability are made place-specific through the reconciliation of the three imperatives; new processes and tools emerge to engage communities in new decision-making processes; and the mobilization of social capital leads to new, less-centralized responsibility for urban sustainability as a goal.

As we argued more than a decade and a half ago (Dale and Robinson 1995), we know enough to act now – we know enough science and have enough information to move from extractive economies to restorative economies to regenerative ones. But we have learned from first- and second-generation responses and the subsequent 'implementation gap' that, to diffuse widely our wealth of principles, practices, strategies, technologies, plans, and tools, we need to engage both form and function, product and process. As the following chapters demonstrate, the processes of widespread community engagement are fundamental to eliminating the implementation gap and closing the ingenuity gap before we cross irreversible thresholds in the absence of strong political leadership and will.

REFERENCES

Agyeman, J., and B. Angus. 2003. 'The Role of Civic Environmentalism in the Pursuit of Sustainable Communities.' *Journal of Environmental Planning and Management* 46, no. 3: 345–63.

Allenby, B., and D. Richards. 1994. *The Greening of Industrial Eco-systems.* Washington, DC: National Academy Press.

Arthur, W. 1994. *Increasing Returns and Path Dependence in the Economy.* Ann Arbor: University of Michigan Press.

Beatley, T., and K. Manning. 1997. *The Ecology of Place: Planning for Environment, Economy, and Community.* Washington, DC: Island Press.

Bell, D., P. Halucha, and M. Hopkins. 2000. 'Sustainable Development Concept Paper.' Toronto: York University.

Benyus, J. 1997. *Biomimicry.* New York: William Morrow.

Berke, P.R., and M. Manta Conroy. 2000. 'Are We Planning for Sustainable Development? An Evaluation of 30 Comprehensive Plans.' *Journal of the American Planning Association* 66, no. 1: 21–33.

Berkes, F., and C. Folke. 1994. 'Investing in Natural Capital for a Sustainable Use of Natural Capital.' In *Investing in Natural Capital: The Economics Approach to Sustainability,* ed. A. Jansson, M. Hammer, C. Folke, and R. Costanza. Washington, DC: Island Press.

–. 1998. *Linking Social and Ecological Systems.* New York: Cambridge University Press.

Bulkeley, H., and M. Betsill. 2005. 'Rethinking Sustainable Cities: Multilevel Governance and the "Urban" Politics of Climate Change.' *Environmental Politics* 14, no. 1: 42–63.

Bush, K. 1990. *Climate Change, Global Security and International Governance.* Ottawa: Canadian Institute for International Peace and Security.

Cordonier Segger, M.-C., et al. 2004. *Social Rules and Sustainability in the Americas.* Winnipeg: International Institute for Sustainable Development.

Cote, R., J. Tansey, and A. Dale. 1995. *Industrial Ecology: A Question of Design.* Vancouver: UBC Press.

Daily, G., ed. 1997. *Nature's Services: Societal Dependence on Natural Ecosystems.* Washington, DC: Island Press.

Dale, A. 2001. *At the Edge: Sustainable Development in the 21st Century.* Vancouver: UBC Press.

–. 2004. Community Research Connections, Research Application Submission. Victoria, BC.

–. 2009. 'Post-Brundtland 2007: Governance for Sustainable Development as If It Mattered.' In *Innovation, Science, Environment,* Special Edition, *Charting Sustainable Development in Canada 1987–2027,* ed. G. Toner and J. Meadowcroft. Montreal; Kingston, ON: McGill-Queen's University Press.

Dale, A., and J. Hamilton. 2007. *Sustainable Infrastructure: Implications for Canada's Future.* Victoria, BC: Royal Roads University, Community Research Connections.

Dale, A., and L. Newman. 2005. 'The Role of Agency in Sustainable Local Community Development.' *Local Environment* 10, no. 5: 477–86.

–. 2008. 'Social Capital: A Necessary and Sufficient Condition for Sustainable Community Development?' *Community Development Journal* 45, no. 1: 5–21.

Dale, A., and J. Onyx, eds. 1995. *A Dynamic Balance: Social Capital and Sustainable Community Development.* Vancouver: UBC Press.

Dale, A., and J. Robinson. 1995. *Achieving Sustainable Development.* Vancouver: UBC Press.

Dale, A., and J. Sparkes. 2010. 'The "Agency" of Sustainable Community Development.' *Community Development Journal* 46, no. 4: 476–92.

Daly, H.E., and J.B. Cobb. 1989. *For the Common Good. Redirecting the Economy Toward Community, the Environment, and a Sustainable Future.* Boston: Beacon Press.

Frankl, V. 1985. *Man's Search for Meaning.* Washington, DC: Washington Square Press.

Freeman, R. 1984. *Strategic Management: A Stakeholder Approach.* London: Pitman.

Funtowicz, S., and J. Ravetz. 1991. 'A New Scientific Methodology for Global Environmental Issues.' In *Ecological Economics: The Science and Management of Sustainability*, ed. R. Costanza. New York: Columbia University Press.

–. 1993. 'Science for a Post-Normal Age.' *Futures* 25, no. 7: 735–55.

Grunwald, A. 2007. 'Working Towards Sustainable Development in the Face of Uncertainty and Incomplete Knowledge.' *Journal of Environmental Policy & Planning* 9, no. 3: 245–62.

Gunderson, L., and C.S. Holling. 2001. *Panarchy: Understanding Transformations in Human and Natural Systems.* Washington, DC: Island Press.

Hawken, P. 1993. *The Ecology of Commerce: A Declaration of Sustainability.* New York: Harper Business.

Hawken, P., A. Lovins, and L. Lovins. 1997. 'Natural Capitalism.' *Mother Jones*, April, 40–53.

–. 1999. *Natural Capitalism: Creating the Next Industrial Revolution.* Boston: Little, Brown.

Hempel, L. 1999. 'Conceptual and Analytical Challenges in Building Sustainable Communities.' In *Towards Sustainable Communities: Transition and Transformations in Environmental Policy*, ed. D. Mazmanian and M. Kraft. Cambridge: Cambridge University Press.

Holling, C.S. 1986. 'The Resilience of Terrestrial Ecosystems: Local Surprise and Global Change.' In *Sustainable Development of the Biosphere*, ed. W.C. Clark and R.E. Munn. Cambridge: Cambridge University Press.

–. 1993. 'Investing in Research for Sustainability.' *Ecological Applications* 3, no. 4: 552–5.

–. 1994. 'Simplifying the Complex: The New Paradigms of Ecological Function and Structures.' *Futures* 26, no. 6: 598–609.

–. 2001. 'Understanding the Complexity of Economic, Ecological, and Social Systems.' *Ecosystems* 4, no. 5: 390–405.

Holling, C.S., and S. Sanderson. 1996. 'Dynamics of (dis)Harmony in Ecological and Social Systems.' In *Rights to Nature: Ecological, Economic, Cultural and Political Principles of Institutions for the Environment*, ed. S. Hanna, C. Folke, and K.-G. Maler. Washington, DC: Island Press.

Homer Dixon, T. 2000. *The Ingenuity Gap: Facing the Economic, Environmental, and Other Challenges of an Increasingly Complex and Unpredictable World.* New York: Knopf.

Kemp, R., S. Parto, and R. Gibson. 2005. 'Governance for Sustainable Development: Moving from Theory to Practice.' *International Journal of Sustainable Development* 8, nos. 1–2: 12–30.

Ling, C., K. Hanna, and A. Dale. 2009. 'A Template for Integrated Community Sustainability Planning.' *Environmental Management* 44, no. 2: 228–42.

McDonough, W. 1998. 'The Next Industrial Revolution.' *Atlantic*, October, 82–92.

Mitchell, G. 1996. 'Problems and Fundamentals of Sustainable Development Indicators.' *Sustainable Development* 4, no. 1: 1–11.

Newman, L., and A. Dale. 2005. 'Sustainable Development, Education and Literacy.' *International Journal of Sustainability in Higher Education* 6, no. 4: 351–62.

–. 2007. 'Homophily and Agency: Creating Effective Sustainable Development Networks.' *Environment, Development and Sustainability* 9, no. 1: 79–90.

Norgaard, R. 1994. *Development Betrayed: The End of Progress and a Co-evolutionary Revisioning of the Future.* London: Routledge.

Onyx, J., and P. Bullen. 2000. 'Measuring Social Capital in Five Communities.' *Journal of Applied Behavioural Science* 36, no. 1: 23–42.

Parkinson, S., and M. Roseland. 2002. 'Leaders of the Pack: An Analysis of the Canadian "Sustainable Communities" 2000 Municipal Competition.' *Local Environment* 7, no. 4: 411–29.

Regier, H. 1995. 'The Limits of Ecological Carrying Capacity.' In *Reconciling Human Welfare and Ecological Carrying Capacity: A Series of Workshops*, ed. A. Dale, J. Robinson, and C. Massey. Vancouver: Sustainable Development Research Institute.

Regier, H., and G. Baskerville. 1986. 'Sustainable Redevelopment of Regional Ecosystems Degraded by Exploitative Development.' In *Sustainable Development of the Biosphere*, ed. W.C. Clark and R.E. Munn. Cambridge: Cambridge University Press.

Robert, K.-H. 1993. *The Necessary Step.* Stockholm: Ekerlids forlag.

–, et al. 2002. 'Strategic Sustainable Development: Selection, Design and Synergies of Applied Tools.' *Journal of Cleaner Production* 10, no. 3: 197–214.

Robinson, J. 2004. 'Squaring the Circle? Some Thoughts on the Idea of Sustainable Development.' *Ecological Economics* 48, no. 4: 369–84.

Robinson, P. 2008. 'Urban Sustainability in Canada: The Global-Local Connection.' In *Environmental Challenges & Opportunities: Local-Global Perspectives on Canadian Issues*, ed. C. Gore and P. Stoett. Toronto: Emond Montgomery.

Roseland, M. 1999. 'Natural Capital and Social Capital: Implications for Sustainable Community Development.' In *Communities, Development and Sustainability across Canada*, ed. J. Pierce and A. Dale. Vancouver: UBC Press.

Saha, D. 2009. 'Factors Influencing Local Government Sustainability Efforts.' *State and Local Government Review* 41, no. 1: 39–48.

Saha, D., and R.G. Paterson. 2008. 'Local Government Efforts to Promote the "Three Es" of Sustainable Development: Surveys in Medium to Large Cities in the United States.' *Journal of Planning Education and Research* 28, no. 1: 21–37.

Salwasser, H. 1993. 'Sustainability Needs More than Better Science.' *Ecological Applications* 3, no. 4: 587–9.

Smith, A., and A. Stirling. 2010. 'The Politics of Socio-Ecological Resilience and Socio-Technical Transitions.' *Ecology and Society* 15, no. 1: 1–13.

United Nations. 2010. *We Can End Poverty 2015: Millennium Development Goals*. New York. http://www.un.org/millenniumgoals.

WCED (World Commission on Environment and Development). 1987. *Our Common Future: Report of the World Commission on Environment and Development*, chaired by Gro Harlem Brundtland. Oxford: Oxford University Press.

Willard, Robert. 2002. *The Sustainability Advantage*. Gabriola Island, BC: New Society Publishers.

Williams, K. 2009. 'Sustainable Cities: Research and Practice Challenges.' *International Journal of Urban Sustainable Development* 1, no. 1: 128–32.

Winter, G. 1988. *Business and the Environment: A Handbook of Industrial Ecology*. Hamburg; London: McGraw Hill.

World Bank. 1992. *World Development Report, 1992: Development and the Environment*. New York: Oxford University Press.

Young, O.R. 1989. *International Cooperation: Building Regimes for Natural Resources and the Environment*. Ithaca, NY: Cornell University Press.

2 Sustainability and Integrated Approaches to Regional Planning

KEVIN HANNA AND D. SCOTT SLOCOMBE

Over the past three decades, urban and regional planning has moved through several iterations, from the dominance of rational comprehensive models (weighing options to solve planning problems and selecting the one with the greatest net benefit) to the development of communicative and deliberative theories of action (based on cooperative action through mutual deliberation and argumentation) to the recent fashion of *real politik* (considerations based on practical and material matters) as the basis for informed planning practice. Sustainability has also been embraced by planning, though, as with other realms, it has proven difficult to define and apply. Common to these and other recent approaches is an interest in conflict mitigation and the integration of diverse interests, values, and knowledge into decision-making (as discussed elsewhere in this volume by Dushenko). These are qualities inherent in notions of sustainability. Integrated urban and regional planning, like integrated resource and environmental management, draws on scientific and other forms of knowledge, information and other forms of technology, and collaborative processes to foster better planning through improved integration of disciplines, governments, sectors, perceptions and values, ecosystems, and actors. As we note elsewhere (Slocombe and Hanna 2007), the identification of integration as an important component of planning is perhaps not especially new; it was a key part of McHarg's (1969) approach with respect to regional planning using natural systems, and has been reconsidered regularly since, often linked to a systems perspective, considering systems and their component parts and interactions and behaviour in the environmental context (for example, Petak 1980; Barrett 1985; Cairns 1991; Born and Sonzogni 1995; Margerum and Born 1995). Regional perspectives –

implicit and implied, and centred on the notion of natural regions – were also a key theme with McHarg (1969).

Although integration has often been discussed as a component of resource and environmental management, it has rarely been the primary focus of planning theory. In part, this may reflect the strong home for integration that has developed within modern resource and environmental management (Slocombe and Hanna 2007), while integration has tended to be a 'visitor' to regional and rural-urban planning. Despite this lack of disciplinary connectivity, integration is an implicit concept in planning practice. Many pervasive challenges in planning have stemmed from weak sustainability due to a lack of its consideration by such disciplinary solitudes, a situation also found historically in resource and environmental management. At the same time, there is growing interest in local and regional control and action as a basis for sustainability at those scales (see Dushenko, in this volume) and as a base for national and global sustainability as part of third-generation responses.

Integration can mean different things within the diverse approaches that characterize land use management and planning. In terms of the components of resource and environmental management, it is often thought of as integrating interests and demands, actors, disciplines, and even different dimensions or perceptions of sustainability. The applied implications and specific methods of integration, however, can also vary greatly depending on what is to be integrated or the degree to which integration is desired or appropriate. Despite the chasm between theories and ideas in resource management, and the evolving realm(s) of planning theory and practice, there are clear advantages to making connections between the thinking, ideas and lessons such areas of interest offer (Slocombe and Hanna 2007).

A key challenge in the sustainability discourse is to illustrate practical approaches to putting sustainability into practice, especially in planning. We propose that integrated resource management examples can offer valuable experience in implementing sustainability objectives. Sustainability is characterized as the confluence of disciplines, resources, and systems – themes long evident in integrated resource management. We begin this chapter with a brief overview of integration based on our recent conceptual work (Slocombe and Hanna 2007), which sets the stage for three brief narratives of integrated land use planning. Each of these cases has a strong region-based focus evolved from conflict settings, and each embraces integrative elements from the planning phase to varying degrees through implementation and into operation. The scales at which these programs operate are diverse, but they share common elements and illustrate the practical nature of integration. They also show the potential for integration through their application across settings and at different scales required as part of third-generation responses. Two of the examples are set in complex urban regions, while the third encompasses a large rugged, rural landscape with many small communities. We also present an overview, based on regional planning approaches, of lessons and implications for integrated land use planning systems.

An Inclusive Definition of Integration

While approaches to defining integration certainly vary, there seems to be an implicit consensus that integrated resource management contains common elements. These elements, as exemplified by Child and Armour (1995, 116–19) include multiple means and multiple purposes; multisectoral blending; the incorporation of multiple professions and perspectives into planning; public participation, which enhances political will, contributes expertise and knowledge, and fosters bottom-up approaches; and accommodation and compromise among affected interests.

Although models of integration vary, two themes, comprehensiveness and a strategic approach, are common – indeed, dominant. Comprehensiveness emphasizes broad consultation, participation, and engagement among all stakeholders and the consideration of an extensive range of issues and solutions. Despite its integrative elements, comprehensiveness poses application challenges – it can consume excessive time and resources among implementing agencies (Barrow 1999). The second theme, a strategic or tractable approach, is based on a more defined process of interagency cooperation with more limited jurisdictions and physical boundaries – in essence, a more defined regional approach (Hanna 2000). While the scope of comprehensiveness may often simply be too large, strategic approaches concentrate on developing a structured and consistent forum for policy development and implementation. The focus is on a distinct range of issues and options, emphasizing practical planning solutions while concentrating on key components and linkages within a problem area (Mitchell 1997). Strategic approaches may also be less inclusive as a by-product of the 'focusing' imperative (Slocombe and Hanna 2007). Under either theme, integration is a process of increasing organization and order across interests in a decision-making system (Walther 1987).

Integration in both the strategic and comprehensive contexts assumes the perception of deliberative process, where negotiation assumes an integral role. Indeed, integration may be very much about the co-creation of a common setting within which stakeholders create a social basis for action, with shared objectives, knowledge, and even program language. Parallels of this common setting and social capital development theme are also demonstrated through map-making as place-making (Lister, in this volume) and agency (Dale, Chapter 6 in this volume). The perception of deliberative process is particularly appropriate to the intent of integrative management. Dominant themes or contexts aside, the broad concept of integration is embodied through coordination and cooperation. Within this framework, integrated planning can best be defined as a process based on several dynamics as follows:

- reaching a mutual understanding of issues and approaches;
- coordinating action, socializing participants (agencies, the public, non-governmental organizations);
- embodying a regional scale of attention; and
- reaching an integrative understanding of problems and solutions.

The socialization dynamic is ultimately expressed in the language of planning as seen in policy statements, common definitions of issues, problems, and solutions, and the plan. Although appearing somewhat ethereal, it is integral, reflecting the capacity of process and participants to coordinate, or integrate, activities and to strategize. The regional emphasis recognizes the interconnected nature of places and systems (both human and non-human) and the need for a new scale of awareness to better address issues that are rarely defined as overriding administrative goals. An example of this emphasis on regional scale is ecological integrity in the Canada National Parks Act for the management of national parks.

Such integrated settings can become a new form of institutional reality, breaking down silos and, from a critical perspective, creating a new set of rules for interaction whereby power is no longer exercised separately by agencies but within a new integrative setting where, in a more emergent environment, agencies are not always explicitly aware of the impact of the new rules of deliberation (Hanna 2007). Negotiation imparts influence and power to the process, and participants use the integrative setting to seek common ground, rather than advantage through conflict.

Although there may be no single model, there is an implicit consensus that integration means the reduction of agency fragmentation, the injection of cooperation into organizational culture, the use of diverse information sources and knowledge, participation, and accommodation and consensus rather than conflict (Lang 1986; Child and Armour 1995; Slocombe and Hanna 2007). Where integration, as Walther (1987) suggests, is introduced as a conflict management mechanism, as opposed to accommodation and consensus, too-great expectations can arise. The conflict setting can be poisoned to the extent that the new management model, no matter how well conceived, cannot address simmering issues or create a new sense of cohesion and collaboration. Both, we propose, are qualities most helpful for achieving sustainability.

The context of agency domains, which dominate government stovepipes, reinforces agency self-interest, rather than support for integration and cooperation, which can make the cooperative decision-making and planning process challenging to say the least. This is especially true if resources are limited and departments must compete for what is available. From a critical perspective, these elements highlight the potential for implementation challenges since even modest forms of integration require a change in power relationships – a potentially significant obstacle in any implementation process. This stovepipe approach has certainly been one of the great obstacles to place-based decision-making in Canada and elsewhere. Different levels of government and other policy actors rarely enter into relationships on an equal basis or with equal resources at their disposal, and they can have disparate policy goals in mind, both stated and unstated. Although there is the perception that power will be ceded through integrated planning – and indeed it may be – power also may be gained. There are greater opportunities for efficiencies through shared resources, shared authority, and power to all, to better achieve individual or collective institutional goals. Such a setting ultimately may provide a strong foundation for the ongoing, stable support of environmental programs, even when political will wanes.

Integrated Planning

Fragmentation, the planning equivalent of silos and solitudes, is the opposite of integration and remains a substantial obstacle to improving approaches to sustainable planning based on ecological, regional, and systems-based thinking. The fragmentation of power, information, responsibility, resources, governance, and social and ecological systems contribute to failed planning, a theme Dushenko (in this volume) examines in rural communities. Addressing the pervasive fragmentation challenge, as seen in the various manifestations of institutional approaches, is an essential part of realizing fundamental changes to the ways that humans manage their communities, landscape interactions, and relationships with nature (Slocombe and Hanna 2007). As noted above, fragmentation also limits the potential for creating governance systems that effectively respond to sustainability imperatives at the social, economic, and ecological scale. The notion of sustainability and its imperatives, although somewhat reactive, is something planners worry about when things begin to go wrong. Sustainability in the planning environment can be ethereal in that it is deliberately vague and all too appealing to many, as exemplified in some of the challenges of second-generation responses (see Dale, in the Introduction to this volume). Nevertheless, sustainability certainly calls for connectivity among disciplines, resources, and systems (economic, social, and ecological) and is, therefore, inherently integrative. The most promising aspect of this integrative dynamic is the attention paid to the importance of natural systems and the sustainability of ecosystems that also support human well-being.

With the new prominence of ecosystem concepts and recognition of ecological functions has also come the understanding that planning, with natural systems in mind, requires biophysical knowledge. There is an acknowledgment that environmental degradation is unavoidably tied to the failure of an ecological system to support biological and, more specifically, unsustainable human processes that impair function (Karr 1992; Slocombe and Hanna 2007). Based on this acknowledgement, Norton (1992, 2005) has argued forcefully for some time that environmental management is moving – slowly, it may seem – towards a paradigm based on the hierarchical complexity of ecosystems, and with the adoption of the self-organizing character and functions of ecosystems as the centrepiece of management. This idea also proposes that fairness to future generations, a tenet of sustainability, requires the maintenance of large, self-organizing natural systems that function ultimately to provide the life-giving context for human well-being. As sustainability and ecosystem concepts are complementary and intertwined (see, by way of comparison, Norton 2005), it is logical that the integrity of ecosystems should become the basis for decision-making.

Although such planning approaches are difficult to implement, they certainly are not impossible (Hanna et al. 2007). Effective planning should be dictated by the real constraints that nature imposes, including limits to consumption and development – that is, carrying capacity, in ecological terms, and the boundaries necessary to protect the self-organizing and self-regulating functional components of the system. These can provide a strong context for decision-making (Norton 1992). In practice, however, such frameworks appear to have assumed the character of a two-stage management system. The first is resource management, which is concerned with economic criteria and the annual cycles of production and consumption. The second is environmental management, which attempts to apply criteria based on an ecological understanding of a system either to mitigate, and sometimes remediate, the impacts of development, as in the outcomes of many environmental assessment processes; or to define permissible limits to degradation, as in the growing use of thresholds in land-use planning and environmental assessment (see, for example, North Yukon Planning Commission 2007). Unfortunately, planning sits, sometimes uncomfortably, between these two solitudes. On the one hand, planning ideally provides the vision for development but, in practice, it emerges more commonly as reactive and geared to approving developments. If planning were actually visionary, prescriptive, anticipatory, or, for that matter, integrative, would we see so many of the problems that define contemporary landscapes?

Regardless of how integration is defined, the tenets of truly integrated planning are that landscapes should provide multiple benefits for nature and humans alike, and that our communities should grow in ways that reflect an understanding and acknowledgement of, and respect for, the complexity of natural processes and human systems (Slocombe and Hanna 2007; see also Ndubisi 2002). The challenge for planning may lie not so much in defining the concept or accepting its necessity as in putting into operation realistic, consistent, and effective approaches or processes (Hanna 1999). Although integration explicitly incorporates ecosystems as a primary consideration, the importance of supporting societal and economic demands cannot be forgotten, as people are integral to the ecosystem approach (Slocombe and Hanna 2007). The use of landscapes, regardless of planning or governance systems, reflects the values held by society – or at least by some of the more powerful elements of society. Ideas from communicative and deliberative planning models can be linked to the importance that planning practice, at least normatively, places on consultation, shared decision-making, pluralistic processes, and deliberative action. Although integration shares these values, the language of integration theory may be different.

Within the broad and interconnected realms of sustainability and integrated management we see several recurrent themes: origins of conflict; consultation and participation; multiple-use, shared resources; and the desire for new efficiencies and meaningful change. With these notions in mind, we turn to three case studies from Canada to illustrate the potential, challenges, and practicality of integrated approaches to planning. Each example is drawn from empirical work examining integration at a complex regional scale (Hanna 2007; Hanna et al. 2007; Hanna, Webber, and Slocombe 2007), and is framed with our recent conceptual work in mind (Slocombe and Hanna 2007). Each illustrates an effort to develop an integrated approach, and strong sustainability themes are present; however, none should be considered the perfect model of third-generation sustainability planning. There is no halcyon vision here – indeed, it is the resulting dialogue that makes them interesting. They illustrate the challenges inherent in changing institutional approaches and relationships, and the imperfect road to sustainability.

A Regional Approach to Managing Land and Water Interactions: The Fraser River Estuary

The Fraser River estuary on Canada's Pacific coast includes the City of Vancouver, and has a regional population of about two million people. Over the past three decades, the region has seen one of the highest urban growth rates in North America. Despite such pressure, it still contains large areas of rural land and long stretches of relatively untouched river and estuarine shoreline. The estuary also hosts a range of industrial activities, many of which impact the river. The Fraser is one of the world's great salmon rivers, perhaps the last undammed salmon river of significance, and the estuary region plays a key habitat role for the inward and outward migration of Pacific salmonids. Though the Fraser may be in good health relative to other large rivers, it appears to be on the threshold of harmful change (Hanna 2007).

Three levels of government (federal, provincial, and regional-municipal) are responsible for estuarine management and planning, for both water and land areas in this region. As this has led to periodic conflict about managing the river's resources, a low-key cooperative framework was formed in the 1980s – the Fraser River Estuary Management Program

(FREMP) – to help address interagency differences and, more important, the reluctance of federal and provincial politicians to cooperate. The FREMP was created after a period of study and debate over what kind of integrative entity should be formed. In the end, it was decided by governments that a system based on cooperative planning and facilitation of planning was preferred, but one without any real authority. Instead, the FREMP would be a clearinghouse for information, development reviews, and the study of estuary issues. It would have an office, staff, and resources, but, although the entity would help with planning, it would have no planning authority. The boundaries of the FREMP were limited to the estuary's waters and upland areas only as far as the river side of the dykes or the shorelines – a tight boundary without significant upland links.

Even without the creation of physical projects, the FREMP has been influential as a venue for integrated decision-making, even though formal decision-making power remains vested in the supporting agencies (Hanna 2000, 2007). As a planning entity, the FREMP has focused on enhancing the social significance and strength of technical/planning activities and on reducing the potentially adversarial nature of interagency linkages. In this way, the program has achieved impact and influence despite its lack of direct power. The implementation process has evolved in terms of hierarchical integration, regional-scale planning for estuary uses, and the allocation of collective resources from the participating agencies. Links to upland activities have been developed through an estuary plan that integrates estuary activities and needs into municipal and other agency planning within established land-use planning systems. Integration has been negotiated and has not required a realignment of authority.

Ideally an integrated approach not only addresses the activities of a broad range of agency actors, it is also inclusive (Hanna 2007). While the FREMP concentrates on agencies and a few key departments, participation by those outside government is ad hoc. The program, therefore, is not pluralistic in accounting for a full range of different perspectives. The FREMP's impacts are indirect, and have been achieved by facilitating actions – for example, coordinated planning policy and collaborative environmental development reviews – rather than direct in creating, say, new capital projects or regulations (Hanna 2000). As a result, explicit cause-and-effect relationships between policy and physical or social outcomes are not always easily apparent where capital works or new regulations are not the dominant instruments. Success can be difficult to measure, therefore, in settings where the links between program actions and environmental change may be indirect. This somewhat emergent approach also poses a challenge for policy-makers and analysts interested in examining the impacts of integration and seeking unambiguous evaluations of success.

The discreet approach of the FREMP was influenced at a very early stage by an understanding that implementation of any change to the administrative status quo would be difficult. Although agencies have certainly cooperated, it is difficult at the political level to cede power or create a new agency with overarching authority, or to create a program with an expansive boundary. Agencies more readily recognize the importance of developing an integrated approach using existing institutional structures that can be applied successfully within a locale that is environmentally and jurisdictionally complex. This has resulted in improved efficiency in estuary management and planning, reduced conflict, and the facilitation of integration (links) among planning activities and upland/water uses to sustain estuarine resources. All the while, tractability has remained a key feature and objective in the FREMP's design. This is very much the product of an approach that enhances institutional relationships by creating a setting where cooperation can be fostered without the perception of threatening power or resources. While the FREMP and its predecessors originated at a time of high interest in sustainability, this has not been a core part of the discourse. Rather, the program has focused on the ecological foundations and biodiversity of a critical part of the Greater Vancouver region. As such, the FREMP is a key part of overall work towards sustainability in the region, with more specific details and actions around this having been taken up by municipal and regional governments.

The model of integration created by the FREMP illustrates a setting where power is not necessarily exercised individually by agencies, but more within a collaborative setting. Although agencies may not always explicitly acknowledge this, their support for the program, their deference to it as an avenue for problem-solving, and their support for program enhancement all suggest an undeclared and unrecognized exercise of power through the program. This has promoted an inherently integrative approach to land/water resource management (Hanna 2007). Despite its failure to include participation by those outside government beyond an ad hoc basis, the primary success of this approach is likely in its emergent nature, arising through the aforementioned collaborative setting. This environment has allowed for some flexibility in ideas and the determination of common outcomes by the individual agency players, thereby reducing the occurrence of competing interests and probability of future conflict.

Integrating Complex Rural-Urban Uses: The Oak Ridges Moraine Region

The Oak Ridges Moraine region stretches some 160 kilometres across the northern edge of Toronto. A landscape with a well-defined physiography, the moraine is also a complex urban-rural region, having experienced high growth pressures as Toronto expands in the most populated region of Canada. Over the past three decades, impacts such as sprawl, loss of wildlife habitat, and urbanization of farmland have fed a level of land-use conflict that became quite acrimonious. In May 2001, the Ontario government announced a six-month moratorium on development in the region and created an advisory committee to help develop a long-term plan for managing the moraine region's growth. The committee was composed of stakeholder representatives from the provincial government and the civil conservation/environment and development sectors. Although this format brought together people who had been at great disagreement about the future of the moraine, the approach worked (Hanna, Webber, and Slocombe 2007). The committee was given six months to develop a plan that would replace the moratorium. In this plan, the committee developed key ecological criteria in designating land use and a broad integration element that balanced uses, growth, and ecological information-based planning. The new plan was turned into legislation by the Ontario government (the Oak Ridges Moraine Conservation Act), which gave the new Oak Ridges Moraine conservation plan substantial legal force.

The conservation plan designates four land-use areas, each with well-defined boundaries that limit the potential for manipulation. Natural Core Areas cover 38 per cent of the moraine and are designated to 'protect those lands with the greatest concentrations of key natural heritage features which are critical to maintaining the integrity of the moraine as a whole.' Natural Linkage Areas represent 24 per cent of the moraine and 'protect critical natural and open space linkages between the Natural Core Areas and along rivers and streams.' Countryside areas account for about 30 per cent of the moraine and 'provide an agricultural and rural transition and buffer between the Natural Core Areas and Natural Linkage Areas and the urbanized Settlement Areas.'

This also includes rural settlements representing existing hamlets and small, long-established communities. Settlement Areas cover about 8 per cent of the moraine and represent 'a range of existing communities planned by municipalities to reflect community needs and values.' This latter area is the only portion of the Oak Ridges Moraine eligible for development within the parameters specified in the municipal official plans (Ontario 2002).

The goal of planning based on ecological information on a wide regional level is an innovative aspect of the plan, whose objectives centre on maintaining ecological integrity. The protection of ecological integrity is advanced by requiring the integration of environmental objectives into formal land-use planning to maintain and, where possible, improve or restore ecological integrity, while also reconciling this need with social and economic needs associated with development. This intention of regenerative capacity, where improving or restoring ecological integrity is concerned, is an important aspect of third-generation responses to sustainable development (see also McDonald; and Newman and Waldron, both in this volume). Another key part of the plan is supporting the maintenance of connectivity – the areas where habitat corridors and other ecologically connective areas exist.

The plan has four substantial sustainability components with integrative qualities. The first component is the spatial basis for planning – a striking biophysical feature that transcends institutional boundaries. Based on this natural region, there is a set of common planning criteria that all local governments in the Oak Ridges Moraine area must follow, including technical documents providing definitions and criteria to guide ecologically based planning. The second integrative aspect relates to the balancing of urban growth, rural land use, and conservation uses through a definitive set of land-use designations, consistent rules for development, and preservation of countryside and key natural features. The third component is the conservation plan, which seeks to foster a collaborative setting based on ongoing integrative research and administrative activities across institutions, agencies, and disciplines (Hanna, Webber, and Slocombe 2007). The last component has, perhaps, the most evident sustainability qualities of third-generation responses. A range of human actions, ecological functions, and planning policies was brought together and reconciled in once piece of legislation, one plan – a radical departure from the more common fragmented approaches to legislative land-use planning, habitat conservation, and water resource management familiar across North America and elsewhere.

The Oak Ridges Moraine conservation plan is a recent example that explicitly seeks an integrated approach to sustainability, particularly in terms of participation, local and regional ecosystem and landscape protection, and maintenance of quality of life in peri-urban areas (see, for example, Whitelaw and Eagles 2007; Whitelaw et al. 2008). Its more pluralistic approach to planning by engaging a wider range of stakeholder participants to develop a unifying conservation act, compared with the largely interagency approach in the FREMP case, is likely to result in a decidedly more integrated approach, reducing the probability of outside conflict and increased collaborative stewardship over time in the region.

Integration at the Scale of Large Regions: British Columbia's North and Central Coast

Bitter conflict has been one of the most notable characteristics of land-use policy debates in British Columbia. In 1993, after a decade of clashes among government, environmental groups, and business over forest industry practices, the British Columbia government initiated an innovative province-wide collaborative planning process consisting of Land and Resource Management Plans (LRMPs). This initiative was designed to help address the disagreements and prepare a set of comprehensive land and resource management plans based on defined regions. The LRMPs system was one of several policy outcomes emerging from the conflict period, but it is arguably the most integrative, influential, and broad in terms of geographic and thematic scales of attention. This novel model of collaborative planning delegated the responsibility for preparing plans to stakeholder roundtables representing First Nations, government, and other key players. In the LRMPs setting, participants engage in face-to-face negotiations to reach consensus agreements on plans that address long-term land management, account for a range of traditional and emergent uses, and provide for participatory plan development, implementation, and operation (for details, see Owen 1998; Gunton, Day, and Williams 2003; British Columbia 2007).

The LRMPs are regionally based integrated resource management plans in that they define a vision for the use and management of public lands and resources that seeks to sustain a regional economy and the landscape qualities that support it. In terms of content, LRMPs generally provide broad land-use zones defined on maps; specific objectives that guide the management of natural resources in each zone; strategies for achieving objectives; and a socio-economic and environmental assessment that evaluates the plan. Decisions about use and preservation reflect social choices – they are negotiated – and diverse values are presented and debated within the LRMPs setting.

In practice, the LRMPs process has emerged as highly participatory in that communities express a profound sense of ownership over the outcomes through engagement. As a result, this has ensured the longevity of the process. Although work on the LRMPs arguably has been slow, progress has been made, and the implementation and monitoring of approved LRMPs continues across the province. British Columbia's Protected Areas Strategy, which helps identify areas deserving park or similar status, is also implemented, in part, through LRMPs.

While the LRMPs process is advancing across British Columbia and several are now operational, only recently has consensus agreement been reached on plans for some of the most significant regions of contention. These include the Central and North Coast and Haida Gwaii (formerly the Queen Charlotte Islands) regions, whose LRMPs contain several features that combine to make a unique experiment in land and resource planning and provide a first-time opportunity to develop and assess new approaches to achieving economic, social, and environmental sustainability. Three innovative features distinguish the coastal LRMPs:

1 a new co-management process involving First Nations, government, and other stakeholders to manage implementation;
2 the first systematic adoption in Canada of ecosystem-based management as the preferred route to addressing conflicts over forest land use and accommodating diverse values; and
3 a comprehensive community economic development component to facilitate the transition of the regional economy to achieve social and economic sustainability in a manner consistent with ecological sustainability.

Co-management delegates the responsibility for implementation of the plans and ongoing resource management to new agencies and affected stakeholders. This is a fundamental shift in management and decision-making structures from centralized models to community-based, stakeholder-controlled models. The approach is integrative in that a range of resource uses, communities, and management regimes has been brought together – not just in the planning process, but carried through in the implementation and operation stages as well.

Given that ecosystem-based management is not primarily about managing ecosystems, but about managing human behavior by using ecosystem processes as a guide for the societal use of natural resources, there are clear connections to the notions of balance and social-ecological integration in third-generation responses to sustainability. Ideally, ecosystem-based management seeks to transcend arbitrary political and administrative boundaries using a systems approach that searches for more effective, integrated resources management and looks at ecosystems at regional and landscape scales. In 2001, the province and non-government and First Nations organizations developed a consensus for a unique definition of, as well as the principles and goals of, ecosystem-based management, emphasizing the human dimension rather than the natural one: '[it is] an adaptive approach to managing human activities that seeks to ensure the coexistence of healthy, fully functioning ecosystems and human communities. The intent is to maintain those spatial and temporal characteristics of ecosystems such that component species and ecological processes can be sustained and human well-being supported and improved' (Coast Information Team 2004).

The significant community economic development aspect included in LRMPs also provides for the transition to a sustainable economy that meets economic, social, and environmental needs. This component also entails new management structures and new models of community-based development consistent with social and ecological sustainability – essentially institutional transformation consistent with third-generation responses. The end result is an enhancement of the integrative potential of the overall approach.

Taken together, the integrative aspects of the LRMPs system across British Columbia represent an important experiment in sustainability and cooperative planning to meet and reconcile broad ecological, social, and economic objectives. The scale of attention, consisting of very large regions encompassing many communities and landscapes, also provides a unique example of integration in practice. The challenges in achieving successful implementation of the LRMPs model are certainly large, and the opportunities to learn from the experience and advance knowledge on sustainable development will be significant (see Frame, Gunton, and Day 2004; Gunton et al. 2006). In many respects the LRMPs process represents the potential for achieving integrative sustainability in large regions with substantial legacies of land-use conflict. Of the three cases presented here, this recent process likely provides the best example of efforts to link human well-being and societal sustainability, and ecological or ecosystem sustainability, at a regional scale using new management structures and development models based on communities. Perhaps not coincidentally, this region's residents likely have the strongest sense of place of the three cases discussed here as a result of the high level of engagement and integrative planning processes.

Concluding Comments: Dynamics of Integration and Sustainability in Planning Programs

Each of the three cases described here has an origin in conflict. For each, formal and informal relationships between agencies and non-government organizations have played an important part in addressing conflict. In two of the cases, the Oak Ridges Moraine and British Columbia's LRMPs, civil society had an overtly important instigating role in creating the planning process and defining the outcomes; in both cases, conflict was public, overt, and acrimonious. In the Fraser River Estuary Management Program case, conflict was originally between agencies and levels of government; while conflict was present, it was also understated. In the Oak Ridges Moraine case, conflict was widespread among interests and sectors, and attained a high profile among Toronto journalists. The Land and Resource Management Plans were one of several policy developments that the British Columbia government introduced to address longstanding land-use conflicts, mostly centred on the use of forest resources; these discussions were also public and often bitter. The LRMPs arguably have emerged as the most integrative and influential planning response, where integration is introduced as a problem-solving mechanism and a way to provide a systematic process for addressing complex or divergent expectations in the development of a multiple-use plan.

Ideally, integrative approaches should include a substantive consultation and participation component, which is extended to all affected stakeholders. The cases presented here differ in how and to what degree they apply this engagement process. In the FREMP case, consultation was based on agency participation, with very limited opportunities for participation by the community at large. This reflects, in part, the time when the FREMP was formed: in the 1980s, public participation expectations were perhaps not as strong as in later decades. It also reveals the interagency and intra-governmental nature of conflict in the estuary region. With a tightly controlled participation process, agencies were able to develop an integrative system that they believed would be most salable to political masters and across the bureaucracy. Tractability was a significant issue in the FREMP development, and it is reflected in the participation approach. Despite the largely ad hoc engagement of stakeholders outside these government agencies, civil society has had some influence, in part, through pressure placed on FREMP member agencies to reach consensus and through direct connections with FREMP planning activities and public consultation forums.

In the Oak Ridges Moraine case, participation was achieved through an advisory committee composed of broad representation from affected and interested sectors. This might be described as participation by proxy. Although these representatives consulted with and had the support of their constituencies, there were few substantive opportunities for broad consultation before the final Oak Ridges Moraine conservation plan was introduced. The timeline was simply too short, but the product developed by this approach nonetheless has been widely accepted (Hanna, Webber, and Slocumbe 2007), due largely to the opportunity for the engagement of stakeholder representatives and aforementioned support of their peers.

The LRMPs process is perhaps the most participatory example of the three cases, embodying the highest level of engagement and integration in the planning process. This process developed within a context of substantial conflict and has since become the focal point for stakeholder participation. Even with the use of the tables, which are akin to participation by proxy, a profound sense of ownership has gradually developed in communities through engagement. Beyond the tables, the LRMPs process also provides substantial ongoing opportunities for information dissemination, consultation, and plan-refinement discussions for the broader public. This ultimately strengthens the decisions reached within the LRMPs setting, as documented in the case of the Lillooet LRMP (Gunton et al. 2006).

Each of the cases described here has yielded a multiple-use product, realized in different plans for balancing uses, demands, and values. The culture of multiplicity is reinforced through processes whereby the integration and engagement of a range of disciplines and stakeholders contributes to the development of plans, and new organizational customs are formed to overcome institutional and societal barriers. The latter occurs gradually, often emergently, as common outcomes are realized and, as a result, not always explicitly. Such opportunities for the transformation of institutionalized approaches are inherent in third-generation responses. In the FREMP case, the program itself has acted as the venue for new approaches to information development and interagency planning. The Oak Ridges Moraine conservation plan, by comparison, is embedded in law, but has not created a specific program. Agencies cooperate, refer, and collaborate, as required by the law. In the LRMPs process, the plans defined by the engagement of communities are enacted by the British Columbia government and implemented through existing and new agency structures as a 'need' defined by the process.

The LRMPs and Oak Ridges Moraine cases illustrate the importance of an inclusive process to successful integrated planning. These cases also help illustrate connections between theories of civil society influence and impacts on practice and policy – particularly evidenced in the LRMPs and Oak Ridges Moraine processes (on the latter, see Whitelaw and Eagles 2007). These dimensions reflect current thinking on sustainability (see Dale 2001; Dale and Onyx 2005), which present sustainability as a bottom-up process of engagement, where the transition of informal relationships and influence becomes formalized in new planning systems. They also illustrate recent progress in urban and regional planning for sustainability via the integration of ecosystem and landscape ecology (for example, Forman 2008).

While each of our examples has a strong biophysical boundary, significant differences demonstrate the diverse nature of how regions are conceived and defined. The Fraser River estuary provides a convenient, if narrow, definition: it certainly encompasses a broad landscape, including large settled areas, but it is defined as a fairly tight water and foreshore area for program administration. The Oak Ridges Moraine is a well-defined region, certainly biophysically and, in many respects, by the assorted cultural attributes of its landscape. As for the LRMPs, these large regions are physiographic, but they are also very much defined by history, economy, and community (see, for example, the rural communities on Vancouver Island, discussed by Dushenko, in this volume). All three cases with their regional focus illustrate the need to engage and make links with other scales – the local or municipal, provincial, and federal levels – in an integrated fashion to design and implement planning programs successfully. Although the objective of sustainability reflects global needs, its dependence on regional and local action necessitates its application at a range of scales. While it is neither feasible nor necessarily desirable to undo existing institutional structures wholly, sustainability objectives will have to be integrated creatively into existing social, economic, and political systems as part of third-generation responses.

An integrated approach to planning emerges in part as a process of engagement, yielding a socially defined multiple-use plan as the outcome. Although the nature of who may contribute to the process is variable, the cases illustrate the different ways that integration in pursuit of sustainability can emerge. The illustrative value of such planning cases to sustainability serves as possible templates for putting an essential, but elusive and difficult, concept into practice. The examples outlined here illustrate not only the variable approaches to integration at regional scales, but also the very real potential the concept holds for fostering sustainability through environment and resource planning, and for mitigating conflict through engagement and the establishment of mutually shared outcomes that lead to success. Such processes are permeable to a range of ideas and concepts – from adaptive to ecosystem-based approaches – that ultimately support sustainability objectives. If such integrated approaches, in these case studies and elsewhere, can also be extended in practice beyond the planning process and into the implementation and operation stages across a range of settings to support success, we may be well on our way to embracing third-generation responses to sustainable development in Canadian communities.

REFERENCES

Barrett, G.W. 1985. 'A Problem-Solving Approach to Resource Management.' *BioScience* 35, no. 7: 423–7.

Barrow, C.J. 1999. *Environmental Management: Practice and Principles*. London: Routledge.

Born, S.M., and W.C. Sonzogni. 1995. 'Integrated Environmental Management: Strengthening the Conceptualization.' *Environmental Management* 19, no. 2: 167–81.

British Columbia. 2007. Integrated Land Management Bureau. 'Land and Resource Management Plans (LRMPs) and Regional Land Use Plans in BC.' Victoria.

Cairns, J., Jr. 1991. 'The Need for Integrated Environmental Management.' In *Integrated Environmental Management*, ed. J. Cairns Jr and T.V. Crawford. Chelsea, MI: Lewis Publishers.

Child, M., and A. Armour. 1995. 'Integrated Water Resource Planning in Canada: Theoretical Considerations and Observations from Practice.' *Canadian Water Resources Journal* 20, no. 2: 115–26.

Coast Information Team. 2004. 'Ecosystem-Based Management Framework.' Victoria, BC. http://www.citbc.org/c-ebmf-fin-03May04.pdf.

Dale, A. 2001. *At the Edge: Sustainable Development in the 21st Century*. Vancouver: UBC Press.

Dale, A., and J. Onyx. 2005. *Social Capital and Sustainable Community Development: A Dynamic Balance*. Vancouver: UBC Press.

Forman, R.T.T. 2008. *Urban Regions: Ecology and Planning beyond the City*. Cambridge: Cambridge University Press.

Frame, T.M., T.I. Gunton, and J.C. Day. 2004. 'The Role of Collaborative Planning in Environmental Management: An Evaluation of Land and Resource Management Planning in British Columbia.' *Journal of Environmental Planning and Management* 47, no. 1: 57–80.

Gunton, T.I., J.C. Day, and P.W. Williams, eds. 2003. 'Collaborative Planning and Sustainable Resource Management: The British Columbia Experience (Special issue).' *Environments* 31, no. 3.

Gunton, T.I., M.B. Rutherford, P.W. Williams, and J.C. Day, eds. 2006. 'Evaluation in Resource and Environmental Planning (Special issue).' *Environments* 33, no. 3.

Hanna, K.S. 1999. 'Integrated Resource Management in the Fraser River Estuary: Stakeholder Perceptions of the State of the Estuary and Policy Influence.' *Journal of Soil and Water Conservation* 54, no. 2: 490–8.

–. 2000. 'The Paradox of Participation and the Hidden Role of Information.' *Journal of the American Planning Association* 66, no. 4: 398–410.

–. 2007. 'Implementation in a Complex Setting: Integrated Environmental Planning in the Fraser River Estuary.' In *Integrated Resource and Environmental Management: Concepts and Practice*, ed. K. Hanna and D.S. Slocombe. Oxford: Oxford University Press.

Hanna, K.S., R.W. Negrave, B. Kutas, and D. Jojkic. 2007. 'Conflict and Protected Areas Establishment: British Columbia's Political Parks.' In *Transforming Parks and Protected Areas: Policy and Governance in a Changing World*, ed. K. Hanna, D. Clark, and D.S. Slocombe. London: Routledge.

Hanna, K.S., S. Webber, and D.S. Slocombe. 2007. 'Integrated Ecological and Regional Planning in a Rapid-growth Setting.' *Environmental Management* 40, no. 3: 339–48.

Karr, J.R. 1992. 'Ecological Integrity: Protecting Earth's Life Support Systems.' In *Ecosystem Health: New Goals for Environmental Management*, ed. R. Costanza, B.G. Norton, and B. Hakell. Washington, DC: Island Press.

Lang, R., ed. 1986. *Integrated Approaches to Resource Planning and Management*. Calgary: University of Calgary Press.

Margerum, R.D., and S.M. Born. 1995. 'Integrated Environmental Management: Moving from Theory to Practice.' *Journal of Environmental Planning & Management* 38, no. 3: 371–91.

McHarg, I.L. 1969. *Design with Nature*. New York: Doubleday/Natural History Press.

Mitchell, B. 1997. *Resource and Environmental Management*. Harlow, UK: Longman.

Ndubisi, F. 2002. *Ecological Planning: A Historical and Comparative Synthesis*. Baltimore: Johns Hopkins University Press.

North Yukon Planning Commission. 2007. 'Draft North Yukon Regional Land Use Plan.' Whitehorse. October.

Norton, B.G. 1992. 'A New Paradigm for Environmental Management.' In *Ecosystem Health: New Goals for Environmental Management. Washington*, ed. R. Costanza, B.G. Norton, and B. Hakell. Washington, DC: Island Press.

–. 2005. *Sustainability: A Philosophy of Adaptive Ecosystem Management*. Chicago: University of Chicago Press.

Ontario. 2002. Ministry of Municipal Affairs and Housing. *Oak Ridges Moraine Conservation Plan*. Toronto.

Owen, S. 1998. 'Land Use Planning in the Nineties: CORE Lessons.' *Environments* 25, nos. 2–3: 14–25.

Petak, W.J. 1980. 'Environmental Planning and Management: The Need for an Integrative Perspective.' *Environmental Management* 4, no. 4: 287–95.

Slocombe, D.S., and K.S. Hanna. 2007. 'Integration in Resource and Environmental Management: Towards a Framework.' In *Fostering integration: Concepts and Practice in Resource and Environmental Management*, ed. K.S. Hanna and D.S. Slocombe. Oxford: Oxford University Press.

Walther, P. 1987. 'Against Idealistic Beliefs in the Problem Solving Capacities of Integrated Resource Management.' *Environmental Management* 11, no. 4: 439–46.

Whitelaw, G., and P.F.J. Eagles. 2007. 'Planning for Long, Wide Corridors on Private Lands in the Oak Ridges Moraine, Ontario, Canada.' *Conservation Biology* 21, no. 3: 675–83.

Whitelaw, G., P.F.J. Eagles, R.B. Gibson, and M. Seasons. 2008. 'Roles of Environmental Movement Organizations in Land Use Planning: Case Studies of the Niagara Escarpment and Oak Ridges Moraine, Ontario, Canada.' *Journal of Environmental Planning and Management* 51, no. 6: 801–16.

3 Map-making as Place-making: Building Social Capital for Urban Sustainability

NINA-MARIE LISTER[1]

The map is not the territory.

– Alfred Korzybski (1931)

Maps, or visual representations of spatial territory, are as much a part of human history as the written word. Human societies have always preoccupied themselves with developing a spatial representation of nature and the physical space we occupy on the earth. From physiography to geology, from nation-states to ethnic enclaves, our space and our place within our communities and our world have long been the common subject of maps, and the art and science of their making.

Today, mapping is an exercise typically associated with scientific analyses of spatial territory, often for the purpose of directional navigation and way-finding. Enhanced by the current era of brilliant visual technology and million-pixel colour graphics, the map is preoccupied with precision, scale, and *Truth*. For many people, the contemporary map is a tool to get somewhere, perhaps via Google Earth's latest interactive StreetView of the city, town, or street; or a quick click on MapQuest to find the fastest route to somewhere. Others may rely on the Global Positioning System that comes with a smartphone or a new car. Even the vernacular paper map today is predominantly a way-finding tool, as the well-thumbed copy of the local street index kept in the car or the dog-eared tourist maps collected from last year's vacation. Modern cartography is all but defined by the tool that makes the map, whether geographic information systems (GIS) or computer-based spatial analyses that allow the mapping and interactive querying of increasingly complex phenomena. The advent of these powerful visual aids arguably has become the reality for many users today.

Fundamentally, the map has never been merely a tool, nor ever has it been a true representation of the world. Scholars of geography and cartography have long acknowledged that maps are essentially social constructions (see, for example, Harley 2001). Even the most modern, scientifically precise, state-of-the-art cartography involves some fundamental distortion of reality through the act of representing a three-dimensional space on a flat (two-dimensional) surface. Many historical maps are a testimony to various societies' desires to bend perception, distort scale, and persuade location.[2] In its most elemental state, a map is a heuristic or conceptual art form used to tell the story of a place – a place one is not necessarily meant to find, but rather to explore, experience, or envision.

Alfred Korzybski's (1931) famous observation that 'the map is not the territory' is a reminder that the concept cannot logically be the thing it represents. The truth lies not in the representation or its product, but in the process of its making. As a process, mapping is ultimately a creative act of design and agency in defining and describing both space and place.[3] As James Corner observed, mapping is 'a collective enabling enterprise [that both] reveals and realizes hidden potential' (1999, 213).

Map-making is very much about storytelling; through the collection of place-specific stories, the map becomes an agent in place-making. As a dynamic blend of fact and anecdote, stories impart meaning about those who tell them. If viewed as a collection of stories, the art of map-making is as much about place-making as it is about the geospatial location or topographic description of that place. Indeed, a map can be seen as the culmination of a process of exploration, discovery, meaning-making and storytelling – what Carruthers (2005) has called 'a campaign of discovery.' In the pursuit of urban sustainability, humans necessarily engage in navigating the confluence of natural and cultural landscapes – both physical landscapes and psychological 'mindscapes.' Together, these are the ecological, economic, and socio-cultural realms that overlap, integrating our physical territory (space) and our relationship to it through our emotional, spiritual, and cultural attachments to it (our place). Other manifestations of this concept are observed elsewhere in this volume by Dushenko in the rural context (Chapter 9) and by Luka on cottage country (Chapter 8). It is here, in this layered context, that maps and map-making may hold significant untapped potential in both the process and practice of urban sustainability and its agent, social capital.

As the contributors to this volume collectively theorize, urban sustainability is both process and goal (see Robinson, Chapter 4). It is,

according to Dale (2001; and Chapter 6), fundamentally about the reconciliation of personal, ecological, economic, and socio-cultural imperatives. Robinson (2008; Robinson and Dale, Chapter 1) further categorizes
sustainability approaches as first-generation approaches – those characterized by a focus on outcomes (that is, environmental and economic
performance); and second-generation approaches – those characterized
by a focus on processes (that is, strategies of civic engagement, empowerment, and collaboration in decision-making). It is in this second-
generation context, as a process, that map-making may be a useful guide
towards urban sustainability.

This chapter explores the notion that map-making, as both a
tool and a discourse, is used not merely to describe places, but, in a
richer, deeper way, to articulate, envision, reinvent, reinforce, and
ultimately reconnect us to the idea of place. Places ultimately sustain us
– ecologically, economically, culturally, spiritually, personally, and collectively. These concepts are inherent elements of third-generation responses. Place-making is central to the pursuit of urban sustainability:
without an appreciation for and attachment to the uniqueness of location, landscape, and community, there can be no hope for the reconciliation of the ecological, economic, social-cultural, and personal
imperatives that underpin sustainability as described by Dale (2001)
and developed by others in this volume (see Luka, Chapter 8; and Dushenko, Chapter 9). Intertwined exercises of map-making and place-
making are opportunities to build social capital and, in so doing,
advance the bonding, bridging, and networks necessary for urban
sustainability. This chapter investigates these interdependent phenomena, first, through an exploration of the theoretical aspects of mapping
and place-making; and, second, by illustration through an action-
research case study of map-making and place-making on the Toronto
waterfront.

Social Capital and Urban Sustainability

Bourdieu (1986) has argued that there are four kinds of human-based
capital – economic, cultural, symbolic, and social – which take the
form of 'connections' or social obligations that are subject to political
motivations and structures of power. In the context of sustainability,
Dale (2005) observes that different capitals exist at different scales, and
identifies four fundamental forms: natural (ecological), human (individual), social (collective), and, economic. All of the essential forms of

capital that Bourdieu and others have described have limited value independently. As Dale (2001, 2005) emphasizes, these are essentially intertwined and mutually dependent in the context of our planet. Sustainability demands the reconciliation of these capitals as part of second-generation responses, particularly in the case of natural (or ecological) capital, which subsumes and bounds all others by virtue of its finite nature, on which we depend. Much of society tends, however, to value this capital least, followed by social capital in its current structures of power and institutions of governance. Sustainable action cannot exist without reconciliation between and the rebalancing of these fundamental capitals. In particular, Dale argues, social capital is the most critical capital to activate the reconciliation required for sustainability precisely because 'changes of the magnitude necessary for sustainable development require collective mobilization of people in communities worldwide' (2005, 15). From this assertion, Newman and Dale (2005) have argued that agency becomes paramount, as it is fundamental to the mobilization of social capital.

Social capital has been described and analysed as a community asset – in particular, as an asset that can be accessed or created through participation in community-based planning (Manzo and Perkins 2006). Dale and Onyx (2005) argue there is a clear link between social capital and sustainable community development and that the basis for this notion has been long resonant in the community planning literature (see, for example, Gans 1968).[4] In fact, urbanist Jane Jacobs was among the first theorists to refer to the idea of social capital as a resource and an essential component of urban vitality (Smith and Kulynych 2002). In her now-classic work, *The Death and Life of Great American Cities,* Jacobs observed that social capital is necessary for the 'civilized self-government' of urban neighbourhoods (1961, 117) and that this capital is mobilized by the linking of social relations that are fundamental to urban life. The linking of these relations across geographical scales from the street to the neighbourhood to the city itself is the mechanism by which citizens build networks and break down barriers with increasing power to influence planning decisions that affect their communities. This is also a central feature of integrated approaches to regional planning, as illustrated by Hanna and Slocombe (in this volume) and an important component of third-generation responses.

While some have criticized the concept of social capital as merely a by-product of demographics and wealth (see, for example, Middleton et al. 2005), other scholars dispute this claim. In particular, Manzo and Perkins note that, in many 'place-based communities,' social capital is thriving and that 'there is substantial evidence of citizen participation, informal neighboring, and other bases of social capital across a wide range of demographics [and] socio-economic status' (2006, 342). In their detailed review of the community planning literature, Manzo and Perkins observe that social capital has important implications beyond its usual economic and political contexts – in particular, for 'physical capital,' or the assets of place and the built environment (see also McDonald, in this volume). While the decline of social capital popularized by Putnam in *Bowling Alone* (2000) refers specifically to the landscapes of suburban America and the proliferation of urban sprawl in homogenous 'non-places,' there is in fact good evidence that social capital is an important contributor to place-based communities (Taylor 2000; Manzo and Perkins 2006).

As Manzo and Perkins (2006) also observe, an improved understanding of the nature and value of social capital may foster more successful participatory planning processes that many argue are critical to urban sustainability (see, for example, O'Riordan 1998; Dale 2001; Tippett, Handley, and Ravetz 2007). Indeed, there is a rich literature on the theory and practice of community planning and development that explores the relationships of social capital to community vitality and engagement, often with particular reference to the important associated notions of place and environment (for example, Kemmis 1990; Speer and Hughey 1995; Flora and Flora 1996). In this context, I explore the role of mapping as a tool to operationalize and engage social capital in the timely pursuit of place-making towards urban sustainability, including the bridging of barriers required in third-generation responses.

The Role of Mapping Place in Urban Sustainability

We are all creatures of place, embedded in a complex spatial context that is at once ecological, social-cultural, and political-economic. Yet our collective understanding of place has changed dramatically over the past twenty years, with significant implications for planning. Smith (2007) observes that static conceptions of place have now given way to interpretations emphasizing relationships, such that the character of place is always under (re)construction (7). In particular, our association with place, and with *particular* 'experienced' places, is more complex than previously imagined and is considerably less rigid and more fluid in expression. Jivén and Larkham (2003; see also Dushenko, in this volume) also note that an individual's and a community's values and attitudes towards place may change over time, with some elements being valued now but not in the future, or the reverse. Literatures on environmental psychology, community planning, and landscape studies are all concerned with understanding and navigating this fluid interface. Indeed, the human relationship to, and interactions with, place have been well documented,[5] from the study of individuals' emotional and psychological perceptions of place to meanings of place to the role of civic engagement in place-making and community-building.

Tuan (1974) was one of the first scholars to identify and study the notion of place and human attachment to it, using the term 'topophilia' (literally, 'love of place') to describe a strong sense of identity with place, and the powerful emotional connections between humans and their physical environment that create this identity. Tuan argued that, over time, unremarkable physical spaces become 'places' through the gradual 'accretion of sentiment' (1974, 33) – that is, the acquisition of deep meaning through human attachment, achieved primarily through lived experience. This emphasis on human learning and cognition in relation to physical space – particularly landscape and urban design – is now central to environment-behaviour research.

In general, environment-behaviour research is concerned primarily with *how* place matters to people, in terms of three broadly defined dimensions: thinking, feeling, and acting (Luka 2006). Across the disciplines, from urban planning to cultural geography, there now exists a diversity of concepts and models that explore each of these dimensions of the human connection to place. Among them are place-attachment theory (Altman and Low 1992), sense of place (Relph 1976), rootedness (Vitek and Jackson 1996), place legibility (Lynch 1960), and place identity (Proshansky 1978). The common ground across these concepts is the critical importance of the human connection to place, and the role this relationship plays in shaping our communities.

The notion of 'place legibility' was developed first by noted urban planner Kevin Lynch. His observations of how citizens perceive, interpret, and navigate urban space (1960) led to the idea of place legibility and, from it, to the development of a standard method of analysis and the conceptual basis for good urban design. Through his research and practice, Lynch observed that people understand urban spaces in consistent and predictable ways, and that they tend to form mental maps of their perceptions of the spaces that are known to them according to a set of common elements. Lynch also coined the term 'imageability' to imply the extent of uniqueness of a given place and its subjective, non-measurable character. Notably, according to Lynch, 'imageable' places are not necessarily limited to physical spaces, and they may include memory and emotional context of a place. This is particularly strong in rural contexts (see, for example, Luka, Chapter 8; and Dushenko, Chapter 9 in this volume). In this context, Lynch's work was the precursor of a rich literature exploring the notion of place – as distinct from undifferentiated space – and its relationship to built form and landscape.

The concept of place has been the subject of seminal works in urban design and planning. In this context, 'good city form' is understood to be to a function of human-place relationships (see, for example, Rapoport 1977; Whyte 1980; McDonald, Chapter 10 in this volume). In particular, Amos Rapoport, an anthropologist and architect, studied human reactions to physical space and recognized that humans make sense of their surroundings by way of a complex continuum of sensory, cognitive, emotional, and evaluative processes. Similar to Lynch (1960), although based on a more rigorous empirical method, Rapoport observed that the human relationship to space and place was both orderly and complex, as well as predictable – in other words, that it was based on observable, distinct patterns. In this context, Rapoport's work was instrumental in relating the notions of physical space and meaning to urban design specifically, and to city form more generally.

It should be noted that place attachment and meaning are not limited to individual perceptions, experiences, or feelings. Attachment to community and shared places is of particular interest in the context of urban sustainability and identity, and is an important component of social capital. While it has been long recognized that a sense of community – or the connection and bonds between people within a community – is a vital component of healthy, vibrant cities (Jacobs 1961), there is also a growing awareness that attachment to community places is an important component of sustainable urban areas. This link is evident in research that examines neighbourhood character and demographics – for example, ethnic enclave studies that explore ethno-cultural diversity and homogeneity across various neighbourhoods or villages in relation to the city (see Abrahamson 1996; Qadeer and Kumar 2006). In this context, the concept of place is important to sustaining a community, in terms of both individual and collective bonds, from both inside and outside a physical community (see Dushenko, Chapter 9 in this volume).

Highlighting the critical connection between place and community, David Harvey's (2000) work on 'spaces of hope' discusses various utopian urban planning projects that failed, in part, because they were confined to spatial form. He calls instead for a utopianism of social process, with attachment to place as a central theme in what he terms 'dialectical utopianism' or visionary thinking and creative planning for how sustainable, equitable, and just cities could work. Akin to Harvey's call for visionary planning, the emphasis on social process, and, with it, the recognition of the value of place, is a common call among the authors in this volume in their various pursuits to activate and engage urban sustainability.

In a similar context, the act of mapping is very much a social activity. In gathering, representing, and interpreting spatial data, the act of making a map always tell a story – often implicitly but sometimes explicitly, whether about one's self, terrain, or place. Historically, cartographers focused their studies on the map itself, as both artefact and representation, but contemporary cultural geographers, ethnographers, anthropologists, and other social scientists have come to recognize mapping less as an individual response to territory and more as a social activity. This is one of a suite of cultural and material processes involved in the production of place-based knowledge (Cosgrove 1999; Perkins 2004). A community map-making process in which place-specific stories are recorded spatially and visually is shown in Figures 3.1 and 3.2.

Abrams and Hall reflect that mapping has 'become foregrounded as a cultural concern – a mode of gathering, presenting, perceiving, and reconceiving knowledge of the world and our place in it' (2006, 17). They note that neither the process of mapping nor the mapped product is static or fixed, but ongoing, incomplete, and indeterminate. This observation is particularly relevant in our contemporary digital culture, in which real and virtual worlds increasingly are represented as seamless and dynamic. This phenomenon is powerfully demonstrated by popular and proliferate Internet-based social networking sites such as Facebook, MySpace, or Second Life. Today, 'mapping is the conceptual glue linking the tangible world of buildings, cities and landscapes with the intangible world of social networks and electronic communications' (Abrams and Hall 2006, 12).

In the context explored in this chapter and the case study that follows, both maps and mapping are seen as fundamentally social constructions. Crampton (2001, 237) makes the case for 'an alternative landscape of cartography,' in which maps are not merely a system of

Figure 3.1. Community map-making process in Belleville, Ontario. Nina-Marie Lister

Figure 3.2. Community map-making results on Toronto's waterfront. Carruthers (2005)

communication, but more widely recognized as post-structural social constructions that reveal discourses in power relations, knowledge, and the complex phenomena of community. The sentiment that maps, like other texts, symbols, and their communications are cultural productions open to a variety of interpretations is resonant in the writings of a number of post-structural cultural theorists, from Baudrillard to Barthes and Foucault.[6] As Harley (2001, 35) observes, 'far from holding up a simple mirror of nature that is true or false, maps redescribe the world – like any other document – in terms of relations of power and of cultural practices, preferences, and priorities.' In this context, maps and map-making have the potential to engage or repel a community, whether through truth or fiction, humour or gravitas.[7] No matter the guise, maps clearly have a role as agents of social capital and as catalysts in creating (sustainable or other) communities.

Contemporary spatial analyses are dominated by sophisticated digital mapping using geographic information systems and digital visualization simulations. As a result of this and other aspects of society's reliance on traditional science, we tend to associate 'better' maps with precision and with more scientifically accurate data, usually in the context of way-finding or ground-truthing (Edney 1993; Crampton 2001). Digital colour mapping is deemed to be more accurate, and thus 'better,' than a to-scale hand rendering of a similar site, no matter the skill or artistry of the cartographer. It can be argued, however, that this same reliance on accuracy and precision also warrants a look beyond what is often a false sense of objectivity and distance. Monmonier (1991, 1995) has written extensive critiques of the dangers of relying on digital colour mapping as an indicator of precision, noting that mapping is an activity that is precisely about power and control (about marking 'territory' or 'property'), whether accurate or not. Of course, notions of accuracy also vary over time: what was considered precise in the explorers' maps of the pre-colonial medieval world would not pass for more than an antique artefact today. This is evident in Pietro Vesconte's *Mappa Mundi*, ca. 1320 (Figure 3.3), which was considered highly accurate at the time, but did not take into account the curvature of the earth. Yet, by understanding the map and the process of its making as a social and cultural (and for that matter, political and economic) practice, we avoid privileging certain forms of spatial information as 'better' merely because they are more scientific, and we open ourselves to the power and diversity of cartographic forms and the stories they tell (Crampton 2001).

Figure 3.3. Pietro Vesconte's Mappa Mundi, ca. 1320. Oriented east, this is one of the earliest world maps projected as a sphere. Wikimedia Commons

Cartography has long been subject to the myth of 'representation-as-reality.' That is, we pretend that the authority of the map is a function of its resemblance to the real world. This pretense, Wood (1993) argues, explains modern cartography's obsession with precision and accuracy. Yet for most of human history, maps have been ephemeral, scratched in sand, snow, caves, or on a tree, as needed. Even today, as impromptu way-finding devices, maps are often no more than hasty sketches on the back of an envelope or napkin, quickly consulted and tossed away. As Wood, a self-described 'psycho-geographer,' observes, maps for many cultures have an aura of permanence; he argues that this permanence and graphic quality ironically ends the map's authority '[arising] directly from the *certainty* guaranteed by the map's object quality, by its being . . . *a thing in the world*' (1993, 83; emphasis in original).

This observation highlights the schism within cartography between mapping as 'truth-object' (emphasizing technique and method) and a critical cartography or ethnographic approach to mapping as a social process (emphasizing context and discourse). Critical approaches to mapping include bioregional mapping (Aberly 1992), traditional aboriginal mapping (Tobias 2000), and community asset mapping (Carruthers 2005; and in the case study in this chapter), and other forms of alternative or subversive cartographies. These also range from humorous maps (Caquard and Dormann 2008) to emancipatory post-colonial maps.[8]

The recent proliferation of so-called alternative cartographies may be a reaction, in part, to the digital age and its concentration of power through access to information. Aberly observes that the result of increasingly object-oriented scientific mapping is nothing less than a sinister activity, 'primarily reserved for those in power, used to delineate the "property" of nation states and multinational companies' (1992, 1). Indeed, the digital age abounds with opportunities for those with access to technology to gather and manipulate spatial data for purposes of corporate profit, social exclusion, surveillance, and other exercises of power. The result is that, although we have unprecedented access to maps, we may be losing the self-reliance that comes with conceptualizing, making, and using images of place as we experience it. Aberly argues that '[digital maps] aid in attaching legitimacy to a reductionist control that strips contact with the web of life from the experience of place' (1992, 2). In a sentiment resonant with Aberly's sinister view of modern cartography, Wood claims, 'the map's power derives from the authority the map steals from its maker' (1993, 81). In other words, the human memory and cognition of physical space and its complex cousin, place, are what is real for us. The map is merely our representation of the process by which we understand and interpret, or make meaning from, place.

Through a return to focus on place, maps can play a significant role in social change. Cartographic depictions of a vision for the future, alternative development, or strategies of resistance and empowerment can serve as demonstrations of the possible, not merely the inevitable. Monmonier (1995) has shown how deliberately distorted maps have been used to steal property, how military maps have been used to crush opposition, and how popular maps can galvanize or decimate public support for an election candidate. However, democratized mapping need not pertain to physical or even existing terrain at all: it can be imaginary, visionary, or inspirational, with complete regard or disregard to territory, memory, or experience. Aberly observes, 'images of place can make the actual building of an alternative a possibility' (1992, 5). Through the use of maps as visioning devices or tools for imagination, for example, community engagement and social capital can be fostered and activated in the building of a convivial, sustainable future – whether in place, process, or both.

Maps increasingly are making socially and culturally relevant meaning from imaginary places. Virtual geographies have become commonplace on the Internet, including imaginary but highly detailed places central to the growing number of so-called Massive Multiplayer Online fantasy games such as *World of Warcraft*, *Rise of Nations*, and *Runescape*, or, more famously, literary worlds such as J.R.R. Tolkien's *Lord of the Rings*. Indeed, to the engaged reader and the active player, the imaginary lands of Mordor and Rohan in Middle Earth or WoW's Ironforge or Stormwind are no less 'real' communities than New York's SoHo, Toronto's Annex, London's Hyde Park, or a village in Tanzania. Katherine Harmon's *You Are Here* (2004) is an acclaimed collection of inventive maps of places one is not expected to find; rather, they are imaginary journeys and explorations – provocative examples include the ideal country estate from a dog's perspective, a love-making map of seduction, a trip down the road to success, or the world as imagined by an inmate of a mental institution.

In another similarly imaginative context, popular culture television series such as *Lost*, *Star Trek*, or *The Sopranos*, have developed online cult followings that number in the millions of subscribers and viewers. These and many other series often have multiple fan-based Web sites that act as virtual communities, in which members collectively and collaboratively map the characters' worlds, plotlines, timelines and neighbourhoods, often with impressive (or obsessive) detail. In the contemporary world, popular culture, through vernacular media, facilitates diverse and unprecedented opportunities for the intertwined exercise of place-making through map-making.

Although it may be tempting for scholars to dismiss the popularizing force of the Internet and of mass media, to do so would overlook the significant potential of vernacular media for social-cultural mapping. While critics (Aberly 1992; Wood 1993) have warned of the pitfalls of a singular reliance on precision digital mapping, others see potential in visualization tools and mass access to digital mapping.[9] Although cartographers have always been preoccupied with visualization and graphic communication, the digital age has provided a far more powerful ability to visualize spatial data. For example, Crampton (2001) notes that the powerful capabilities of interactive mapping software include the ability to rotate data in three dimensions, to add or sequentially delete data layers during analysis, and to query the map interactively. The sophistication of current graphic techniques in user-friendly mapping packages breaks down barriers to information access and makes it relatively easy, even for lay people, to see many spatial relationships that would otherwise go unnoticed or be inaccessible.

Similarly, various authors and cartographers (for example, Crampton 2001; Carruthers 2005) have argued that there is significant potential for online or distributed, Web-based mapping to engage social processes. Indeed, there is a groundswell of evidence that mapping is being democratized through online or distributed mapping using the Web and commonly available interfaces, such as Google Map (Carruthers 2005; Abrams and Hall 2006; Caquard and Dormann 2008). Perkins (2004) and others have noted there is also contemporary evidence of mapping practice in Web-based environments where production and consumption of visualization is increasingly collaborative. Practice indicates that, through situating maps within their social and cultural power relations – that is, online and easily accessed by virtually anyone anywhere – a richer and more meaningful interpretation of a map's purpose and audience, as well as any ethical implications, may be possible (Crampton 2001).

Crampton (2001) has also described a transition or an 'epistemic break' between a model of cartography as a communication system and one in which it is seen in a field of power relations, between maps as the presentation of stable, known information, and exploratory mapping environments in which knowledge is constructed' (235–6). Others (for example, Bell and Reed 2004) suggest that, increasingly, multi- and interdisciplinary geographic research tends to include a broader diversity of information types – tourist photos, sound files, audio narratives – into traditional proprietary geographic information systems. Furthermore, the effect of open-source software applications (such as Google and Skype) coupled with the rise of more user-friendly platforms has been to democratize and make readily accessible these and other emergent mapping technologies. In the hands of citizens and community groups, this newfound freedom to map may hold significant potential to contribute to both place-making and the (re)establishment of social capital.

It is in this emerging context that the case study of The Explorer's Map of the Toronto Bay is situated and in which the citizen's knowledge of place and community is explored, constructed, and communicated. In this democratized and vernacular context – decidedly apart from the convention of the map as truth-telling – one can explore the merit of the map as 'alternative cartography.' Specifically, the case study considers the utility of a community map in building social capital in the context of urban sustainability on the Toronto waterfront, a community that has been undergoing a thirty-year transition from industrial to post-industrial to residential.

The Explorer's Map of the Toronto Bay

The Explorer's Map of the Toronto Bay is the result of a classroom-to-community learning effort in the context of sustainability, guided by one community's exploration of a special place within the urban landscape. It is a place that exists as much in real time as it does in the hopes, dreams, and imaginations of a growing number of residents and visitors. The map is also an investigation in the practice of mapping as agency, moving beyond way-finding towards reflexive knowledge of our place and ourselves. It also serves as a democratizing act to construct and explore the knowledge of place to which we share a powerful attachment and the aspects about which we know both a little and a lot. Set on the urban waterfront in downtown Toronto, this project is both a case study in community-based mapping and an action-research exercise in building social capital for sustainability through the art and practice of map-making.

The Explorer's Map project is an action-research-based[10] case study of a university-community partnership that has two purposes evident in two distinct phases: to teach sustainability through ecological design and map-making to undergraduate students in urban planning at Ryerson University; and to foster community-based learning and action in urban sustainability through the process of collectively uncovering, revealing, and relating the story of a place and its community through time.

The project began in September 2005 with a partnership between Ryerson University's School of Urban and Regional Planning and a local community group, the Toronto Bay Initiative (TBI). Established in 1997, TBI is a local non-profit charitable organization that develops and promotes community-based projects and programs that improve the health and integrity of Toronto Bay. The community group targets its activities on five specific aspects of Toronto Bay's health and functionality: 1) improving water quality; 2) regenerating habitat; 3) ensuring public access to the water; 4) partnering with other watershed groups; and 5) educating the public on the ecological and historical importance of Toronto Bay. The group fulfils its mission by developing and delivering an annual slate of events for its members and the wider community. Regular events include guided natural and cultural heritage tours, canoe and boat tours of the bay, and shoreline clean-ups. TBI also undertakes longer-term projects, including habitat regeneration, restoration, and creation; shoreline stabilization; parkland naturalization; and stewardship and education programs.

As part of its mandate in education and stewardship, TBI became the client for a course in ecological design offered through Ryerson University's School of Urban and Regional Planning. The course was designed as a forum for senior students to undertake environmental action research, or research on a real-world problem for which the students would design a solution, process, or advocacy strategy for positive change in the context of sustainability. Funding to facilitate the university-community partnership and, from it, to produce The Explorer's Map was obtained from the HIVA Environmental Fund and the Metcalf Foundation – two local charitable foundations with an interest in environmental health and sustainability. An advisory committee provided creative oversight, technical and management advice, and constructive feedback. Two other key partners were PlanLab Ltd., a private sector community planning and mapping firm, and Bruce Mau Design Inc., an internationally recognized, multidisciplinary design studio. These partners,

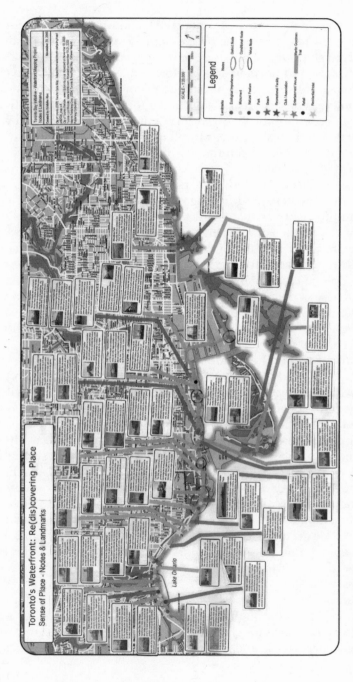

Figure 3.4. Map by K. Alex, the format of which was selected for The Explorer's Map. PlanLab Ltd.

as discussed later, were instrumental in contributing substantively and financially to the mapping process and the resulting map products.

In partnership with TBI, students produced a series of prototype maps, later used to develop The Explorer's Map. Students were challenged first to create a map as a communication strategy for the Toronto waterfront. As a post-industrial area undergoing a gradual transition to a residential community, there is a small but growing, active, and vocal residential community on site, as well as a larger and passionate – albeit spatially dispersed – community of dedicated waterfront users. In the context of ecological design, the map was 'to communicate broadly about the opportunities and barriers to (re)connect, (re)discover, (re)-integrate, (re)mediate, and (re)engage the cultural and natural land-scapes and their places that characterize the waterfront' (Lister 2005). Engaging the notions of place and community, the students' maps narrate, explore, and reflect various ways in which the cultural and natural places on the waterfront intersect, repel, and sometimes collide; they also explore the identity and tensions in the notion of place for the express purpose of engaging a diverse community of residents and their constituencies. The overall purpose of the maps was to provide a larger narrative within the context of ecological design and sustainability for the waterfront area.

More than one hundred wide-ranging assets pertaining to the space and place of the waterfront were identified, including natural and cultural heritage elements (such as fish habitats, rare orchids, wildlife sightings, beaches and dunes, cafes and museums), historical events and landmarks, recreational opportunities, anecdotes of place, and planned and spontaneous trails. The prototype maps effectively created a bioregional atlas of the waterfront, including natural, cultural, political, economic, imaginary, and historical data. Based on the assessment of a jury of designers, planners, and community representatives, one map was selected as the style most conducive to engaging the wider community in a place-based mapping exercise. The map, by student K. Alex (Figure 3.4), depicts historical and natural points of interest mapped along the Waterfront Trail as a 'storyboard,' a format that was used as a prototype for the next phase of the project to develop The Explorer's Map.

In February 2006, PlanLab Ltd. and Ryerson University held a mapping workshop that brought together fifteen waterfront residents and sectoral experts, including ecologists, fisheries biologists, recreation specialists, historians, and sailors. In a graphic style described by

Figure 3.5. Community map of Toronto Bay, used to develop the subsequent interactive online and print versions of The Explorer's Map. PlanLab Ltd.

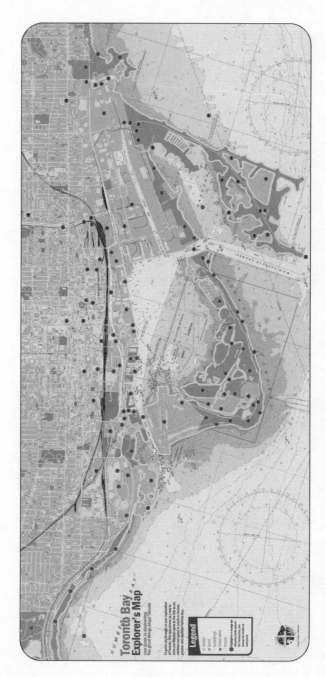

Figure 3.6a. Place-making: The Explorer's Map, Print Version. PlanLab Ltd.

Figure 3.6b. Place-making: The Explorer's Kit, jackdaw folio created by Bruce Mau Design Inc. PlanLab Ltd.

Aberly (1992), the workshop participants became co-researchers in an exercise that quickly became as much about place-making as it was about mapping. The team mapped together their collective knowledge into a single graphic repository of data (Figure 3.5) that would become the master file for both the online interactive digital version and the future print version (Figure 3.6a). Connected by points, lines, and places, the map was a repository of previously untold stories, little-known anecdotes, historical events, timelines, fish tales, landmarks, and lore – all of it superimposed on a 2.5-metre base map both to scale and geospatially accurate in terms of urban infrastructure and street references. Bruce Mau Design Inc. then produced the final mapped product, which was designed on the principle of the jackdaw – a folio designed to be carried in a hip pocket and containing a variety of information devices, including, but not limited to, several maps (Figure 3.6b). The common themes that emerged from the mapping workshop were used as the organizational framework for the jackdaw, which included fold-out historical timelines, thematic maps, a deck of ecological playing cards featuring native and invasive species, a 'ruler' detailing development progress and pitfalls, and various fact sheets.

Figure 3.7. Explore Toronto Bay online at http://www.ExploreTorontoBay.ca. PlanLab Ltd.

The Explorer's Map identifies and interprets the rich natural and cultural resources in the Toronto Bay area and the interrelationships among them, to encourage citizens, community members, and visitors alike to explore and understand these place-based relationships. Inspired by a cartoon-like vernacular map – *The People's Guide to the Toronto Waterfront* produced in 1971 by the Faculty of Environmental Studies at York University – The Explorer's Map uses both text and graphics to depict the major elements of Toronto's unique natural and cultural waterfront landscape and to identify potential future opportunities to create a healthier, sustainable Toronto Bay. The map is not intended to be an exhaustive collection of stakeholders' perceptions, nor was it created with the input of representative commercial and industrial sectors. Rather, it was deliberately targeted at residents and citizens, with the aim of engaging people in assessing, valuing, and inventorying the assets of place – a place that might be sustained in part, through the knowledge gained through the act of mapping.

Central to its application in place-making, The Explorer's Map has a built-in capacity for – indeed, an expectation of – evolution. PlanLab Ltd. created the custom interactive Google Map application (Figure 3.7) as a platform for the full digital version of The Explorer's Map. The site is a layered series of maps that can be queried by the user. TBI owns and administers the site, verifies data, and adds, deletes, and edits 'stories' or place-identifiers. The Web site can accommodate growing the map, as well as stories of and attachments to place that the wider community submits over time. In this way, the map is a living, evolving entity – a collective product of its place and an on-going process of place-making.

Reflections

From the outset, TBI envisioned The Explorer's Map as a living testimony to the Toronto waterfront as a special place – in particular, as a place that, until recently, had been largely forgotten by the residents of Toronto. The past decade of revitalization initiatives has resulted in a growing number of residential communities and a wide range of stakeholders on the waterfront, but stakeholders were limited to special interests associated principally with recreation (for example, boating, fishing), industry (for example, Redpath Sugar, the Toronto Island Airport, the Harbour Commission) or resources conservation (through Fisheries and Oceans Canada, the Conservation Authority, the Ontario Ministry of the Environment). More recently, the establishment of new communities has brought renewed attention to and engagement in the waterfront as a *place* – for living, working, and playing – not merely a fragmented collection of industrial areas, a port, and a seasonal tourist destination.[11] Given the influx of new local residents and growing numbers of Torontonians who visit, steward, and invest in the area, TBI saw The Explorer's Map as a device to engage citizens in the rediscovery of a place that helps to define the city.

In this context, the map was designed as both tool and method – an innovative product for and a creative process towards community engagement and public education around issues of sustainability that pertain to the reconciliation of ecological, social, cultural, recreational, and historical assets. The map was meant to foster users' understanding of the unique places along the waterfront and the relationship of the bay to the rest of the city. It was intended to activate and facilitate an ongoing narrative and, from this, a dialogue among residents, citizens, and stewards about the assets and the identity of place. In so doing, The Explorer's Map is an important educational device that could contribute to a wider, deeper understanding of the issues and tensions of sustainability for the waterfront. In that sense, the map is as much social process as it is both a cultural product and a representation of spatial data.

Through inviting more of Toronto's citizens to explore the city's unique waterfront location and the special places around the bay, the map capitalizes on a nascent existing community network and the social bonds between and among various waterfront citizens. Although not yet empirically observed, these networks are thought to be growing deeper and more resilient, tied into a wider number of inter- and intra-waterfront user communities, and that both the virtual (online) and tangible networks are linked, in part, to The Explorer's Map. As the number of waterfront communities, parks, and public spaces continues to grow, so too does the number of stakeholders and potential contributors to the map repository. Given this dynamic, it is hoped that The Explorer's Map will become a key resource for residents and citizens to continue the story: the act of mapping place may help identify issues central to sustainability while engaging the growing community in shaping the future of this particular place. In short, it is expected, through follow-up research, to be able to evaluate the utility and efficacy of map-making as an agent of social capital in place-making. For now, anecdotal evidence in print media, residents' comments, participation at community meetings, and online presence suggests a renewed sense of stewardship towards, and civic engagement in this evolving urban landscape.[12]

While representing the experience of one community in charting the complexities of place, The Explorer's Map is but one small product of a complex learning process towards urban and community sustainability. The map, for all its vitality and engaging potential as a process, will remain only an artefact without consistent interaction and the nurturing and cultivation of social capital on which its learning potential depends. Most important, in working towards sustainability, the expertise of a map cannot be relied on solely; an understanding is needed of the powerful social process that created it. More specifically, these processes are what Dale (2001) has called the silo-bonding, solitude-bridging, and stove-pipe-networking social processes that have defined place in Toronto Bay, in the community, and in its vibrant urban landscape. As Wood (1993, 85) poignantly observes, 'underneath it all the map is still no more . . . than a voice on the wind.' Perhaps, in the pursuit of third-generation responses to urban sustainability, our task is to engage our collective voice and to recover the understanding that we *are* the place in which we dwell.

NOTES

1 I am indebted to David Carruthers of PlanLab Ltd. for his cartographic
   expertise, creative perspective, and good humour in bringing The
   Explorer's Map to life. I am grateful to Jason Globus-Goldberg my Research
   Assistant at Ryerson University's School of Urban & Regional Planning,
   for his capable and persistent pursuit of the background literatures, and
   to Chris Beck of PlanLab Ltd. for his thorough research on Toronto Bay.
   I thank Joanna Kidd, Chair of the Toronto Bay Initiative for her shared
   vision and co-direction of The Explorer's Map project, from concept
   to completion. Sincere thanks to the students of my *Ecological Design*
   class (Fall 2005) who worked with me to make their studio a creative
   learning space for The Explorer's Map concept, and to the members of
   the Toronto Bay community who, as co-researchers, contributed to the
   mapping workshop that shaped the emergent product. I appreciate the
   contribution of time and the design talents of Kevin Sugden and Marc
   Lauriaut of Bruce Mau Design in the creative packaging of the map. The
   George Cedric Metcalf Foundation, the HIVA Foundation, Bruce Mau
   Design Inc., and the Ryerson Faculty of Community Services are gratefully
   acknowledged for their generous funding and in-kind support of this joint

university-community project. Finally, this chapter has been improved
thanks to the sharp eyes and insights of several anonymous reviewers and
the talents of the editors.

2 For accounts and examples of deception in cartography, see Carlucci
   and Barber's *The Lie of the Land* (2001), and Monmonier (1991, 1995) who
   has written popular accounts of strategies for designing deliberately
   misleading maps, as well as guidebooks to understanding cartographic
   distortion and its impacts.

3 'Space' is used here in the geographic sense, as in spatial territory. It is
   distinct from 'place,' which is used here in the context, defined by Tuan
   (1974), of geographic space to which humans attribute meaning.

4 The basis for this link is clear as early as the 1960s in the urban planning
   literature, insofar as the relationship between attachment to place and
   the importance of social networks was well recognized – indeed, studied
   as a precondition for healthy communities; see, for example, the works
   of Lynch (1960, 1981); Jacobs (1961); Gans (1968); and Whyte (1980). This
   earlier literature, however, does not use the language of social capital and
   sustainable development explicitly, as these are relatively recent terms
   originating in the late 1980s; see, for example, Bourdieu (1985); WCED (1986).

5 There is an established scholarship in geography and related social
   sciences in place attachment theory; see, for example, Tuan (1974); Relph
   (1976); Hayden (1995); and Vitek and Jackson (1996).

6 It is perhaps unsurprising that many post-structural critiques have
   taken aim at mapping, both literally and figuratively, whether of space,
   language, culture, or literary works; see, for example, Barthes (1957);
   Baudrillard (1968).

7 Social commentary using humour is common in contemporary maps;
   see, for example, 'A Simplified Map of London.' http://bigthink.com/
   ideas/21251 (accessed 14 October 2011).

8 See for example, 'United States of Canada vs. Jesusland,' a humorous map
   of the United States made popular during the 2005 US election. http://
   strangemaps.wordpress.com/2006/09/10/3-united-states-of-canada-vs-
   jesusland/ (accessed 14 October 2011).

9 See, for example, the rise of municipal cultural planning (Baeker 2010)
   as an exercise rooted in cultural mapping, undertaken by stakeholders
   with little or no experience in cartography but with a keen interest in
   understanding and identifying the cultural landscape of their communities
   (Baeker and Brown 2010).

10 'Action research' as used here is a research method characterized as
   'learning by doing.' It is used in the same context discussed by Stringer

(1996), in which reflexive and progressive research is undertaken by a researcher and his or her study participants, who work together as co-researchers, collectively learning their way through an applied problem in a real-world setting in which the underlying purpose of the research is to advocate for positive change or improve a situation.

11 As the agency charged with revitalizing the waterfront, WATERFRONToronto is engaged in multiple projects and plans for new communities, parks, and public spaces. These range from RiverCity (the first development in the West Donlands, beginning construction in 2010) to precinct plans for the whole East Bayfront-Port Industrial lands to the reconfiguration of the mouth of the Don River, Don Park, and the 980-hectare Lake Ontario Park Master Plan. The full range of current plans and associated designs is available at http://www.waterfront oronto.ca/.

12 For example, the mapping exercise explored issues of conflict and tension around waterfront development, from the relocation of a boating club in the Lake Ontario Master Plan to the planned expansion of the Toronto Island Airport. In each case, contributors reported being made more aware of the issues underlying these conflicts through engagement in the mapping activity. In several instances, creative solutions were offered when participants were asked specifically to identify aspects of a sustainable waterfront.

REFERENCES

Abrahamson, M. 1996. *Urban Enclaves: Identity and Place in America*. New York: St. Martin's Press.

Abrams, J., and P. Hall. 2006. *Else/Where: Mapping – New Cartographies of Networks and Territories*. Minneapolis: University of Minnesota Design Institute.

Aberly, D. 1992. *Boundaries of Home: A Guide to Bioregional Mapping*. Gabriola Island, BC: New Society Publishers.

Altman, I., and S. Low. 1992. *Human Behavior and Environments: Advances in Theory and Research*, vol. 12, *Place Attachment*. New York: Plenum Press.

Baeker, G., ed. 2010. *Rediscovering the Wealth of Places: A Municipal Cultural Planning Handbook for Canadian Communities*. Toronto: Municipal World.

Baeker, G., and D.T. Brown. 2010. 'Mapping Community Identity: The Power of Stories.' *Municipal World*, September.

Barthes, R. 1957 [1972]. *Mythologies*, trans. Annette Lavers. London: Hill and Wang.

Baudrillard, J. 1968 [1996]. *The System of Objects*, trans. James Benedict. London: Verso.

Bell, S., and M. Reed. 2004. 'Adapting to the Machine: Integrating GIS into Qualitative Research.' *Cartographica: The International Journal for Geographic Information and Geovisualization* 39, no. 1: 55–66.

Bourdieu, P. 1986. 'The Forms of Capital.' In *Handbook of Theory and Research for the Sociology of Education*, ed. John Richardson. New York: Greenwood.

Caquard, S., and C. Dormann. 2008. 'Humorous Maps: Explorations of an Alternative Cartography.' *Cartography and Geographic Information Science* 35, no. 1: 51–64.

Carlucci, A., and P. Barber. 2001. *The Lie of the Land: The Secret Life of Maps.* London: British Library.

Carruthers, D. 2005. 'Mapping Workshop Lectures and Notes to Students of PLE 835, Ecological Design.' Toronto: Ryerson University, School of Urban and Regional Planning. October–November.

Corner, J. 1999. 'The Agency of Mapping: Speculation, Critique and Invention.' In *Mappings*, ed. D. Cosgrove. London: Reaktion Books.

Cosgrove, D., ed. 1999. *Mappings.* London: Reaktion Books.

Crampton, J.W. 2001. 'Maps as Social Constructions: Power, Communication and Visualization.' *Progress in Human Geography* 25, no. 2: 235–52.

Dale, A. 2001. *At the Edge: Sustainable Development in the 21st Century.* Vancouver: UBC Press.

–. 2005. 'A Perspective on the Evolution of e-Dialogues concerning Interdisciplinary Research on Sustainable Development in Canada.' *Ecology and Society* 10, no. 1: 37–45.

Dale, A., and J. Onyx, eds. 2005. *A Dynamic Balance: Social Capital and Sustainable Community Development.* Vancouver: UBC Press

Edney, M.H. 1993. 'Cartography without "Progress": Reinterpreting the Nature and Historical Development of Mapmaking.' *Cartographica* 30, nos. 2–3: 54–68.

Flora, C.B., and J.L. Flora. 1996. 'Creating Social Capital.' In *Rooted in the Land: Essays on Community and Place*, ed. W. Vitek and W. Jackson. New Haven, CT: Yale University Press.

Gans, H. 1968. *People and Plans: Essays on Urban Problems and Solutions.* New York: Basic Books.

Harley, J.B. 2001. 'Text and Contexts in the Interpretation of Early Maps.' In *The New Nature of Maps: Essays in the History of Cartography.* Baltimore: Johns Hopkins University Press.

Harmon, K. 2004. *You Are Here: Personal Geographies and Other Maps of the Imagination.* Princeton, NJ: Princeton Architectural Press.

Harvey, D. 2000. *Spaces of Hope.* Edinburgh: University of Edinburgh Press.

Hayden, D. 1995. *The Power of Place.* Cambridge, MA: MIT Press.

Jacobs, J. 1961. *The Death and Life of Great American Cities.* New York: Random House.

Jivén, G., and P.J. Larkham. 2003. 'Sense of Place, Authenticity and Character: A Commentary.' *Journal of Urban Design* 8, no. 1: 67–81.

Kemmis, D. (1990. *Community and the Politics of Place.* Norman: University of Oklahoma Press.

Korzybski, A. 1931. 'A Non-Aristotelian System and Its Necessity for Rigor in Mathematics and Physics.' Paper given before the American Mathematical Society at the American Association for the Advancement of Science, New Orleans, 28 December. Reprinted in A. Korzybski, *Science and Sanity: An Introduction to Non-Aristotelian Systems and General Semantics.* 1933.

Lister, N.-M. .2005.. 'PLE 835: Ecological Design.' Course syllabus, School of Urban and Regional Planning, Ryerson University.

Luka, N. 2006. 'Placing the "Natural" Edges of a Metropolitan Region through Multiple Residency: Landscape and Urban Form in Toronto's "Cottage Country".' Unpublished PhD diss., Department of Geography, University of Toronto.

Lynch, K. 1960. *The Image of the City.* Cambridge, MA: MIT Press.

–. 1981. *Good City Form.* Cambridge, MA: MIT Press.

Manzo, L.C., and D.D. Perkins. 2006. 'Finding Common Ground: The Importance of Place Attachment to Community Participation and Planning.' *Journal of Planning Literature* 20, no. 4: 335–50.

Middleton, A., A. Murie, and R. Groves. 2005. 'Social Capital and Neighbourhoods that Work.' *Urban Studies* 42, no. 10: 1711–38.

Monmonier, M.S. 1991. *How to Lie with Maps.* Chicago: University of Chicago Press.

–. 1995. *Drawing the Line: Tales of Maps and Cartocontroversy.* New York: Henry Holt.

Newman, L., and A. Dale. 2005. 'The Role of Agency in Sustainable Local Community Development.' *Local Environment* 10, no. 5: 477–86.

O'Riordan, T. 1998. 'Civic Science and the Sustainability Transition.' In *Community and Sustainable Development,* ed. D. Warburton. London: Earthscan.

Perkins, C. 2004. 'Cartography – Cultures of Mapping: Power in Practice.' *Progress in Human Geography* 28, no. 3: 381–91.

Proshansky, H.M. 1978. 'The City and Self-identity.' *Environment and Behavior* 10, no. 2: 147–70.

Putnam, R.D. 2000. *Bowling Alone: The Collapse and Revival of American Community.* New York: Simon and Schuster.

Qadeer, M., and S. Kumar. 2006. 'Ethnic Enclaves and Social Cohesion.' *Canadian Journal of Urban Research*, Special Issue on Immigration and Cities 15, no. 2: 1–17.

Rapoport, A. 1977. *Human Aspects of Urban Form: Towards a Man-Environment Approach to Urban Form and Design.* New York: Pergamon Press.

Relph, E. 1976. *Place and Placelessness.* London: Pion.

Robinson, P. 2008. 'Urban Sustainability in Canada: The Global–Local Connection.' In *Environmental Challenges and Opportunities: Local-Global Perspectives on Canadian Issues*, ed. C. Gore and P. Stoett. Toronto: Emond Montgomery.

Smith, D.M. 2007. 'The Moral Aspects of Place.' *Planning Theory* 6, no. 1: 7–15.

Smith, S., and J. Kulynych. 2002. 'It May Be Social, but Why Is It Capital? The Social Construction of Social Capital and the Politics of Language.' *Politics & Society* 30, no. 1: 149–86.

Speer, P.W., and J. Hughey. 1995. 'Community Organizing: An Ecological Route to eEmpowerment and Power.' *American Journal of Community Psychology* 23, no. 5: 729–48.

Stringer, E. (1996. *Action Research: A Handbook for Practitioners.* Thousand Oaks, CA: Sage.

Taylor, M. 2000. 'Communities in the Lead: Power, Organizational Capacity, and Social Capital.' *Urban Studies* 37, nos. 5–6: 1019–35.

Tippett, J., J.F. Handley, and J. Ravetz. 2007. 'Meeting the Challenges of Sustainable Development: A Conceptual Appraisal of a New Methodology for Participatory Ecological Planning.' *Progress in Planning* 67, no. 1: 9–98.

Tobias, T. 2000. *Chief Kerry's Moose: A Guidebook to Land Use and Occupancy Mapping, Research Design and Data Collection.* Vancouver: Union of BC Indian Chiefs and Ecotrust Canada.

Tuan, Y.F. 1974. *Topophilia.* Englewood Cliffs, NJ: Prentice-Hall.

Vitek, W., and W. Jackson. 1996. *Rooted in the Land: Essays on Community and Place.* New Haven, CT: Yale University Press.

WCED (World Commission on Environment and Development). 1987. *Our Common Future: Report of the World Commission on Environment and Development*, chaired by Gro Harlem Brundtland. Oxford: Oxford University Press.

Whyte, W. 1980. *The Social Life of Small Urban Spaces.* Washington, DC: Conservation Foundation.

Wood, D. 1993. 'What Makes a Map a Map?' *Cartographica* 30, nos. 2–3: 81–6.

PART II

Social Capital and the Built Environment

4 Planning for Sustainability: Moving from Plan to Action

PAMELA ROBINSON

Sustainability is the new imperative for cities in the 21st century and the Toronto waterfront will be distinguished by its leadership on sustainability. The question is not if we will do it but how we will do it.
– Robert A. Fung, Chairman, Toronto Waterfront Revitalization Corporation (2005)

Toronto's vast waterfront has been a source of both pride and lament in Canada's largest city. While the waterfront area has been the focus of a number of studies since the early 1900s, visions of redeveloping this 809-hectare, 47-kilometre swath of prime real estate persist in modern local politics. The waterfront's myriad complexities were significant enough to warrant the appointment of the Royal Commission on the Future of Toronto's Waterfront, which operated under the chairmanship of former Toronto mayor the Hon. David Crombie from 1988 to 1992. The Commission's groundbreaking work *Regeneration* (Canada 1992) proposed an ecosystem approach of integrated planning as a means of ensuring that the future of the waterfront would be ecologically sound while also dynamic for Torontonians. Still, a decade later, the waterfront's potential remained a work in progress. In March 2000, the Toronto Waterfront Revitalization Corporation (TWRC) was established by the federal government, the Ontario provincial government, and the City of Toronto as the lead organization on waterfront planning and revitalization initiatives. This followed the release in 1999 of the report of the Toronto Waterfront Revitalization Task Force, a business plan with recommendations for the development of the waterfront. In 2006, the TWRC was renamed WATERFRONToronto.

Through the development of its sustainability framework (2005), the TWRC embedded the principles of urban sustainability in its long-term revitalization plans. In the past decade, pairing urban sustainability with redevelopment has grown in popularity, including in Toronto, where sustainability principles were, and continue to be, guiding forces in projects such as the Downsview Park and Regent Park redevelopment projects. Further afield, we see similar uptake with the Vancouver Olympics; the Victoria (British Columbia) Docklands (Dockside Green); Montreal's strategic plan on sustainable development; Lloyds Crossing in Portland, Oregon; the London 2012 Olympics; and China's many eco-cities. The international examples, among many, demonstrate the proliferation of urban sustainability goals and objectives into significant and influential urban development plans. But how are these principles being operationalized?

This chapter explores the TWRC/WATERFRONToronto sustainability framework, an early example of what the contributors to this volume classify as a third-generation urban sustainability response. It is one in which a place-based approach has been deployed to advance the deep and integrated reconciliation of sustainability's three imperatives in the specific context of the social, ecological, economic, and political characteristics of the Toronto waterfront. I begin with an overview and evaluation of how successfully sustainability principles are translated into local development processes through the articulation of development plans with sustainability goals and objectives. I examine the sustainability framework's process of development, and review and evaluate its key substantive elements as to potential positioning as a third-generation response. This evaluation reveals that, while the process and positioning of the sustainability framework had the potential to influence and guide the work of WATERFRONToronto, as of 2010 the framework has not been used even though WATERFRONToronto has moved forward on other innovative sustainability-oriented projects. I consider the reasons the framework has not been put to active use, and offer 'lessons learned' for those communities active in the development of their own sustainability plans. I conclude with a reflection on the significance of moving from plan to action, in order to deliver the paradigmatic transformation of institutions and communities required to make real progress towards urban sustainability.

Planning for Sustainability

The success of any urban sustainability plan, framework, or strategy is dependent in part upon how sustainability is positioned or defined

(Robinson 2008). The now-twenty-year-old simple definition of the Brundtland Commission (WCED 1987, 43, and noted in this volume's introduction) is still commonly used, but it fails to capture the complexities of urban sustainability, particularly when it is used as a foundation for informing action. Given that simplistic definitions drive simplistic approaches, the future success of sustainability necessitates strategic initial positioning. The challenges that Canadian communities face in responding to urban sustainability were recognized as early as 1996 by Environment Canada in its *State of the Environment* report:

> Urban sustainability is not a clearly defined, concrete objective to be reached by a certain deadline. It is an idea, a vision, to be used as a guide for sustained, multifaceted efforts over an indefinite period. It demands a long-term, comprehensive, and integrated perspective. For many people, including some politicians and public officials, these are new and difficult ideas, and they constitute an approach to urban management that does not fit well with traditional political and administrative systems. An issue of long-term, fundamental importance can easily be obscured by the apparently urgent immediate problem. (Environment Canada 1996)

Here again, we are reminded that complex problems cannot be solved with simplistic responses.

The contributors to this volume characterize first-generation responses as too tidy in their segmentation of sustainability's three constituent parts. Practitioners and scholars, in responding to these reductionist efforts, soon realized the significance of the process of *reconciliation* of social, economic, and environmental imperatives of sustainability (Dale 2001). Dale's work, among others, reminds us that sustainability is more than the simple addition of its social, economic, and ecological elements, and more than good environmental performance. The emphasis on reconciliation reminds us that the *process* of achieving sustainability has a direct influence on the outcomes (Robinson 2008). The outcomes are a fundamental product of the process; more inclusive, ecologically sound society cannot be accomplished using undemocratic processes. While first-generation responses favoured the use of sustainability indicators and scorecards to track progress, the second generation gave rise to the search for a wider range of voices to add to the sustainability table. This was also achieved through the mobilization of social capital and other new resources from which to leverage response. In the transition from second- to third-generation responses, the emergence of formalized plans with high-order sustainability goals and principles developed in multi-stakeholder processes and grounded in place-specific targets and benchmarks is commonplace. That is, if the principles of equity embedded in the sustainability paradigm are to be advanced, we must adhere to these principles in our processes of envisioning, planning, designing, and building for sustainability. The question arises as to how these principles have been translated into action at the local scale in development-oriented plans and the eventual creation or revitalization of real communities.

From the first Earth Summit in Stockholm in 1972 to the release of the Brundtland Commission report to current practice, the need to reconcile community, environmental, and economic imperatives to ensure that the 'needs of the future can be provided for without compromising the needs of the present' (WCED 1987) has been at the top of the agenda for governments. Over time, the global conversation about how sustainable development might be practically mobilized focused on the roles that urban regions would play if the transition to a more equitable, greener, and more financially viable future were possible (Robinson 2008). This task of planning for the future is not new to Canadian communities; they have a long-standing tradition of developing long-range, comprehensive land-use plans as a means of articulating how and where growth will be directed. As the role that local governments potentially could play in mobilizing sustainability efforts was realized, sustainability plans, frameworks, and strategies were developed as a comprehensive means of articulating and coordinating sustainability action.

As both contributors to the problem and incubators of capacity and infrastructure, communities and local governments recognized the fundamental role they might play in the broad urban sustainability agenda through the development of these plans. While local governments internalized their urban sustainability mandate, academic research explored the process by which practice has unfolded. In North America, there are some surprising and consistent findings about how urban sustainability, thus far, has manifested itself on the ground in the transition from second- to third-generation approaches. First, in practice, actions taken under the umbrella of 'urban sustainability' are typically actions with an environmental focus (see, for example, Berke and Conroy 2000; Parkinson and Roseland 2002; Portney 2002), or actions that do not adequately integrate action towards advancing intra- and intergenerational equity (Saha and Paterson 2008). Second, local and regional governments continue to be challenged by how to address the social, economic, and equity dimensions of 'sustainability' simultaneously, and how to move beyond sustainability's being equated with predominantly ecological concerns (Robinson 2008; Robinson and Dale, in this volume). These findings reinforce the need to position these elements effectively and appropriately in the substance of plans from the outset. Otherwise, when activities commence with an environmental focus, it is challenging to later 'scale up' to the more robust challenge of sustainability (Pediaditi et al. 2006). With these challenges in mind, the positioning and substance of the TWRC sustainability framework, in 2005, is noteworthy.

The Sustainability Framework: Purpose, Goals

The TWRC sustainability framework was the product of an eighteen-month collaboration, with stakeholders from the federal, provincial, and local levels of government, the Regional Conservation Authority, academics, consultants from planning, design, architecture, and engineering firms, the public, and a team of experts from Sweden consulted to inform the multiple stages of framework development. External consultants provided leadership for the process. The framework document (TWRC 2005) is publicly accessible and can be downloaded from the corporation's Web site. Seeking to demonstrate leadership internationally, the TWRC drew from other 'world class' cities such as London, New York, and Barcelona for their experiences in waterfront revitalization success. In 2005, the TWRC's mission was '[t]o put Toronto at the forefront of global cities in the 21st century by transforming the waterfront into beautiful, sustainable new communities, parks and public spaces, fostering economic growth in knowledge-based, creative industries and ultimately re-defining how the city, province and country are perceived by the world.'[1] To achieve this mission, the TWRC developed the following vision statement: 'Working with the community, and public and private sector partners, the Corporation will create waterfront parks, public spaces, cultural institutions and diverse and sustainable commercial and residential communities. We will strive to ensure that Toronto becomes the city where the world desires to live.'[2]

In its Development Plan and Business Strategy, the TWRC stated that its leadership on sustainability issues would be *the* defining feature of the revitalized Toronto waterfront. As an illustration, this excerpt from the framework highlights the Corporation's approach to using urban sustainability to drive waterfront revitalization efforts:

> Building a sustainable community means paying attention to several important aspects of revitalization at the same time. It is widely agreed that development is not moving in the direction of sustainability unless it is characterized by:
>
> - achieving exemplar standards of functional and beautiful urban design;
> - minimizing resource consumption and waste production;
> - ensuring that participation in governance is as broad as possible;
> - encouraging innovation that addresses conservation and building technologies;
> - increasing economic opportunity and self-sufficiency; and,
> - focusing on development that supports diversity of all types along with a strong sense of community (TWRC 2005, 1–4).

Recognizing the complex nature of urban sustainability, the framework 'translates general commitments to sustainability into a clear vision, concrete goals, actions and targets' (1–1). The substance and format of the framework were designed specifically to respond to the challenge of integrating sustainability principles into all aspects of the TWRC's operations and work, with the goal of the development of sustainable communities on Toronto's waterfront.

One deliberate omission from the document was a formal definition of sustainability. Instead, the TWRC chose to state that a precise definition was not 'critical' (TWRC 2005, 1–3), opting instead to take advantage of the ambiguity often associated with the concept of urban sustainability. Similarly, Hempel notes that, '[l]ike other transformative ideas, the concept of sustainability promises to remake the world through reflection and choice, but its potential to engage people's hopes, imagination, and sense of responsibility may depend more on strategic uses of ambiguity than on conceptual precision and clarity' (1999, 44). Dale (2001) suggests, furthermore, that the vagueness of urban sustainability is what has kept the idea afloat for so long and that its vague nature has allowed stakeholders with little common ground to remain at the table. The framework's authors, recognizing the complex stakeholder relationships required for implementation, wisely steered clear of a detailed and lengthy debate over a definition that, in practical terms, might have resulted in stakeholders debating whether the three-legged stool or the Venn diagram depiction was more effective (see also Dale, and Robinson and Dale, in this volume). Furthermore, the absence of a definition should not be taken to mean that the TWRC lacked a clear direction. The characteristics of an integrated sustainable community (Figure 4.1) demonstrate the TWRC's vision of sustainability as moving beyond strong environmental performance alone to incorporate elements such as diversity, sense of place, and high-quality design, consistent with what we would now categorize as a third-generation approach.

Another notable element of the framework is the link between goals and action. Five sustainability outcomes were proposed to inform action and delineate the TWRC's positioning of urban sustainability. The first outcome is 'Sharing the Benefits of NetPLUS,' the term used to convey the inclusive notion that the implementation of sustainability principles should deliver sustainability benefits beyond the waterfront district to the city of Toronto as a whole (TWRC 2005, 2–8). Second, the Toronto waterfront should emerge as a 'Global Hub of Creativity and Innovation' (2–9), serving as an international demonstration city for the celebration of cultural diversity and environmental stewardship. Third, the waterfront should serve as an 'Urban Cottage' by providing recreational opportunities, a healthy ecosystem, and an aesthetic break from

---

Sustainable Waterfront Revitalization:

Characteristics of an Integrated Sustainable Community:
- vibrant, diverse, economically thriving community
- efficient use of power, green energy
- green space, green buildings
- green water, wastewater, and stormwater infrastructure
- extra ordinary design
- reuse, recover and recycle land, facilities and waste
- strong sense of place
- transit, bike, pedestrian water access

Figure 4.1. Sustainable waterfront revitalization
Source: Author's adaptation from TWRC (2005).

the high energy of the city (2–10). Fourth, the new waterfront should be a place that 'Feels like Home' (2–11). And fifth, sustainability of the waterfront depends, in part, on '[Ecological and Economic] Strength through Diversity' (2–12).

In the framework, urban sustainability is operationalized through a series of 11 goals, 44 objectives, 99 actions and 28 targets in the following substantive areas: energy, land use, transportation, sustainable buildings, air quality, human communities, cultural resources, natural heritage, water, materials and waste, and innovation. Specific targets were established for each area. For example, '[n]ew buildings must be designed to maximize the longevity of their systems: structural systems, 500 years; plumbing systems, 150 years; and building envelope, 150 years' (3–26). It is noteworthy that the framework balanced short-term measurable outcomes with the goals of long-term paradigmatic shifts similar in intent to those identified by Dale (2001). These more significant decision-making and management-oriented changes are communicated in the framework in a section entitled 'What the TWRC will do.'

By demonstrating that progress towards sustainability must include more than measuring emissions reductions and installing alternative energy and water systems and green roofs (see also McDonald, in this volume), the TWRC distinguished itself from other organizations pursuing sustainability. The TWRC's approach is a decidedly society-oriented approach to implementing sustainability, whereby the management of relationships with stakeholders, the process of making decisions, and the internal management of the TWRC must all be reconsidered in light of proposed sustainability commitments. This emphasis on inclusive relationships and interactive decision-making with stakeholders is consistent with social capital building. While it might be expected that an urban redevelopment sustainability strategy would narrow its focus to quantifiable development-oriented initiatives such as green building standards, the approach of TWRC/WATERFRON-Toronto to sustainability has been as much about state-society relationships as it has been about development outcomes. From the top leadership of the organization through accounting and procurement to expanding current and future staff members' capacity, the framework positions sustainability as a priority. Its proposed plans to internalize the principles of urban sustainability suggest that the TWRC was serious about its commitments in 'walking its talk.' Based on this approach, Dale's (2001) research suggests that the likelihood of the TWRC's succeeding is increased by its efforts to break down 'silos, stovepipes, and solitudes' inherent in institutional and other social systems.

The framework's 'Sustainability Checklists for Project Management, Planning and Design' signalled the TWRC's intention to internalize the principles of sustainability into its decision-making, noting, '[m]anagers have a particular responsibility to ensure that sustainability guidelines are adhered to in all decision-making processes' (2005, appendix 2, 1). The inclusion of the checklist tool demonstrates the TWRC's important recognition that the development of a wide range of decision-making tools is more likely to be successful than an approach that seeks to advance sustainability only through the use of benchmarks and indicators. During its short, three-year existence (2000 to 2003), the City of Toronto's Sustainability Roundtable also experimented with the development of a toolkit for implementation by creating draft versions of tools that included a sustainability capacity audit, a sustainability decision-making checklist for councillors, a sustainability indicators series, and a budget process that would have resulted in a sustainability 'bottom-line' similar to a triple bottom-line approach.

Thus, the TWRC/WATERFRONToronto sustainability framework presents an important integration of outcome-driven and process-oriented approaches to urban sustainability. How does its positioning compare with other sustainability initiatives?

Prospects for the Success of the Sustainability Framework

TWRC/WATERFRONToronto's approach to framing sustainability has built a sophisticated, complex, and integrated foundation upon which the sustainable waterfront revitalization effort is based. As noted, the framework was designed to avoid the tendency to link sustainability primarily with strong ecological principles, instead offering a broader approach that seeks to integrate cultural principles with ecological and technological ones. As I note in an earlier publication, '[t]heir approach is instructive because it links the basic elements of sustainability with design excellence and the processes needed to achieve sustainability being new governance structures and inclusion in decision making' (2006, 14).

When considered in the context of other sustainability efforts at the local scale, the TWRC/WATERFRONToronto sustainability framework is distinctive. First, the inclusion of benchmarks and indicators gives it a precision that other plans lack. Second, the comprehensive nature of the framework stands in contrast to the piecemeal, ad hoc approaches embodied in other responses. Third, the holistic, integrative, and process-oriented nature of the document differs from those with a more segmented approach. While there are efforts in the framework to address equity issues, environmental issues are still dominant, consistent with the range of the aforementioned plans. With the substantive potential of this framework established, a question arises in terms of implementation: what are the prospects for its success?

One method of measuring the success of the framework's implementation would be simply to track the progress made towards meeting its goals. While significant progress would seem to be a strong indicator of success if one uses a goal- or outcome-oriented approach, sole reliance on such accomplishments would fail to shed light on the broader, more complex nature of paradigmatic change. This change includes integrating sustainability principles into decision-making, planning, and implementation, as part of a more process-oriented approach. For example, through technological advances, improvements in air quality and reductions in greenhouse-gas emissions could be measured without any overt corresponding shift in thinking, decision-making, or behaviour by individuals or institutions. If the process by which sustainability is pursued bears relevance to the accomplishment of sustainability outcomes, then we also need new, more process-oriented measures with which to assess the potential for future success.

Previous research suggests the following criteria are prerequisites for progress in implementation and success in the context of process-oriented sustainability (Robinson 2006, 2008):

1 Sustainability principles must be an integral part of the planning, design, and building processes; they cannot be added on at the end.
2 Meaningful citizen engagement is an essential element of any sustainability strategy throughout all phases of project conceptualization, planning, design, building, and operation (see also Hanna and Slocombe, and Dushenko, in this volume).
3 The value of leadership (community, professional, institutional) emerges when early sustainability success stories are examined. Sustainability efforts require a champion for success.
4 A series of buildings with good environmental performance (strong energy efficiency, low-to-zero wastewater discharge, and so on) does not collectively add up to a 'sustainable community.'

Good design is not a natural outcome of projects designed to improve environmental performance, as McDonald illustrates (in this volume).

5 Cookie-cutter approaches to sustainability are less successful than place-based ones; sustainability projects from other jurisdictions cannot simply be inserted into another community (accompanied by a simple name change).

6 An effective strategy must be developed to address the tension between the need to plan effectively and the pressure to produce demonstrable results quickly.

In applying these criteria and evaluating TWRC/WATERFRONToronto's experience to date, what can one predict about the potential success of the implementation of its framework? In the first case, the sustainability framework clearly recognized the need to internalize sustainability principles at all phases of the revitalization process. A 'start-to-finish' approach for integrating the principles is in the framework, but moving beyond the document to practice is the next step. Unfortunately, one of the challenges the TWRC faced in the development of the framework was that planning and design projects were concurrently proceeding while the framework was being developed. Thus, for the earlier projects, the goals, objectives, actions, and targets were not in place for the consideration of the design and development teams. After the public release of the framework, the TWRC required all respondents to Requests for Qualifications to demonstrate prior experience with sustainability initiatives.

There are challenges to infusing sustainability principles in an organization's decision-making processes. In 2005, the TWRC created the position of director of sustainability, which has great potential, but there are other considerations beyond simply creating such a position. Confronted with the task of implementing new initiatives, organizations often consider appointing an expert, advocate, or champion as an agent of change or authority. This option is attractive because it designates responsibility for sustainability issues to one internal catalyst, presenting an active voice in all decision-making processes. For sustainability initiatives to be realized, the champion, expert, or advocate needs to be located within the organization's power structure – reporting, for example, directly to the chief executive officer – and to be supported at the corporate level. With such an approach, however, the organization runs the risk that sustainability initiatives will be perceived as the responsibility of one individual or office, without an acknowledgement or assumption of this responsibility by other people and areas throughout the organization. As a result, efforts to integrate sustainability by institutionalizing responsibility in one position actually may lead simultaneously to both segmented and integrated outcomes.

Another measure of the degree of infusion of sustainability principles into the TWRC and its development plans is the degree to which the TWRC/WATERFRONToronto adheres to the framework in public competitions and plan development stages. The process of reconciling sustainability imperatives is a challenge in the waterfront's revitalization, as developers advocate and lobby for the economic imperative over social and ecological imperatives. Between 1995 and 2005, there was significant weaker adherence to sustainability principles in the planning and development of new communities in Ontario – a result of loosely worded provincial policy statements that provided strategic direction to municipal governments on all land-use planning decisions. More recent policy statements, however, include sustainability-oriented language for which all communities must 'have regard.' TWRC/WATERFRONToronto's willingness to address the competing economic and sustainability imperatives is a strong test of its commitment to urban sustainability.

With regard to the second prerequisite, previous experience suggests that meaningful citizen engagement is imperative to sustainability success. As discussed by both Lister and Dushenko (elsewhere in this volume), citizens need to play a fundamental role in changing paradigms rather than just being consulted about proposed changes. Interestingly, the 'What the TWRC will do' section of the framework makes no explicit mention of the role of citizens in decision-making, yet WATERFRONToronto's Web site does have a 'Public Consultation' link that provides information about upcoming meetings. The framework's policy statement and principles demonstrate, however, that TWRC/ WATERFRONToronto is committed to consulting the public about its revitalization process, and the inclusion of background documentation speaks to the corporation's commitment to transparency.

TWRC/WATERFRONToronto has routinely held meetings to consult the public on its views of new development. In summer 2006, it hosted 'Quay to the City,' showcasing the winning design of the Central Waterfront Innovative Design Competition (TWRC 2006). The corporation spent $900,000 on the ten-day installation, which replaced car traffic with new bicycle lanes, picnic grass, and flower plantings. An outdoor art installation and waterfront trail were also featured, along with a series of events geared to increase public visitation of the installation. Rather than relying on the standard exhibition and lecture detailing the winning work, the corporation allowed the public to experience a taste of what the winning design would look and feel like. Public reactions were documented in two opinion surveys and a local business survey. This innovative approach to public consultation resulted in strong public support for the winning design.

TWRC/WATERFRONToronto's emphasis on consultation, rather than engagement, could be explained in part by the complicated position it holds in being accountable to three levels of government. In Ontario, the provincial government imposes requirements on local governments for minimal public consultation on planning and development matters, while the provincial and federal governments typically rely on stakeholder consultation processes. Accordingly, there may be less of a political imperative to develop creative engagement processes and more of a reliance on standard consultation. As development continues, previous experience, such as the 'Quay to the City' event, suggests that creating new opportunities for citizens to contribute to agenda-setting and decision-making in planning and design would strengthen the implementation of the sustainability framework.

TWRC/WATERFRONToronto's consistent efforts to consult and, at times, to engage the public in constructive dialogue about the future of Toronto's waterfront is noteworthy in light of the intense politics surrounding the development of the waterfront and the long time frame over which this revitalization process is unfolding. The rationale for including citizens in local land-use planning processes is generally driven by both philosophical and pragmatic imperatives. With respect to the former, the effective design and creation of local policy and programs must consider and respond to the needs, concerns, and priorities of those who will be affected, emphasizing the significance of citizen participation in local democratic processes. With respect to the latter, top-down, centralized approaches to local problem solving are less effective than those that emerge from the affected communities (Chaskin and Garg 1997). Planning literature, in general, provides an effective descriptive foundation for the criteria of 'good' citizen participation practices. Consensus planning, a popular approach guiding planner-citizen relationships since the 1960s, places heavy emphasis on the importance of the citizen in the planning process and seeks to distribute power among a wide range of actors (Woltjer 2000). One subset of consensus planning involves a process of collaboration and learning between the planner and the citizen (Innes 1996, 1998; Healey 1997; Woltjer 2000). Planning's recent embrace of sustainability in the context of community planning has internalized elements of consensus-based planning, and this influence is apparent in the following generalized characteristics of 'good' community planning: purpose driven, inclusive, voluntary, flexible, fair, respectful of diverse interests, accountable, time limited, and implemented (Roseland 2005). Yet for all of these good intentions, conflict is a normal and constant element of land-use planning processes.

With respect to the public's role in planning process, Susskind and Field (1996) offer many remedies to responding to an 'angry public.' Their work is diagnostic in its evaluation of the bad behaviours of government and business officials that have resulted in public anger emerging through episodic, reactive inputs into the planning process. WATERFRONToronto has certainly encountered its share of dissent and conflict around development-related issues on the waterfront, but it has made persistent efforts to continue the dialogue about redevelopment.

In the case of the third prerequisite, the role of leadership must be considered when assessing the future potential success of the framework. Robert Fung, chairman of the Board of Directors from 2001 to 2006, was an early advocate of sustainability. John Campbell, president and chief executive officer, has also been a strong public and internal supporter of the sustainability framework, stating, '[w]e want sustainability to define us and be the standard against which we are judged.'[3] And, as noted above, the corporation also now has a director of sustainability. In addition, a Waterfront Design Review Panel was charged with offering its professional advice about the quality of design of new waterfront projects, and included architects and engineers with a strong track record on sustainability projects. This inventory of key WATERFRONToronto actors suggests that there is strong leadership to advance sustainability.

WATERFRONToronto's robust interpretation of sustainability issues has been somewhat at odds with the more generic marketplace equation of sustainability with Leadership in Energy and Environmental Design (LEED) standards (see McDonald, in this volume). The corporation took some steps towards accelerating market transformation through a partnership with Natural Resources Canada, which had developed an integrated design process workshop geared to expanding the capacity of the development community to respond to robust sustainability expectations. WATERFRONToronto also may have to lead in terms of defining, through its requests for qualifications, new partnerships to allow the framework to be implemented. Through the inclusion of partnership-oriented language in its Request for Qualifications and Requests for Proposal processes, successful bidders may need to assemble new groups of consultant teams and build new relationships among developers, academics, professionals, and community and not-for-profit groups in order for a true paradigm transformation to occur.

In the fourth criterion, the positioning of the framework signals that the corporation has avoided distilling sustainability down to the more easily achieved task of demonstrating good environmental performance. With the proliferation of LEED standards, technological advancements in green building technologies (see McDonald, in this volume), long-standing success with financial mechanisms to fund such projects – for example, the Toronto Better Buildings Partnership and the Federation of Canadian Municipalities' Green Infrastructure Fund – and new-found public interest in global climate change, the future for a reduced ecological footprint from built-form exists. Although these advances are important, they cannot be considered, in and of themselves, interchangeable with urban sustainability advances. Green buildings do not necessarily equal excellence in design, nor do they necessarily form the building blocks of welcoming, vibrant communities. The corporation's early participation in the US Green Building Council's Leadership in Energy and Environmental Design for Neighbourhood Development (LEED ND) process indicates that it understands the importance of scaling sustainability to neighbourhood and community levels.

In the fifth prerequisite, Dale's (2001) emphasis on the process of reconciliation of sustainability imperatives reminds us of the need to root sustainability initiatives in the ecological, cultural, and economic conditions of our communities, as community-based sustainability solutions have a stronger potential for success. TWRC/WATERFRONToronto has balanced best-in-show lessons learned from elsewhere with its 'made-in-Toronto' approach. In the collective haste to respond to the challenge of urban sustainability, there is often a temptation to borrow significantly from the efforts of others and then import 'best practices' into new jurisdictions. The framework's authors, however, were clear that they were not interested in this 'cut-and-paste' approach (TWRC 2005, 2–1). Instead, the 'made-in-Toronto' approach required that the framework be in concert with the city's Central Waterfront Secondary

Plan (Toronto 2003a), the Official Plan (Toronto 2006a), the Environmental Plan (Toronto 1999), the Economic Development Strategy (Toronto 2006b), the Social Development Strategy (Toronto 2001), and the
Culture Plan for the Creative City (Toronto 2003b).

Finally, with regard to the sixth criterion for success, one conclusion
that can be drawn from the evaluation of the framework is that time is a
complicating variable in the process of reconciling urban sustainability
imperatives, particularly in the context of urban development. TWRC/
WATERFRONToronto has been criticized routinely that its revitalization process is taking too long (recall the debate in spring 2011 when
Toronto Mayor Rob Ford introduced his new vision for the waterfront;
see Alcoba and Kuitenbrouwer 2011), but previous experience shows
that good planning takes time even without the added complexity of
urban sustainability. Indeed, the framework recognizes that 'sustainability does not happen overnight' (2005, 1–11), and realizes that the
pace of implementation will be affected by knowledge and capacity levels, technology options, partnership opportunities, and the availability
of funding. The corporation's intention to represent 'best-in-show' examples, the desire to be market transforming, and its commitment to
strong consultation are all in potential friction with the public's and
other levels of governments' interest in getting the development ball
rolling. In the end, will the desire to demonstrate leadership slow down
implementation or will it facilitate leadership through the determined
pursuit of ambitious goals? The framework, furthermore, adds a new
layer of complexity to the revitalization process: will political and market pressures to demonstrate progress lead to compromises in terms of
urban sustainability implementation? Or will the integrated, process-
oriented approach to urban sustainability embodied in the framework
build the political capital necessary to allow for robust implementation?

These questions and the associated intergovernmental jurisdictional
battle over the Toronto waterfront prompt one additional prerequisite:
lead institutions must have the political capital necessary to transcend
or mediate the complex multijurisdictional challenges that urban sustainability actions require. This tactical experience and knowledge differs from the third prerequisite of needing 'leadership' in that having
a vision does not necessarily mean the institution has the jurisdictional
authority to implement it. The federal, provincial, and local governments have jurisdictional control over different elements of the framework, and the ongoing issue over the future of the Toronto Island
Airport is an example of the lack of jurisdictional capacity on the part of

WATERFRONToronto, and the City of Toronto to fight a land use that is widely recognized as being fundamentally at odds with the sustainability of the waterfront.[4] Furthermore, all three levels of government have wavered in their political and economic support of the corporation and its goals throughout its existence. If the corporation is able to navigate this complex situation and build the political capital needed to advance, the prospects for urban sustainability on the Toronto waterfront are promising; without this support, implementation will likely be 'watered down.'

How Has the Sustainability Framework Fared?

Given the process by which it was developed, the significant positioning of sustainability within it, and its practical use of benchmarks and targets, the TWRC/WATERFRONToronto sustainability framework had a strong potential to translate ideas into practice. The current status of the framework implementation suggests, however, that an eighth criterion for success is necessary: the use of innovative and progressive plans. Although the framework is readily available on the WATERFRONToronto Web site, accompanied by two implementation-oriented appendix documents,[5] the framework, despite its progressive third-generation positioning, has not found its way into active use within the organization. What accounts for the framework's inactive status?

One explanation emerges from the original allocation of responsibility for the framework's completion. During the corporation's early days, a team of outside consultants was instrumental in developing the framework and managing the corporation's sustainability initiatives. Once the framework was completed, there was a short pause until late in 2005 when the corporation hired its first director of sustainability, responsible for mobilizing its sustainability initiatives. Given that the framework was developed by outside consultants, the new director inherited a sustainability strategy in which they had no hand in developing. This situation sheds new light on the need for connectivity and continuity between process and outcome: in third-generational sustainability practice, the outcome from an earlier process, regardless of its positioning, does not necessarily form an easy starting point for a new process if the conditions (people, the political climate, ecosystem change) change significantly along the way.

A second explanation is evident when we consider the relationship between the framework and other plans and legislation that also

influence development outcomes. TWRC/WATERFRONToronto's creation was the product of three levels of government cooperating on
a revitalization initiative: federal responsibility for inland waters and
ports and building codes, provincial land-use planning, and local government plans and zoning bylaws. There is a multitude of legislative
requirements to which new waterfront plans must adhere. Yet despite
the framework's precise suite of benchmarks, goals, and objectives, it
had no legislative 'teeth.' So even if the framework were in active use,
the corporation would have to be persistent and vigilant in accessing
and aligning the legislative mechanisms with which to bring together
the framework's requirements. To speed the implementation of place-
based outcomes as part of third-generation responses, we need to find
new strategies among these more robust, voluntary, bottom-up plans
to inform and challenge, in progressive ways, the legally binding plans
and restrictive policies that dominate the planning hierarchy.

The inactive use of the framework is not a signal that WATERFRON-
Toronto has stepped away from its pursuit of sustainability initiatives;
other sustainability efforts continue to move ahead. For example, in
September 2009, WATERFRONToronto achieved LEED ND Gold certification under a pilot program established by the US Green Building
Council for development plans on the East Bayfront, West Don Lands,
and North Keating in the Lower Don Lands.[6] Notably, of the twenty-
three Canadian projects that participated in the pilot phase of LEED
ND, WATERFRONToronto was the only one to submit, and be approved, with an affordable housing component. This accomplishment
is important from the perspective of spatial justice when we recall that
across North America sustainability efforts routinely fail to deliver on
equity outcomes (Saha and Paterson 2008). The imperative to include
affordable housing is a strong example of a place-based approach in
light of Toronto's long-standing challenge to provide such housing. Yet,
despite this success, the framework was not used to inform the submission for the LEED ND process.

What can we learn from this experience? Why is the story of a single
governmental agency and its five-year-old progressive, yet seeming-
shelved, sustainability plan worth considering now? One lesson is
that well-defined plans that meet the characteristics of third-generation approaches with good process-oriented prospects for success do
not necessarily translate into plans that inform practice. In 2010, the
implications of a 'robust plan that we're not using' warrants further
consideration in a province in which a flurry of sustainability plan

development is under way, partly as a result of the signing in 2004 of the federal gas tax agreement, which established a 'new deal' for federal-to-local-government transfers of funds in Ontario for the period from 2005 to 2015.[7]

To be eligible for the gas tax transfer, municipal governments must develop plans that advance sustainability principles in community development, a requirement that has led to communities across Canada to develop Integrated Community Sustainability Plans (ICSPs). The potential for these plans rapidly to expand the uptake of sustainability-based planning in Canada is tremendous (de Heer 2010). Moving beyond the federal government's suggestions about how to operationalize sustainability efforts, Ling, Hanna, and Dale (2009) have created a template to inform more robustly the process by which ICSPs are developed and the substance around which they are formed. Their recommendations, if followed, would lead communities to create plans consistent with third-generation approaches. Through a strong commitment to community engagement practices such as community-based mapping tools (see Lister, in this volume), the template seeks to embed place-based approaches in new community development funded by gas tax transfers. These ICSPs, however, have two strong implementation parallels with WATERFRONToronto's sustainability framework. First, in many communities, such plans are being developed by outside consultants hired by local governments; second, there is no legal or binding requirement to implement these plans once developed. Whether the ICSPs will face similar challenges to those seen with WATERFRONToronto's sustainability framework remains to be seen.

Practice Demands a Third-Generation Approach, but Will We Use It?

As Dale tells us in the Introduction to this volume, third-generation approaches emerged from gaps in practice as a means of refining how we position sustainability relative to the goal of accomplishing more robust sustainability outcomes. Yet the experience of WATERFRONToronto demonstrates that an inclusive process with a substantive third-generation plan is no guarantee that the plan will be put into play; similar concerns arise with regard to the ICSP process (see, for example, Canada 2006; Hanna 2007; Ling, Hanna, and Dale 2009). While research in North America thus far has tracked the extent to which sustainability content has been integrated into strategic plans, we need new research that explores how and whether these plans, without legislative standing, can and do actually inform planning, development, and design processes dependent on complex interjurisdictional legislative contexts.

Ultimately, as humans and ecosystems are dynamically co-evolving (Norgaard 1994), we need, in third-generation responses, to continue efforts to transform the political and institutional ecosystems on which sustainability implementation depends. One challenge of sustainability plans is that they can be static policy or strategic planning documents imposed on dynamic ecosystems. The lessons of the TWRC/WATER-FRONToronto sustainability framework illustrate that plans need to be linked fundamentally to implementation processes. Otherwise, sustainability plans that use third-generation responses will suffer from the same problems as second-generation responses in failing to move from plan to action.

NOTES

1 See 'About Us,' http://www.waterfrontoronto.ca/about_us.
2 Ibid.
3 John Campbell, news conference, 27 September 2004, Toronto.
4 For more information about one side of the debate regarding the Island Airport, see http://communityair.org, a Web site hosted by a community group against the continued operation of the airport. For the other side of the debate, see the Web site of the Toronto Port Authority (http://www.torontoport.com/, a federal government agency that is the leading proponent of the airport's future operation and expansion.
5 See TWRC (2005) and the corporation's Web site at http://www.waterfrontoronto.ca/our_waterfront_vision/our_future_is_green/sustainability_framework (accessed 29 September 2010).
6 See the corporation's Web site at http://news.waterfrontoronto.ca/2009/09/waterfront-toronto-achieves-leed-gold-for-neighbourhood-plans/ (accessed 28 September 2010).
7 See the Infrastructure Canada Web site at http://www.infrastructure.gc.ca/alt-format/pdf/gtf-fte-on-eng.pdf (accessed 4 October 2010).

REFERENCES

Alcoba, N., and P. Kuitenbrouwer. 2011. 'Waterfront Toronto is moving too slowly: critics.' *National Post*, 11 April.

Berke, P.R., and M.M. Conroy. 2000. 'Are We Planning for Sustainable Development? An Evaluation of 30 Comprehensive Plans.' *Journal of the American Planning Association* 66, no. 1: 21–33.

Canada. 1992. Royal Commission on the Future of Toronto's Waterfront. *Regeneration: Toronto's Waterfront and the Sustainable City, Final Report.* Toronto: Queen's Printer for Ontario

–. 1996. Environment Canada. 'State of the Environment 1996.' Ottawa. http://www2.ec.gc.ca/soer-ree/English/SOER/1996report/Doc/1–7–5–6–3–2–1.cfm (accessed 1 October 2004).

–. 2006. Infrastructure Canada. 'The Path towards Sustainability: An Evaluation of the "Sustainability-ness" of Selected Municipal Plans in Canada.' Ottawa: Infrastructure Canada, Research and Analysis Division.

Chaskin, R.J., and S. Garg. 1997. 'The Issue of Governance in Neighbourhood-Based Initiatives.' *Urban Affairs Review* 32, no. 5: 631–61.

Dale, A. 2001. *At the Edge: Sustainable Development in the 21st Century.* Vancouver: UBC Press.

Dale, A., and J. Hamilton. 2009. *Sustainable Infrastructure: Implications for Canada's Future.* Victoria, BC: Royal Roads University, Community Research Connections.

de Heer, L. 2010. 'Sustainability in Communities: Conditions and Strategies for a New Planning Paradigm.' Master's thesis, Utrecht University.

Hanna, K. 2007. 'Implementation in a Complex Setting: Integrated Environmental Planning in the Fraser River Estuary.' In *Integrated Resource and Environmental Resource and Environmental Management: Concepts and Practice*, ed. K. Hanna and S. Slocombe. Oxford: Oxford University Press.

Healey, P. 1997. *Collaborative Planning: Shaping Places in Fragmented Societies.* London: Macmillan.

Hempel, L. 1999. 'Conceptual and Analytical Challenges in Building Sustainable Communities.' In *Toward Sustainable Communities: Transition and Transformation in Environmental Policy*, ed. D.A. Mazmanian and M.E. Kraft. Cambridge, MA: MIT Press.

Innes, J.E. 1996. 'Planning through Consensus Building: A New View of the Comprehensive Planning Ideal.' *Journal of the American Planning Association* 62, no. 4: 460–72.

–. 1998. 'Information in Communicative Planning.' *Journal of the American Planning Association* 64, no. 1: 52–63.

Ling, C., K. Hanna, and A. Dale. 2009. 'A Template for Integrated Community Sustainability Planning.' *Environmental Management* 44, no. 2: 228–42.

Norgaard, R. 1994. *Development Betrayed: The End of Progress and a Co-evolutionary Revisioning of the Future*. London: Routledge.

Parkinson, S., and M. Roseland. 2002. 'Leaders of the Pack: An Analysis of the Canadian "Sustainable Communities" 2000 Municipal Competition.' *Local Environment* 7, no. 4: 411–29.

Pediaditi, K., et al. 2006. 'Sustainability Evaluation for Brownfield Redevelopment.' *Proceedings of the Institution of Civil Engineers: Engineering Sustainability* 159, no. 1: 3–10.

Portney, K. 2002. 'Taking Sustainable Cities Seriously: A Comparative Analysis of Twenty-four US Cities.' *Local Environment* 7, no. 4: 363–80.

Robinson, P. 2006. 'Sustainable Design: Framing a Definition.' *Ontario Planning Journal* 21, no. 3: 13–16.

–. 2008. 'Urban Sustainability in Canada: The Global–Local Connection.' In *Environmental Challenges and Opportunities: Local-Global Perspectives on Canadian Issues*,ed. C. Gore and P. Stoett. Toronto: Emond Montgomery.

Roseland, M. 2005. *Towards Sustainable Communities: Resources for Citizens and their Governments*. Gabriola Island, BC: New Society Press.

Saha, D., and R. Paterson. 2008. 'Local Government Efforts to Promote the "Three Es" of Sustainable Development: Survey in Medium to Large Cities in the United States.' *Journal of Planning Education and Research* 28: 21–37.

Susskind, L., and P. Field. 1996. *Dealing with an Angry Public: The Mutual Gains Approach to Resolving Disputes*. New York: Free Press.

Toronto. 1999. *Environmental Plan*. Toronto: City of Toronto. http://www. toronto.ca/council/environtf_clean_green.htm (accessed 27 November 2008).

–. 2001. *Social Development Strategy*. Toronto: City of Toronto. http://www. toronto.ca/sds/index.htm (accessed 27 November 2008).

–. 2003a. *Central Waterfront Secondary Plan*. Toronto: City of Toronto. http:// www.toronto.ca/waterfront/cwp_2006.htm (accessed 27 November 2008).

–. 2003b. *Culture Plan for the Creative City*. Toronto: City of Toronto. http:// www.toronto.ca/culture/cultureplan.htm (accessed 27 November 2008).

–. 2006a. *Official Plan*. Toronto: City of Toronto. http://www.toronto.ca/ planning/official_plan/introduction.htm#print (accessed 27 November 2008).

–. 2006b. *Agenda for Prosperity*. Toronto: City of Toronto. http://www.toronto. ca/prosperity/index.htm (accessed 27 November 2008).

TWRC (Toronto Waterfront Revitalization Corporation). 2005. *Sustainability Framework*. Toronto: TWRC. http://www.waterfrontoronto.ca/ dbdocs/4a1fe4722fcae.pdf.

–. 2006. *Quay to the City: Summary Report*. Toronto: TWRC. October.

Woltjer. J. 2000. *Consensus Planning: The Relevance of Communicative Planning Theory in Dutch Infrastructure Development*. Ashgate, UK: Aldershot.

WCED (World Commission on Environment and Development). 1987. *Our Common Future: Report of the World Commission on Environment and Development*, chaired by Gro Harlem Brundtland. Oxford: Oxford University Press.

5 Towards Walkable Urban Neighbourhoods

LENORE NEWMAN AND LEVI WALDRON

Cities have always drawn people hoping for a new life, fleeing perse-
cution, or seeking adventure, but never before have the numbers been
so high. As noted by the United Nations human settlements program
(2008), half of humanity now lives in urban areas, a figure estimated to
increase in future years. The shift from dispersed agricultural populations to concentrated urban populations has significant implications,
and, as Soja (2010) argues, in this latter stage it has propelled us into
an age of the spatial. This shift suggests that any serious attempt at
building sustainable societies needs to focus on creating sustainable
urban areas and sustainable urban centres. There is, however, a certain
historical uneasiness among many environmentalists towards cities.
Many regard urban areas as part of the larger and problematic process
of industrialism, and yearn for a return to an idyllic vision of life in villages or small towns (Daly and Cobb 1994, 264). Urban areas are composed, however, of neighbourhoods and communities that face similar
issues to those rural areas face, as Dushenko illustrates in this volume.
To suggest that sustainability means the dismantling of cities is neither
realistic nor does it have a historical or theoretical basis (Newman and
Kenworthy 1999, 17). Cities were particularly ill served by top-down
approaches typical of the second wave of sustainable development; it
was a period when excessive regulation hindered ground-up innovation. As noted in the Introduction to the volume, sustainable development at the local or urban scale requires us to consider the intricacies
and uniqueness of place. It is thus not surprising that cities are also
home to many emerging third-wave sustainable development initiatives; cities, as vibrant sites of human activity, are sites for sustainable development. Cities are not simply 'large small towns'; they are

composed of a number of communities facing local challenges, as evidenced by Vancouver's Eastside (see Dale, Chapter 6 in this volume). Again as noted in the Introduction, meaningful, diverse stakeholder inclusion and widespread community engagement are key to delivering an integrated sustainability effort. In an urban environment, this inclusion can occur as niches for innovation are exploited.

Typically, cities pose interesting challenges and barriers for third-generation responses to sustainable development; infrastructure is expensive, so choices can lead to lock-in, and planning regulations can be a challenge for the new and the innovative. The city, however, is where reconciliation of the three imperatives – the social, the economic, and the environmental – is crucial. Urban dwellers often live in socially and environmentally stressed environments and yet, as hotbeds of social innovation, their leadership in implementing third-generation responses is crucial, given their expanding ecological footprints through urban sprawl and their dominance in shaping the global world future. The discipline of urban planning, as discussed in this chapter, has resulted in the unsustainable development patterns found in many cities worldwide. This is changing, however, as shown in the examples discussed here. That said, the critiques provided in the Introduction remain active barriers to third-wave solutions in urban environments; policy alignment is often absent, and there are not yet structures in place to encourage urban sustainable development models that embrace all citizens.

William Rees, creator of the 'ecological footprint,' expressed unease at the city's endless appetite for resources and waste sinks (Rees and Wackernagel 1996); indeed, urban areas survive on energy and material drawn in from the surrounding countryside or, in many cases, other countries. One classic example is food sources, as Weigeldt discusses (in this volume). Despite perceived negative aspects, cities are important from both a cultural and a societal perspective. As best argued by Jane Jacobs in *The Economy of Cities* (1969), urban areas are the crucibles of innovation, the engines of a region's economy. Today more than ever, urban areas are what Florida (2002) calls the 'creative centers' of society – the places where the creative classes come together. Florida, building on Jacobs's 1969 work, argues that such spaces are necessary to turn ideas into concrete products and actions. Ideally, cities are filled with places that are neither home spaces nor work spaces. Cities are public spaces where people can mingle, interact, and bring new ideas into being. Such spaces include parks, cafes, and, in many cases, the streets themselves. Soja (2010) calls these spaces 'third places'; they have also been referred to as cultural edges, or 'zones of social interaction, cross-fertilization, and synergy' (Turner, Davidson-Hunt, and O'Flaherty 2003, 439). This concept builds on Foucault's 'heterotopias' in *Of Other Spaces* ([1967] 1986), in which he argues that the present epoch will perhaps be, above all, the epoch of space. These edge cultures, by their very diversity, not unlike ecotones at the intersection of natural ecosystems, have increased resilience to environmental, social, and economic challenges (Turner, Davidson-Hunt, and O'Flaherty 2003), as well as being incubation sites for new ideas and new solutions to problems. There are many reasons most of these spaces are urban in nature, among which is that cities have the population base to support research institutes, libraries, and universities. They also tend to house a diversity of people, from the young artist to the retired industrialist. More important, what cities have is population density; they are places where a great number of people interact on a regular basis.

Environmentally, however, cities are sites of enormous use of energy and resources, and thus tremendous producers of waste. Though many urban areas are pioneering new waste-control technologies, they remain sites of intense consumption. The sheer scale of material consumption of an average twenty-first-century urban area, and its resulting forms, is an issue for most environmentalists. Under ideal conditions, however, the urban form has its benefits. Rees and Wackernagel (1996) note that density reduces footprint due to smaller living spaces, shared walls, and shorter travel distances. With more people in a smaller area, shorter pipelines, sewers, and transmission wires are required. It has been suggested that population densities in the traditional downtown core and clusters of neighbourhoods outside of it are key to sustainable development (Kenworthy and Laube 1996). On a deeper level, the innovation Florida (2002) describes as being a hallmark of urban society might also be critical to solving our environmental challenges. Jacobs (1969) argued that innovations (such as refrigeration) that revolutionized country living were forged in urban centres. Ironically, the great environmental innovations of the next century might be emerging in a converted industrial district of one of the world's largest urban centres.

If urban areas are the crucibles of innovation, and the engines of a region's economy, as Jacobs (1969) argued, and if population densities in downtown cores and surrounding neighbourhoods are key to sustainable development, as Kenworthy and Laube (1996) suggest, then cities are an ideal laboratory for third-generation responses to sustainability, especially the reconciliation of place, and innovative spatial planning for diverse transportation modes. The ground-up nature of third-wave approaches is reflected in the neighbourhood-by-neighbourhood adaptation that occurs in urban areas. If innovation is indeed largely an urban phenomenon, the reconciliation of sustainable development with space and place in large centres with access to more diverse resources is critical if we are to achieve third-generation responses in this decade. Many barriers to its implementation exist, even with access to greater resources – for example, Weigeldt (in this volume) discusses the difficulty of reintroducing nature and small food production back to the city, never mind tackling a complex problem such as urban sprawl. Changing the extreme separation of uses will require novel forms of social capital building, to identify the solutions, the necessary transition strategies, and financing options for major redesign of our transportation systems.

The design of our space goes far beyond just the built environment; it is an equally strong determinant of the robustness of our social capital. Social capital is highly dependent upon the design of space in human places for connection. Without opportunities and, one could say, random ways to connect with one another and meet in common spaces – for example, in walkable neighbourhoods – we lose the capacity to engage in meaningful dialogue about the shared meaning of community (Etzionni 2000). Without a shared meaning for community, and connection with place, it is hard to achieve consensus on the characteristics of place we wish to sustain. The case study of Toronto's Kensington Market described below illustrates how the neighbourhood's walkability contributed to residents' connection to the community, which, in turn, contributed to the community's collectively identifying the most important characteristics it wanted to sustain and maintain. The reconciliation of place and space involves being in a relationship with place and with one another, as Dale and Dushenko argue in the Conclusion to this volume.

The Automobile Landscape

The experience of urban life is played out primarily at the neighbourhood level. Local factors have a direct impact on life satisfaction (Brereton, Clinch, and Ferreira 2009) – as echoed in urban-rural fringe environments (Mahon, Fahy, and Ó Cinnéide 2009) – and our location and sense of belonging or 'place' is a major way we can influence our happiness. There is a diverse literature on how spaces can be made

Figure 5.1. A lone pedestrian wheels his groceries through a dreary, car-dominated landscape on Keele Street over Highway 401 in Toronto. Levi Waldron

more liveable (Appleyard 1981; Evans and Dawson 1993; Elliott 2008), walkable (Burden 1995; Southworth 2005), and more human in scale (Calthorpe, Fulton, and Fishman 2001); all of these factors have been discussed with respect to urban form. Whether urban areas will be a model, however, for a sustainable society or ecological disasters will be determined, to a great extent, by one major factor: the car. No factor has changed cities more than the increase in the use of the automobile. Since 1950 cities have planned for the greater speeds and space requirements of the automobile, and now it is almost impossible for city inhabitants to navigate without a car or other vehicle.

Interestingly, the smaller-scale structure has also fundamentally changed, with architecture and signs designed to attract the attention of the fast-paced motorist rather than the slow-paced pedestrian (Freund and Martin 1993). The automobile landscape can be sterile and alienating to citizens (see Figure 5.1); as Matsuoka and Kaplan (2008) observe, urban residents worldwide express a desire for contact with nature and with each other, and for attractive environments and recreation areas. Cities designed around cars, however, do not provide such spaces. Automobile landscapes exist fundamentally for anti-urban reasons; they arose to facilitate the relocation of millions of people out of urban cores into suburban landscapes. One of the greatest challenges facing sustainable development is how to reverse this shift.

The car is one of the major impacts on the urban environment. Its social and environmental consequences are far reaching, from the local to the global scale. Vehicle construction is materials intensive and the construction of vehicle infrastructure more so. Large land areas are needed to facilitate car travel, and large expanses of impervious pavement reduce aquifer recharge and, therefore water quality, increase runoff, and worsen the 'urban heat island effect,' as pavement absorbs heat during the day and radiates it at night (Shutes et al. 1997; Crutzen 2004). Runoff from paved areas is a toxic brew of oil, salt, and other chemicals that have adverse effects on water quality. (See Figure 5.2.)

On a global scale, the transportation sector generates 26 per cent of greenhouse gases, and passenger transportation accounts for 60 per cent of emissions from transportation sources, not including emissions related to petroleum refining, automotive manufacturing, or road-building. In Canada's 13 largest cities, over 75 per cent of the greenhouse gas emissions produced by urban transportation are due to personal transportation and, of this, 97 per cent is from private automobiles (National Round Table on the Environment and the Economy 1998). The Ontario

Figure 5.2. Massive road infrastructure and usage, as seen on Ontario's Highway 401, has a global impact. Levi Waldron

Medical Association estimates that the annual health toll of air pollution in Ontario alone is 5,800 premature deaths, 17,000 hospital admissions, 60,000 emergency room visits, and 29 million minor illness days. The associated cost is estimated at approximately $374 million in lost productivity and $507 million to the health care system, with strongly increasing trends in all health and economic impact figures (Ontario Medical Association 2005).

Cars interrupt the interaction between people and their spaces, or what Soja (2010) calls the social-spatial dialectic. Automobile infrastructure also freezes the natural evolution of cities. In a human-scaled settlement, people and their spaces co-evolve in a process that Jacobs (1961) termed organized complexity. Jacobs noted that 'new ideas must use old buildings' (188) and demonstrated how innovators use portions of the existing cityscape to their own ends, rewriting space as they do. A well-planned city is one with a lot of flexibility of use, or what is often referred to as multifunctionality (Brandt, Tress, and Tress 2000; Ling, Handley, and Rodwell 2007). Automobile infrastructure is notoriously unifunctional: once a space has been allocated to cars, it is seldom useful for anything else. In simple terms, people do not like or feel comfortable on the hot bare expanses created by car culture, as shown in Whyte's seminal Street Life project (1980). What most attracts people is other people, and they gravitate to spaces filled with sun, trees, water, food, and seating. Whyte found that spaces need to be comfortable and walkable, and that there is an emerging realization that these spaces also can have a large impact on human health.

Walkability and Health

Historically, car-oriented suburbs were a response to urban health issues (Frank and Engelke 2005). In the nineteenth and early twentieth centuries, North American cities were dirty, with heavy industrial activity taking place adjacent to residential areas. Slum housing was cramped, dark, poorly built, and lacked indoor plumbing and central heating. As this poorly made housing stock decayed, conditions in many North American cities became intolerable. Planners responded in two ways. Legal separation ensured that residential, retail, and industrial uses were not located near each other, and there was a move towards the development of low-density housing at the city's edge, often referred to today as the 'urban fringe.' Many historical factors have driven urban sprawl within communities of all sizes, but the results have been similar everywhere. The combination of low density and separated use was supposed to provide a means for everyone to enjoy country living; however, the byproduct of this way of life has been that those who live in the urban fringe must drive to perform even the simplest of daily tasks.

Car culture and pedestrian culture do not coexist easily. If buildings have sufficient parking for each tenant, the resulting parking lot increases buildings' footprints to the point where walking from place to place becomes difficult. In most North American urban areas, buildings are islands in seas of asphalt, too far from their neighbours to make foot traffic practical. The shift from a walking culture to a driving culture has also had a serious impact on individual health. Good health requires 'active community environments' where people can take part in daily physical activity (Doyle et al. 2006). Before the widespread adoption of automobile use, most people simply had to walk a good distance each day. Obesity has now become widespread, due in part to a lack of physical activity such as utilitarian walking (Frank and Engelke 2005), and research has shown that people in walkable areas tend to weigh less (Doyle et al. 2006).

Urban planning also directly affects health (Frumkin, Frank, and Jackson 2004). Planning for walkable neighbourhoods could greatly improve the mental and physical health of our sedentary population. A major study by Basset et al. (2008) showed that Americans walk only 0.4 km a day on average, while Europeans walked three times as much per day, largely due to differences in the urban form, suggesting that urban planners could contribute to human health and sustainability by creating more walkable spaces. Care needs to be exercised, however, so that the problems that originally drove people out of walkable urban areas are corrected. Laws control the placement of the worst industrial offenders and regulate housing standards, with implications for some forms of local food production (see Weigeldt, in this volume), but vehicles remain a major source of pollution in today's cities. Some researchers have cautioned that higher-density walkable neighbourhoods could reduce air pollution overall, but increase it locally (Frank and Engelke 2005). While tightening emissions standards, limiting vehicle access to local neighbourhoods, or removing those vehicles entirely might mitigate this, the ideal walkable neighbourhood is likely be a car-free one.

Walkability, Social Capital, and Agency

Physical health is only one aspect of sustainable living. Sustainable societies also foster mental health and well-being for all their members. One measure of a society's mental health is its social capital. Social capital can be defined in a number of ways, including the 'social networks and the norms of reciprocity and trustworthiness that arise from them' (Putnam 2000). Dale (Chapter 6 in this volume) notes that Bourdieu (1986) defines social capital as the aggregate of actual or potential resources, which are linked to possession of a durable network of more or less institutionalized relationships of mutual acquaintance or recognition. Communities with healthy levels of social capital might be known as places where 'people look out for each other' or as communities with high levels of 'activism.' As also defined and discussed by Hanna and Slocombe (Chapter 2 in this volume) and Dushenko (Chapter 9), social capital complements the traditional economy and augments government programs and initiatives. Social capital is found in the individual connections and interactions between people, as well as through networks that a group can use collectively to achieve its objectives. Effective mobilization of social capital involves the creation of networks with a sense of common purpose. Networks are a powerful means of distributing knowledge through social interaction and can lead to the reconciliation of previously competing information, interests, and agendas (Dale and Onyx 2005).

For decades, however, opportunities for the growth and development of social capital have been declining in many communities (Putnam 2000). Some of the decline is the result of poor urban planning, which, without due regard for socio-economic considerations, has been shown to destroy or thwart the development of social capital (Frumkin, Frank, and Jackson 2004). As Reuf, Aldrich, and Carter (2003) note, geography matters. If people live within a nuclear family in detached homes and drive in private vehicles to perform even the most basic of tasks, there is no life on the streets, no chance meeting of neighbours, and no interaction at local stores run by people from the neighbourhood. In short, many of the places where social capital is generated simply will not exist. This intuitive assumption is supported by research that finds social capital to be higher in walkable neighbourhoods and that the decline of social capital is directly related to certain forms of suburbanization (Leyden 2003).

Third-generation responses to sustainable development embrace the social as well as the environmental and the economic. To that end, social capital is critical in creating 'agency' (Newman and Dale 2005), which is 'the capacity of an individual or group to plan and initiate action' (Onyx and Bullen 2000). If community groups are to fight successfully for neighbourhoods designed to improve their physical health, agency is needed. Physical and social environments, however, play key roles in agency maintenance and creation (Horvath 1998). In badly designed neighbourhoods, therefore, it is hard to build the agency needed to challenge that design, a 'catch-22' that suggests that neighbourhood action alone is not enough and that planners must play an active and central role in encouraging walkable urban neighbourhoods.

Granville Mall: Planning and the Pros and Cons of the 'Car-free' Street

One of the easiest ways to create a car-free area in an urban centre is to close a single street to traffic or certain types of traffic, creating a pedestrian mall. This method has proven popular in Europe, and is quite successful. Utrecht, in the Netherlands, for example, has several car-free streets in the old city centre that team with pedestrians during the workweek and host a successful farmer's market on weekends. The North American experience is somewhat different. Of two hundred car-free malls established in the United States between 1970 and 1998, half were subsequently reopened to traffic (Crawford 2002). This significant failure rate suggests changes are needed to North American planning approaches and processes for creating car-free areas.

The physical geography of the North American city street might also be a factor. It is well established that pedestrian streets should be narrow, as wide streets lack a sense of enclosure (Crawford 2002). Many North American streets are too wide in this regard, leaving the pedestrian to feel exposed. Geometry in distance might also play a role. As lot size in North American cities is larger than in European centres, the density of businesses per block is lower. Pedestrians thus find themselves walking correspondingly farther. Frank and Engelke (2005) find that distance is the main determinant of whether people walk. Other studies also show that the number of people who will walk is very sensitive to distance – for example, whether someone will walk to a corner store depends on whether it is two hundred or six hundred metres away (Krizek and Johnson 2006). One factor that is often cited as a disincentive to walking is the extreme winter weather found in much of North America. There are many examples, however, of successful walkable neighbourhoods in Scandinavian cities (Kennedy 2008). The difference is in the thought given to designing for the weather (see McDonald, in this volume).

Another weakness of pedestrian malls in North America is that they are not entirely car free. In Vancouver, a downtown core area was designated a pedestrian mall, the Granville Mall, in 1974 in an effort to revitalize the city's once-thriving theatre strip. As part of this revitalization, trees were planted, the street itself was rebuilt as a series of curves to slow traffic, sidewalk widths were increased to seven metres, and a six-block stretch of the street was closed to automobile traffic. The success of the project has been mixed, however, since there are few attractions to draw pedestrians along much of this stretch. Walkers confront the blank wall of an enclosed mall and a major department store, and for many years one block bordered on a vacant lot. As a result, the project did not have the diversity of businesses, residences, or other draws in close proximity needed to revitalize the area. And although the Granville Mall was closed to cars, it was not closed to trolleybuses, of which as many as 1,900 pass daily through the core (Vancouver 2006). Constant bus traffic and few attractions led to a general decline of the area and, in 1988, the city reopened one block to traffic. The attraction for pedestrians in the remaining blocks has improved as more businesses have opened in the area, and the construction of a new transit line might decrease bus traffic in the area, yet the Granville Mall's future success as a pedestrian area remains uncertain. In many ways the failure of the mall as a public space reflects the weakness of first- and second-wave approaches: although traffic flow and urban form were controlled by the municipality, little thought was given to how the project would fit into the broader context of the neighbourhood and the surrounding land uses.

Planning for Walking

Small blocks encourage walking (Crawford 2002), as they create multiple paths between destinations. People tend to walk more where there are more intersections and blocks are shorter (Doyle et al. 2006). Dense networks create three conditions that fuel vibrant urban form: density, proximity, and connectivity (Frank and Engelke 2005). Atypical street design can also aid pedestrian spaces – T-junction intersections, for example, although not conducive to automobile traffic, provide a natural focal point for an area, and also serve to enclose a neighbourhood; studies have shown that pedestrians prefer communities with clear boundaries (Crawford 2002).

Such neighbourhoods, however, are not easy to find in North American urban areas. Many historic districts meet these requirements, but 80 per cent of buildings in the United States were built in the past fifty years (Kunstler 1993). These new developments sprawl to accommodate road and parking infrastructure, as the amount of space absorbed by urban transport systems has a critical effect on urban form (Crawford 2002). Housing also covers a larger footprint – living area per family member, for example, has increased by a factor of three since the 1950s in the United States (Wilson and Boehland 2005). Also, 63 per cent of Americans now live in single-family dwellings (ibid.), a shift that requires vast amounts of land to accommodate. Interestingly enough, much of the original urban infrastructure (including roads) built in the past fifty years in North America is also beginning to fail, either prematurely or as it reaches its anticipated service life expectancy. This presents challenges as well as opportunities for new forms of urban renewal and sustainable design in cities, as discussed further below.

As the unsustainable nature of current planning and infrastructure choices becomes clear, there is increasing interest in patterns that better accommodate higher densities. One such popular model is that of 'smart growth,' which aims to revitalize community in city centres and established communities through mixed use, transit use, and pedestrian spaces (Barnett 2007). Smart growth provides a mix of commercial, business, and retail uses in order to lower commutes and encourage pedestrian traffic. Smart growth also encourages compact building design. Conventional development is land extensive, often to the point of providing insufficient density for local transit and walkability. Increasing density also decreases the ecological footprint through reduced sprawl and lowers service costs, as discussed earlier. Planning is a key driver in reducing the need for a car (Newman and Kenworthy 1999)

Kensington Market: Pedestrianizing Existing Walkable Areas

One recent site of a car-free initiative in Canada is the Kensington Market community in central downtown Toronto, a thirty-five-hectare area bound by major streets carrying streetcar lines. Though well served by public transit, the area is clogged with vehicle traffic, parked cars, and delivery trucks. Two municipal garages providing ample parking encourage people to drive into the area.

That Kensington Market exists at all is rather remarkable, given that it has faced various renewals and clean-up initiatives, and was almost destroyed completely during a period of freeway development in the city. In the 1960s, planners cleared similar areas across Toronto in order to build blocks of planned housing surrounded by 'dead space' – large, pedestrian-unfriendly landscapes – in a process viewed by some as a terrible failure. The Alexandra Park area to the south of Kensington Market was cleared for such a project, and is now run down and quite intimidating, especially at night. Grassroots opposition stopped a similar restructuring plan for Kensington Market at the time, a demonstration of the strong social capital that exists in such neighbourhood communities.

The streets of Kensington Market were not designed for modern automobiles. They are very narrow, with both T-junctions and high volumes of foot and bicycle traffic that slow car traffic. Lot sizes are very small, leading to a high density of two-storey buildings. Usage is mixed; row housing coexists with converted heritage homes that house retail on the ground floor and residential units above. Rents are also low on the whole. The market area encompasses Bellevue Square Park, an urban green space containing a playground that is often a centre of community activity. Cafe life and shop goods spill onto the sidewalks. More important, residents can walk to purchase almost all of their utilitarian household needs. What is not available in the market proper, such as hardware and alcohol, can be purchased on the main streets near the market entrances.

In many ways, Kensington Market is an ideal example of a walkable urban neighbourhood. It is also, however, an example of the damage that cars can do in a confined space. In the past few years, grassroots interest in making the market car free at least some of the time has led to the tradition of Pedestrian Sundays in Kensington Market. This project began in summer 2002 when a group of employees at an area restaurant expressed concerns about the congestion and pollution in the neighbourhood. They also felt unsafe on the streets, as small fender-benders were common. The employees decided to take action, and gathered friends, neighbours, and activists together in an event they called 'Streets Are for People!: A Celebration of Bikes, Pedestrians, and the Idea of a Car-free Kensington Market.' Organizers paid the parking meters along a section of street, and the resulting 'rented' space was used to have a picnic and play music. The impromptu street party ultimately blocked vehicle traffic, reclaiming the street.

Streets Are for People! held a third, larger, and more formal event consisting of a market-wide parking meter party. This revealed a strong polarization of opinions around the idea of a car-free Kensington. Many merchants feared the potential impact upon their business, concerns that have often been raised during the development of car-free areas in Europe. In summer 2003, Streets are for People! met with the organizers of Red Pepper Spectacle Arts, a local community arts organization that had been planning a Harvest Festival for that fall that would involve all the merchants of the neighbourhood in a street festival of food, culture, music, and art. The two groups collaborated on the building of the Harvest Festival, working closely with merchants to gain their cooperation and support.

With the success of the Harvest Festival, neighbourhood stakeholders gained a new perspective on how the streets could be used. Further plans were developed to have weekly street closures during the next summer on Sundays, the day with the fewest deliveries, so as to be the least disruptive to business. A larger working group, 'P.S. Kensington' or 'Pedestrian Sundays,' was formed to pursue the project. The City of Toronto agreed to collaborate on Pedestrian Sundays, and supported the inaugural year with staff and some funding. Unfortunately, as P.S. Kensington became a city-sponsored event held on city streets, the event became subject to a series of municipal regulations. This included requirements for insurance, paid-duty police officers, barricades, and regulated signage for a special event, which increased the financial burden of running Pedestrian Sundays. Despite these barriers, the events were considered successful. At the grand street opening of the first Pedestrian Sunday, urban planner Jane Jacobs spoke of how this was just the way things ought to happen – the community gets a good idea and the city helps to support it.

Despite a first successful year, the project suffered a serious setback the following year when the city decided to distribute a complex and difficult questionnaire. After receiving a handful of negative responses to the survey, the city concluded that the neighbourhood was not in favour of continuing the event. Community organizers argued, however, that this represented a non-response error; many residents did not even know about the survey, while a small number of critics communicated their opposition effectively. Community organizers explored having smaller block parties, just to keep the spirit of Pedestrian Sundays alive, even if they were not allowed to do full market street closures. Following complaints regarding the cancellation of Pedestrian Sundays, community organizers conducted their own survey to examine the level of support for continuing the project. Results indicated even greater support for the project than the previous year, following a few weeks of individual discussions with merchants and many residents. The decision to continue with a second summer of Pedestrian Sundays, however, came too late to apply for grants or funding. Nonetheless, the organizers forged ahead, raising approximately $2,500 per event from local merchants and environmentally minded Toronto residents to run Pedestrian Sundays, while at the same time planning and running the events. The shift to local funding suggests that, despite early misgivings, area merchants grew to enjoy the events and the business they draw to the area.

P.S. Kensington continues to lead a bipolar existence; the events are hugely popular, but are always at risk of being cancelled for lack of funds. Kensington Market is a natural location for a pedestrian-only demonstration project of many key characteristics of walkable communities within cities. These include narrow streets, short blocks, and T-junctions that help to enclose the streetscape, as well as being very well serviced by rapid (public) transit. Even in such an ideal setting, however, the city's planning rules are a central consideration, in that the longer-term survival or expansion of street closures in the market may rest on changes to government regulations that make the events cheaper and easier to continue. Dale discusses this 'path dependence' by institutions, such as governance bodies, and the requirement of unique stimuli to induce endogenous changes, in the Introduction to this volume.

Equity Issues

Walkable neighbourhoods can improve our quality of life. They increase the health of their residents, encourage and are supported by social capital, and eliminate unpleasant commuting that disconnects us from our environment. Given these positives and that such neighbourhoods are scarce, it might be imagined that such areas are in demand and highly desirable. Although this is certainly true, it raises the possibility that, as long as walkable neighbourhoods remain the exception rather than the norm, they will demand high rents and property values.

Little study has been conducted concerning the 'gentrification' of walkable neighbourhoods, whereby deteriorated neighbourhoods are rehabilitated by new, wealthier residents instead of the long-time residents, resulting in increased housing prices and displacement of the latter. Literature on the subject supports the hypothesis that walkable neighbourhoods inevitably gentrify. In Europe, pedestrian zones have been shown to push out lower-class retail in favour of higher-class chain stores (Leyden 2003). Toronto's Kensington Market has recently experienced the pressures of gentrification as several upscale businesses atypical of the market area have opened in the north end of the area, attracting a different demographic than the vintage clothing and grocery stores they replaced. A similar phenomenon could someday impact Vancouver's Eastside (see Dale, Chapter 6 in this volume). If less affluent neighbourhoods pursue projects that encourage walkability, they might find themselves priced out of their own homes as victims of their own success. This effect should decrease as more walkable neighbourhoods are built in a supply-and-demand relationship. It would also be a function of the original nature of the neighbourhood – that is, commercial, industrial, residential, even small-scale agriculture (see Weigeldt, in this volume) or combination – and the values it supports.

Conclusion

The great walkable cities of the world were actively planned either before cars were developed, or with the express purpose of facilitating foot traffic. They developed following patterns dictated by geography and the limitations of the pedestrian before the widespread use of private automobiles. The self-organized city has proven to be a leader in sustainable, liveable spaces. In the urban context, third-generation responses to sustainable development will require a new sort of urban planning that expressly encourages pedestrian spaces. Planning for mixed use, small streets, and human-scaled places must replace the creation of urban forms designed for the automobile. A reconciliation of place and space is clearly needed, indicative of third-generation responses. Projects such as that in Kensington Market bring forward the social imperative of sustainable development and incorporate it into the urban fabric. Unfortunately, the past half-century has led to a catch-22 situation. In consciously shifting our concept of urban landscape to centre on the car, it will now be difficult to create a sustainable space that is immediately walkable even if we limit or create incentives for reducing automobile traffic. Planning rules need to change in order to create neighbourhoods of the right scale for walking. Conscious demand for such neighbourhoods varies. In Europe, 85 per cent of the population supports drastic limitations on cars in cities (Leyden 2003), but such widespread support is not found in North America. This could be a result of what Jared Diamond calls 'landscape amnesia' (2005, 425); the majority of car-oriented North Americans have never experienced the liveability and 'freedom' of a walkable neighbourhood.

The benefits of walkable urban landscapes are clear. Residents of such areas have smaller ecological footprints, are in better health, and enjoy higher levels of social capital. Walkable neighbourhoods, such as the ones discussed in this chapter, are what Newman and Kenworthy (1999) describe as 'urban villages.' They allow for life on a human scale amid the excitement and energy of a global metropolis. These neighbourhood communities reduce the demand for sprawl, while preserving wild spaces and farmland, and may even contribute to the re-integration of small-scale urban agriculture and local food production in such spaces. Walkable urban spaces are also geographies scaled to people. The best way to increase demand for such spaces is to increase the number of them. As beacons in a sea of sprawl, such demonstrations of integrated planning show how third-generation approaches to sustainable development can use niche accumulation – in which small early examples encourage further examples to develop – to test out approaches from the ground up. Access to enhanced infrastructure choices includes greater access to walkability, which, in turn, could increase the demand for denser, more liveable neighbourhood communities in large urban centres.

REFERENCES

Appleyard, D. 1981. *Livable Streets*. Berkeley: University of California Press.
Barnett, J. 2007. *Smart Growth in a Changing World*. Chicago: American Planning Association.
Basset, D., et al. 2008. 'Walking, Cycling, and Obesity Rates in Europe, North America, and Australia.' *Journal of Physical Activity and Health* 5, no. 6: 795–814.
Bourdieu, P. 1986. 'The Forms Of Capital.' In *Handbook of Theory and Research for the Sociology of Education*, ed. J.G. Richardson. New York: Greenwood Press.

Brandt, J., B. Tress, and G. Tress. 2000. 'Introduction to the Conference Theme.' In 'Multifunctional Landscapes: Interdisciplinary Approaches to Landscape Research and Management: Material for the Conference on "Multifunctional Landscapes",' Centre for Landscape Research, Roskilde, Denmark, 18–21 October.

Brereton, F., J. Clinch, and S. Ferreira. 2008. 'Happiness, Geography, and the Environment.' *Ecological Economics* 65, no. 2: 386–96.

Burden, D. 1995. 'Twelve Steps toward Walkable Communities.' Tallahassee, FL: Department of Transportation.

Calthorpe, P., W.B. Fulton, and R. Fishman. 2001. *The Regional 474 City.* Washington, DC: Island Press.

Crawford, J. 2002. *Carfree Cities.* Utrecht, Netherlands: International Book.

Crutzen, P. 2004. 'New Directions: The Growing Urban Heat and Pollution Island Effect – Impact on Chemistry and Climate.' *Atmospheric Environment* 38: 3539–40.

Dale, A., and J. Onyx. 2005. *A Dynamic Balance: Social Capital and Sustainable Community Development.* Vancouver: UBC Press.

Daly, H.E., and J.B. Cobb. 1994. *For the Common Good,* 2nd ed. Boston: Beacon Press.

Diamond, J. 2005. *Collapse: How Societies Choose to Fail or to Succeed.* New York: Viking Press.

Doyle, S., A. Kelly-Schwartz, M. Schlossburg, and J. Stockard. 2006. 'Active Community Environments and Health: The Relationship of Walkable and Safe Communities to Individual Health.' *Journal of the American Planning Association* 72, no. 1: 19–31.

Elliott, D.L. 2008. *A Better Way to Zone: Ten Principles to Create More Livable Cities.* Washington, DC: Island Press.

Etzionni, A. 2000. 'Moral Dialogues in Public Debates.' *Public Perspective* 11, no. 2: 27–30.

Evans, R., and J. Dawson. 1993. *Liveable Towns and Cities.* London: Civic Trust and Grand Metropolitan.

Florida, R. 2002. *The Rise of the Creative Class.* New York: Basic Books.

Foucault, M. [1967] 1986. 'Of Other Spaces.' *Diacritics* 16: 22–7. Reproduced at http://foucault.info/documents/heteroTopia/foucault.heteroTopia.en.html.

Frank, L., and P. Engelke. 2005. 'Multiple Impacts of the Built Environment on Public Health: Walkable Places and Exposure to Air Pollution.' *International Regional Science Review* 28, no. 2: 193–216.

Freund, P., and G. Martin. 1993. *The Ecology of the Automobile.* Montreal: Black Rose Books.

Frumkin, H., L. Frank, and R. Jackson. 2004. *Urban Sprawl and Public Health: Designing, Planning and Building for Healthy Communities*. Washington, DC: Island Press.

Horvath, P. 1998. 'Agency and Social Adaptation.' *Applied Behavioral Science Review* 6, no. 2: 137–54.

Jacobs, J. 1961. *The Death and Life of Great American Cities: The Failure of Town Planning*. New York: Random House.

–. 1969. *The Economy of Cities*. New York: Random House.

Kennedy, J. 2008. 'Winter Walkability.' Presentation to the Federation of Canadian Municipalities Conference, Ottawa, 15 February.

Krizek, K., and P. Johnson. 2006. 'Proximity to Trails and Retail: Effects on Urban Cycling and Walking.' *Journal of the American Planning Association* 72, no. 1: 33–42.

Kunstler, J. 1993. *The Geography of Nowhere: The Rise and Decline of America's Man-made Landscape*. New York: Simon and Schuster.

Leyden, K. 2003. 'Social Capital and the Built Environment: The Importance of Walkable Neighbourhoods.' *Research and Practice* 93, no. 9: 1546–51.

Ling, C., J. Handley, and J. Rodwell. 2007. 'Restructuring the Post-industrial Landscape: A Multifunctional Approach.' *Landscape Research* 32, no. 3: 285–309.

Mahon, M., F. Fahy, and M. Ó Cinnéide. 2009. 'The Significance of Quality of Life and Sustainability at the Urban-Rural Fringe in the Making of Place-based Community.' *GeoJournal*, November. Online First.

Matsuoka, R.H., and R. Kaplan. 2008. 'People Needs in the Urban Landscape: Landscape and Urban Planning.' *Landscape and Urban Planning* 84, no. 1: 7–19.

National Round Table on the Environment and the Economy. 1998. 'Greenhouse Gas Emissions from Urban Transportation.' Ottawa. http://www.nrtee-trnee.ca/Publications/PDF/ BK_Urban-Transportation_E.pdf (accessed 13 September 2009).

Newman, L., and A. Dale. 2005. 'The Role of Agency in Sustainable Local Community Development.' *Local Environment* 10, no. 5: 477–86.

Newman, P., and J. Kenworthy. 1999. *Sustainability and Cities: Overcoming Automobile Dependence*. Washington, DC: Island Press.

Ontario Medical Association. 2005. 'The Illness Costs of Air Pollution.' Toronto: OMA. http://www.oma.org/Health/smog/report/ICAP2005_Report.pdf (accessed 13 September 2009).

Onyx, J., and P. Bullen. 2000. 'Measuring Social Capital in Five Communities.' *Journal of Applied Behavioral Science* 36, no. 1: 23–42.

Putnam, R. 2000. *Bowling Alone: The Collapse and Revival of American Community.* New York: Simon and Schuster.

Rees, W., and M. Wackernagel. 1996. 'Urban Ecological Footprints: Why Cities Cannot Be Sustainable and Why They Are a Key to Sustainability.' *Environmental Impact Assessment Review* 16, nos. 4–6: 223–48.

Reuf, M., H. Aldrich, and N. Carter. 2003. 'The Structure of Founding Teams: Homophily, Strong Ties, and Isolation among US Entrepreneurs.' *American Sociological Review* 68, no. 2: 195–222.

Shutes, R.B.E., D.M. Revitt, A.S. Mungur, and L.N.L. Scholes. 1997. 'The Design of Wetland Systems for the Treatment of Urban Run Off.' *Water Science Technology* 35, no. 5: 19–25.

Soja, E. 2010. 'After Postmetropolis.' Presentation to the American Association of Geographers Annual Meeting, Washington, DC, 14–18 April.

Southworth, M. 2005. 'Designing the Walkable City.' *Journal of Urban Planning and Development* 131, no. 4: 246–57.

Turner, N., I. Davidson-Hunt, and M. O'Flaherty. 2003. 'Living on the Edge: Ecological and Cultural Edges as Sources of Diversity for Social-Ecological Resilience.' *Human Ecology* 31, no. 3: 439–63.

United Nations. 2008. Statistics Division. 'Population of Cities.' New York. http://www.un.org/unsd/citydata.

Vancouver. 2006. 'Policy Report: Transit and Traffic.' http://vancouver.ca/ctyclerk/cclerk/20060418/documents/ub1.pdf.

Whyte, W. 1980. *The Social Life of Small Urban Spaces.* Washington, DC: Conservation Foundation.

Wilson, A., and J. Boehland. 2005. 'Small Is Beautiful: US House Size, Resource Use, and the Environment.' *Journal of Industrial Ecology* 9, nos. 1–2: 277–87.

6 United We Can: A Street Charity that Makes a Difference

ANN DALE[1]

Some neighbourhoods in large urban areas are marginalized, but they have the same need of equitable access to ecological, social, and economic imperatives as other communities. These communities struggle at a different, more basic scale with homeless and poverty, often as a result of addiction and mental health challenges of their residents. Access to the same ecological, social, and economic capital as other urban communities makes the difference between these communities 'getting by' through basic survival and 'getting ahead' and thriving (Dale and Onyx 2005).

Clearly, urban sustainability will not be achieved as long as there are islands of 'haves' representing more affluent communities and 'have-nots' representing more marginalized communities, particularly when the latter are adjacent to neighbourhoods with greater access to basic resources and other amenities. Nor will third-generation sustainability responses be achieved without integrating spatial justice. As Soja notes, '[t]he geography or "spatiality" of justice is an integral and formative component of justice itself, a vital part of how justice and injustice are socially constructed and evolve over time' (2010, 1). Third-generation sustainability responses place a renewed emphasis on both place (Dale, Ling, and Newman 2008) and equity, captured in the concept of spatial justice (Pirie 1983; Foucault [1967] 1986; Dikec 2001; Soja 2010). Nowhere is the effect of distributional inequality more evident than in Vancouver's Downtown Eastside, often depicted as one of the most marginalized communities in Canada. This dubious distinction is not a contest that any city in the twenty-first century would want to win; paradoxically, Vancouver is described as one of the top five most liveable cities in the world (Mercer 2010).

A community's ability to mobilize collective social capital through bonding, linking, and vertical connections determines its capacity to improve its economic status, one of the imperatives of sustainable development (Robinson and Tinker 1997; Dale 2001). More marginalized communities, however, differ significantly in their capacity for action, and one critical necessary and sufficient condition may be the building of agency prior to the mobilization of social capital (Newman and Dale 2005).

United We Can, created in 1995, is a unique social enterprise formed exclusively around the needs of homeless people to earn a living recovering recyclables from garbage bins, known in Vancouver as 'dumpster divers' or 'binners.' It is a successful example of how a marginalized urban neighbourhood can mobilize collective social capital to increase access to greater economic opportunities.

What factors have contributed to the observed success of United We Can, and can they be replicated in similar communities defined as 'marginal' in large urban centres? This chapter is informed by the results of a three-year detailed case study of United We Can, entitled *Social Capital and Sustainable Community Development*, funded by the Social Sciences and Humanities Research Council of Canada (SSHRC). The case study focuses especially on third-generation responses in marginalized communities. Given the focus on the question of whether this success is replicable elsewhere, the case study is unusually detailed in order to offer lessons that decision-makers, planners, academics, and public servants may choose to apply to their cities. It also demonstrates the important role that agency can play in mobilizing social capital.

Urban Sustainability and the Social Imperative

Social capital, as first defined by Bourdieu (1986, 248), is 'the aggregate of the actual or potential resources which are linked to possession of a durable network of more or less institutionalized relationships of mutual acquaintance or recognition.' He further argued that social networks are not a given, but must be constructed through investment strategies oriented to the institutionalization of group relations, usable as a reliable source of benefits. Putnam (1993, 167) defines social capital as 'those features of social organization, such as trust, norms and networks that can improve the efficiency of society by facilitating coordinated actions.' Onyx and Bullen (2000) explain that social capital consists of networks, reciprocity, trust, social norms, the commons, and social agency. As discussed in the Introduction to this volume and in other chapters (see, for example, Dushenko, Chapter 9; and Lister, Chapter 3), consensus is growing in the literature that social capital represents the ability of actors to secure benefits by virtue of membership in social networks or other social structures (Portes 1998). From another perspective, social capital involves bridging 'structural holes' within society (Burt 2003). In this chapter, social capital is defined as the norms and networks that facilitate collective action (see also Woolcock and Narayan 2000), focusing on the relationships within and between them (Schuler 1996), and the ability of actors to secure greater access to resources because of that social capital. Third-generation sustainability responses explicitly recognize that the mobilization of social capital is critical to the widespread diffusion of sustainable development (Dale and Newman 2005; Dale and Onyx 2005) and social innovation.

A network is composed of actors connected by ties; different ties create different networks (Borgatti and Foster 2003). Many researchers also refer to such networks as social capital, and suggest that an increase in the amount of social capital formed by increasing the size and density of networks will have positive effects on a community (Dale and Onyx 2005; Newman and Dale 2005). Network structure can create enabling conditions for the mobilization of social capital within communities and for people to feel empowered to act (Dale and Sparkes 2008). These effects, however, are often influenced by other factors, notably government policies, and it may be critical for the latter to establish a stable environment within which organizations can sustain and increase the scale of their operations (Dale and Newman 2010). Quite often, the concrete implementation of sustainable community development in third-generation responses is a confluence of political leadership, enlightened governance, and novel network formation, as demonstrated in this case study and others.[2]

Research has also distinguished between 'bonding' and 'bridging' social capital (Narayan 1999; Onyx and Bullen 2000; Putnam 2000; Woolcock 2001). Bonding social capital refers to relations among family members, close friends, and neighbours in closed, interpersonal networks. These networks, by their very nature, however, often lack diversity. Bonding social capital is characterized by dense, multifunctional ties and strong, but localized trust as typified by culturally based communities in urban centres. Meanwhile, bridging social capital connects people (or bonded groups) who share similar demographic characteristics. Bridging social capital may facilitate access to resources and opportunities that exist in one network to a member of another. Thus, such capital can 'connect' people across diverse social cleavages (Putnam 2000), and institutionally across otherwise isolating 'silos' and stovepipes brought on by often narrow and rigidly defined governmental mandates and perspectives (Dale 2001). Bridging social capital can also be characterized as a benefit that allows actors to bring about critical social changes (Newman and Dale 2005). Vertical social capital can be viewed as the ability to link with decision-makers and political leaders to increase access to financial capital and, in some cases, for policy decisions critical to increased sustainable community development. Elements of vertical social capital across different political spheres are also discussed in other chapters of this volume (see, for example, Hanna and Slocombe, Chapter 2).

Agency is the ability to respond to events outside one's immediate sphere of influence to produce a desired effect (Newman and Dale 2005). It is the 'intentional causality and process that brings about a novel state of affairs which would not have occurred otherwise' (Bhaskar 1994, 100). While networks can build social capital, previous research has indicated that agency, at both the individual and collective levels, is needed to mobilize this social capital for sustainable community development (Dale and Onyx 2005). Both agency and social capital must be available in a community to affect meaningful change (Krishna 2001) and to respond to impacts external to a community, often beyond the control of the community to predict. This is also observed in the case of rural communities that mobilize to seek a more effective governance model for sustainability in response to annexation by an external urban centre (see Dushenko, Chapter 9 in this volume). Agency is the key indicator of a group's ability to respond to and identify cohesive solutions to sustainable development challenges (Newman and Dale 2005). Individual agency may be more fungible in marginalized communities, and, therefore, any outside investment in these communities must contemplate building long-term and stable relationships aimed at nurturing the self-organizing properties within the community. Communities achieve agency through a dynamic mix of bonding and bridging ties (Newman and Dale 2005).

The Neighbourhood: Vancouver's Downtown Eastside

The men and women I work with have had every possible negative consequence visited on them. They've lost their jobs, their homes, their spouses, their children and their teeth; they've been jailed and beaten; they've suffered HIV infection and hepatitis and infections of the heart valves and multiple pneumonias and abscesses and sores of every sort. They will not, until something spontaneously transforms their perspective on life, abandon their compulsion to use drugs. The question is only this: How shall we, as a society, respond to their predicament?

– Gabor Mate, a Vancouver physician
(quoted in the *Globe and Mail*, 9 February 2005)

Despite the millions of dollars poured into Vancouver's Downtown Eastside over the past two decades, addiction rates and the level of destitution have continued to increase (Greater Vancouver Regional District 2000). The Downtown Eastside continues to be the centre of the injection drug use epidemic in Vancouver, and disparities persist between area residents' health status and that of other Vancouverites and people in the rest of British Columbia (Buxton 2003). With such marginal outcomes against expenditures, it is surprising that governments at the municipal, provincial, and federal levels are not questioning this failure, the barriers, and how money can be employed more effectively in such communities in need. Between May and September 2004, over two hundred men died in this neighbourhood, most quietly and desperately during the night. In any other community, this would be considered an epidemic; yet it is a simple fact of life in the Downtown Eastside. Compared with British Columbia as a whole, and taking into account the age of the population, this neighbourhood has significantly more observed deaths from all causes than expected (Buxton 2003).

The homeless experience is a vicious cycle of poverty escalation. Unemployment rates, inadequate income, and difficulties with income support have been well documented as contributing factors of people cycling in and out of homelessness (Eberle et al. 2001). In a study of at-risk homeless people, 21 per cent reported being unemployed (Greater Vancouver Regional District 2002). Among those shelter users surveyed, 38 per cent had no current income and only 20 per cent were receiving any welfare support (Tolomiczenko and Goering 1998).

Research Methodology

The research objectives of the three-year SSHRC study were to characterize the properties of networks that generate social capital and of network formation, and to analyse the mechanisms by which social capital contributes to sustainable development. Case study research was chosen as an appropriate methodology because a holistic, deeper investigation was needed (Feagin, Orumund, and Sjoberg 1991) to provide an in-depth discussion of relationships and processes (Denscombe 1998). Five communities were studied in depth, and United We Can was selected to study the role of social capital and network formation in a marginalized community. Purposive sampling and snowball sampling techniques were used to identify interviewees. In-depth interviews were conducted over a three-year period with United We Can's first founding executive director and leader, current board members, the premier of the province at that time, provincial civil servants involved in waste-management policy, private sector representatives, and initial funders.

United We Can: The Genesis

United We Can was founded on the belief of its founder and first executive director, Ken Lyotier, that, in a capitalist economy, access to an economic livelihood is a necessary first condition to attaining individual agency. Other researchers from Vancouver (CS/RESORS 1989) have concluded that employment services for homeless people need to consider helping their clients find housing, emotional counselling, health care, and recreational opportunities. United We Can fulfils the first step in a process of personal reconciliation, engendering economic agency in the Downtown Eastside community and largely independent of any government-sponsored social assistance agencies. This is accomplished by providing employment to people who normally would be considered unemployable, along with flexible working conditions that accommodate a variety of mental and physical conditions unique to the community's residents.

In a short period of five years, United We Can evolved from a loose, ad hoc network of disadvantaged community members into a thriving business enterprise and an increasingly healthy community of workers engaged in providing an essential service to their broader community. As David Driscoll, executive director of the VanCity Community Foundation, recalls, '[t]hey had been scavenging in dumpsters and storing the stuff in their rooms. Their landlords and other tenants in the building were not pleased seeing the growing junk piles' (Caledon Institute of Social Policy 1996, 8).

Prior to the creation of United We Can, dumpster divers were very individualistic and hidden, regarded as the 'lowest of the low' in the community; they operated at night, diving into the big blue garbage bins hidden in the back alleys of downtown Vancouver for recyclables to return to retailers for cash. Owned and operated by the Downtown Eastside dumpster divers or binners, the seeds of the initial recycling depot originated in community resentment and their sense of social injustice around the fairness of retailers. This generalized resentment stemmed from their difficulties in getting retailers to take back recycables, even though Vancouver had a bottle deposit system in place, which spoke to the biases and inefficiencies of the system. In the words of one binner, 'I really don't like it when I go to the store with my empty bottles and they make me buy chewing gum with the money.'

Aside from being averse to having street people come into their stores, many retailers did not have the storage space for the recoverables and equally resented taking back items they did not personally sell. There was also general resentment in the community about the various agencies working to help the Downtown Eastside community. These agencies were very professionalized and, although dominated by well-intentioned people, their professionals were not from the community, did not live there, and did not have a deep understanding of the street dynamics. They were also disconnected from their 'clients' in another basic way: they were an elite bureaucracy controlling how the money flowed, and many were earning a good living from the business of poverty. 'When you are on the bottom, no matter how much the people care who are trying to help, there is a disconnection when they are so fundamentally different and live such different realities than their "clients".'[3]

In 1992, Ken Lyotier and a fellow binner decided to do something about their resentment, and convinced a local church, First United Church, to donate $150.00 to organize a one-day bottle depot in a local park, Victoria Square. The goal was to pay street people to bring in empty cans and bottles, which, at that time, were non-refundable. By organizing this event around a basic issue affecting dumpster divers, the community leaders hoped to highlight the issue publicly. Until then, there was little awareness of the dumpster divers' work, as it was a covert activity viewed by others in the community as distasteful. Small handbills were drawn up and posted on the blue garbage bins and distributed in welfare and food bank lines, the Salvation Army, and other places frequented by the dumpster divers.

The initial one-day bottle depot in Victoria Square attracted divers who lined up along the park and spilled onto the street with shopping carts full of non-refundable bottles and cans. Each person was paid up to $10.00 for his or her non-refundables. The event was a huge success in terms of both its outreach to the 'diver' community and the volume of bottles and cans recovered, even though the organizers had to pay a truck to haul away the 'garbage' in the end. The local media also heavily publicized the event. The fairly new provincial government, led by Premier Mike Harcourt, announced an expanded deposit refund system for beverage containers, which was subsequently critical to the capacity of the organization to achieve greater economic viability.

One unanticipated result of the Victoria Square depot was that the people who had been 'hidden away' working individually in alleyways and sorting through garbage became connected through the success of the event. They also wondered whether there was anything more that could be done. The provincial government, through the human resources ministry, approached the community organizers to learn more about what had happened, and proposed bringing in consultants to organize community workshops. The community organizers suggested instead that the information should come directly from the divers themselves, as paid consultants for their time. Again, street people lined up for the workshops at local community centres and had much to share with the government officials, as they knew the community and the business first hand, as well as its challenges. This also illustrates the emergence of vertical social capital, described earlier, where street people were afforded the ability to link to and access decision-makers in the hope of influencing policy decisions critical to the sustainable development of their community.

The critical learning for the binners from these workshops was the realization that they could create their own deposit system and form networks. Although there was no further money to hold another one-day depot, a small number of people continued to meet regularly to discuss how they could start their own not-for-profit society. Ken Lyotier paid for pizza at the meetings, from his successful earnings as a diver. Although this might seem fairly trivial, it was important for bringing people to the table for bonding social capital. Over time, an increasing number of people were attracted to the meetings and, over five years, the initial core network grew to become a legal non-profit organization.

Following incorporation the group approached VanCity Community Loan Fund, a community savings cooperative, for a line of credit and eventually secured $12,500 from VanCity itself and $12,500 from a benefactor. United We Can was established as a formal depot in 1995, with Ken Lyotier as its first executive director and manager.[4] The operating principle behind the organization was that only less-advantaged people who would never get hired by anyone else would be hired and that there would be no exclusions because of addiction or health issues. This is the innovative feature that demarcates this organization from other social enterprises, such as those supported by government. In that first year, 4.7 million containers were recycled, putting $360,000 back into the community through handling fees. During this start-up phase, the provincial government provided critical support by paying rent and the initial wages of the men and women involved.

There were several operational difficulties in the first years. One was encouraging members of the community to become involved; to overcome this, Lyotier actively knocked on doors and convinced people to leave their rooms. Another difficulty was that businesses in the area were losing money on recycling since the bigger volumes became, the more money was lost, as the handling fees did not cover the costs of collection.

In 1998, the provincial government brought in new regulations to include juice and water containers, and in 1999, added poly-coated containers, which allowed United We Can and other recycling entities to begin to make money. Since United We Can banked all revenues, over time it became self-sustaining, which proved to be a key strategy when, in 1999, government funding was withdrawn. Financial stability also augmented the community group's legitimacy when trying to persuade other funders to support the organization through some lean times.

Over time United We Can has evolved from a loose ad hoc network into a thriving social and economic enterprise with an underlying environmental mandate in redirecting waste streams. Today, the organization employs thirty-three people full time, most of whom had not been previously employable. The enterprise's annual revenue is $1.6 million. On average, between more than seven hundred street people come through every day, three hundred of whom are core binners. United We Can processes more than 16 million cans and bottles a year (see Figure 6.1).

United We Can currently has four other business streams in development. Collection Services, with the use of truck and tricycle hauling, is now offering container collection directly from larger volume commercial and residential consumers in the downtown area. Bike Works

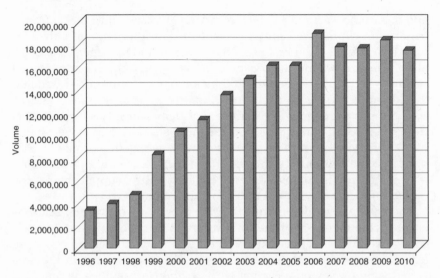

Figure 6.1. Recyclable Volumes, United We Can Bottle Depot, 1996–2010
Note: These figures reflect only beverage containers, non-alcohol and some alcohol, and do not include beer bottles or beer cans, which are also collected by United We Can.
Source: Encorp Pacific (Canada).

provides qualified instruction, sales, and repair tools for low-income residents and depot users who need to maintain their bicycles. Bike Works also maintains a fleet of bicycles for small-scale local pickups. The Bintek Computer Lab involves the recycling of computer equipment, which helps to alleviate the impact of computer obsolescence on the waste stream in support of ecological capital. By acquiring computer parts salvaged out of dumpsters and combining these with outdated components received by donation, the Lab rebuilds consumer-ready systems, which are then sold at affordable prices to low-income residents. A retail plant offering, Happy Plants – originally created by Giovanni Fasciano, later another victim of the Downtown Eastside – takes plant cuttings rescued from the garbage, grows them into larger plants, and essentially 'recycles' them for sale to the wider public. A fourth business stream, the Crossroads and Lanes Community Clean Up campaign, reclaims city lanes and makes them vital links in the urban landscape.

Although the recovery rate for recyclables increased dramatically in Greater Vancouver from 25 per cent in 1994 to 45 per cent by 2004, there is no direct evidence that this can be attributed solely to United We Can. Nonetheless, it is undeniable that the organization has made a significant contribution to reducing the waste stream in the Downtown Eastside, and it has done so through the recovery of recyclables that would not have been recovered even with a conventional deposit system in place.

Evolution from a Network to a Socially Responsible Enterprise

A government-led workshop organized with the leaders of the one-day event and people from the community as advisors evaluated the outcome of the one-day depot held in Victoria Square. Basically, they concluded that the event had been successful because the people from the community understood the nature of the issues in their own community, the event was self-organized and led by the community, and there had been significant media coverage. At the same time, there was a change in government and, in 1991, the province announced expansion of the deposit refund system for beverage containers. As a result of the Victoria Square depot, people previously hidden away, started to connect (novel network formation) and community members began to feel good (agency) about what they were doing. Challenges were evident in the five years it took for the loose ad hoc group of people to organize and obtain legal status, during which time the executive director used his capacity for bridging and vertical social capital extensively to build the organization.

In addition to the expansion of the recoverables system, a number of players (and associated social forces) helped the organization's evolution from ad hoc group to a social enterprise, including VanCity Community Loan Fund (financial capital), which provided the initial line of credit, the provincial government, which paid the rent and salaries in the first years of operation (vertical social capital), enabling changes in recycling policies (governance) and Encorp, a waste management agency, which pays fees to more than two hundred companies to collect, handle, transport and process containers through depot licence agreements. The latter, in particular, has been a critical source of vertical social capital for United We Can. In addition to paying handling fees to United We Can, Pacific (Canada), hereafter referred to as Encorp, has provided financial and logistical support (bridging social capital), including operational tours of other depots, including in Alberta. It has also provided financial support for the Urban Binner utility cart and other activities.

Community members have continued to be committed to the enterprise, which has now evolved into a community of people trying to help one another through their daily struggles – another form of bonding social capital. Although problems of dislocation have not been solved, economic self-sufficiency has ensured that the divers and binners community is at least included in the economic mainstream. Clearly, what the binners had not been able to accomplish as individuals, they were able to accomplish through network formation, by having a common place, and a non-judgmental space. The people associated with United We Can have developed a sense that they belong to a community (place), that they have connection (bonding social capital) to something other than just themselves, and that they have meaning. Individual agency is enhanced when people feel they can make a contribution, which then engenders healthier relationships with the people from whom the Downtown Eastside needs help. Building healthier relationships with those in decision-making authority (vertical social capital) enables both parties to discover the diverse and direct resources needed to reconcile the social imperative fundamental to ecological and economic imperatives; in turn, equitable access to these three imperatives is fundamental to the implementation of sustainable development (Dale 2001).

All interviewees confirmed that Ken Lyotier's personal leadership was crucial to maintaining the loose ad hoc network and in building social capital and a collective sense of community in the Downtown Eastside. As a young boy growing up in one of Vancouver's more established communities, he wondered, when driving through the Downtown Eastside in the middle of such an affluent city, why people were in this state. Somehow it did not seem right that people were so visibly poor. When he became a resident of the Downtown Eastside, he continued his desire to understand how the area worked and how it could be made better. His leadership was thus born out of a deep sense of social justice and, as a resident, out of resentment about how badly the recovery system was working.

> At one of the soup kitchens, I had an epiphany, finally having a sense of belonging, a place where I fit in, where I had meaning. Consequently, I became involved in several projects attempting to involve people from the community, from helping to save a church, to social housing, needle exchanges, and as my disconnectedness decreased, I began to clean up. If you believe it is possible to change, and you act on that belief, at the very least you open up the space for that to happen and in the action, things begin to change. This belief in the possibility of change and that things can happen in ways that are beyond the individual are critical to individual

agency. I began to ask myself how do you make a place where that can happen together?

As a very successful dumpster diver, there is an incredible wealth in the garbage, as an incredibly addicted society we squander so much, consume so much, it is the same as a hole in someone's arm. The straight person is trying to make something fill the gap in them that will not fix the hole over the long term; it is a kind of dislocation. The gap is that we are dislocated as a society, the person in West Point Gray is grateful it isn't happening in their lane, but it is happening there nonetheless. The rest of society projects that the troubled parts of our society are over there behind the door that opens into the Downtown Eastside of Vancouver, where people with difficulties end up concentrating where they can find some grudging tolerance and acceptance, although they don't fit well there either, but it is better if you fit a little than not at all. How do you get to another place that is better from where we are?[5]

In this particular community, at critical points, the timing of key external resources was catalytic to the group's evolution from a loose ad hoc network to a non-profit social enterprise, with respect not just to access to financial capital but also to government policy direction, which facilitated the organization's capacity to realize significant profits through the expansion of the recoverables program. As the Greater Vancouver Regional District (GVRD) plans to overhaul its solid-waste-management plan at some point, timing may again be propitious, to provide direction for additional product stewardship initiatives by the province and resultant revenue opportunities. The GVRD has also embraced the Sustainable Region Initiative to guide a regional approach to sustainable community development. United We Can and other local community groups have used the exposure opportunity of the 2010 Olympics to highlight many urban public policy challenges, notably access to affordable housing. If the momentum from these and other activities is used to develop strategic partnerships between government agencies to integrate social, environmental, and economic policies in organizations such as United We Can, the outcome may well exceed what any one government department with a limited mandate could achieve in isolation, reflecting the integrated decision-making more typical of third-generation responses.

Prior to the United We Can initiative and other locally derived and led projects, the government model of directing significant funding through government agencies working in silos and stovepipes (Dale

2001) had not alleviated problems of addiction, poverty, and home-lessness. Indeed, levels of addiction worsened, poverty became more intractable, and homelessness systemic. What does this government model and the United We Can case study reveal about the dynamics of urban poverty and the implications for third-generation responses? The lack of success of the government model suggests that solutions through external agency intervention alone are not working. United We Can's success was strongly reliant on the Downtown Eastside residents' self-determination and self-organization in finding their own solutions. The community identified the problems, and solutions came from con-nections made within the community, not from social service profes-sionals or external expertise. Agency – the ability to respond to events outside of one's immediate sphere of influence to produce a desired effect (Bhaskar 1994) – occurs within a community, and is a necessary *a priori* condition for social capital to occur (Dale and Sparkes 2011). Sustainable community development can be realized only by recogniz-ing that agency in these kinds of neighbourhoods must be achieved by capacity derived from within, and from the different, often complex social capital dimensions that result.

As Hanna and Slocombe (Chapter 2) and Dushenko (Chapter 9) also demonstrate in this volume, governments need to work in strategic part-nership directly with groups such as United We Can and its employees in order to optimize the self-organizing properties and strengths extant in communities. However, it requires robust, effective, and inclusive governance to enable such possibilities to occur and thrive. United We Can demonstrates two key features of success in a marginalized com-munity. The first necessary step is to increase the connections among people in the community and then to reach out to increase access to more resources. The second critical step is to scale up such enterprises and enhance their sustainability through progressive policy interven-tions directed at enhancing social capital and, thereby, collective social agency.

Agency in Context with Urban Sustainability

United We Can is a leading example of how to create agency and rebuild social capital in some of the more marginalized sectors of our society. An effective way of accomplishing this is by facilitating or 'seeding' self-organization by the members of the community themselves, in-stead of having the solution decided upon and imposed from outside the community. There are, however, place, space, and time elements to the rebuilding of social capital unique to the marginalized. In this case, the 'space' was created by a strategic partnership with the private sector and the need to generate more recoverables from the waste stream, while the 'place' was created by outside seed money at a critical stage in the evolution of the group.

This case also illustrates a social network that uniquely integrates the ecological, social, and economic imperatives for its sustainable community development. It is a concrete example of integrating the three imperatives, by reducing waste through recycling (the ecological), creating jobs (the economic), and thereby augmenting individual agency (the social), all accompanied by a strong and rare element of individual leadership. The transition of this organization from a loose ad hoc network of homeless men and women in the Downtown Eastside of Vancouver to a social enterprise also illuminates the importance of moving from bonding social capital to bridging social capital. This has resulted in the development of a critical mass via network formation that has become a successful organization. Everyone is dependent upon the community to become more than the sum of its parts, and thus to reduce the unsustainable islands that disconnect all of us from what is essential for our future sustainable development.

From a governance perspective, the case study illuminates the following critical policy implications.

1 Marginalized people lack a connection to community.
2 This disconnection from community is a vicious cycle, exacerbating individual challenges.
3 Marginalized communities often lack critical networks to allow them to improve their situation.
4 Access to bridging social capital is critical to marginalized communities and is built through *a priori* network formation.
5 Individual agency is a necessary and sufficient condition before successful network formation and increased social capital can occur.
6 Creating agency takes time, during which governments can help by providing funding support and opportunities for self-organizing activities.
7 Governments can play a key role in facilitating access to vertical social capital through more integrated policy implementation.

8 The timing of government interventions is sometimes essential in making the difference between 'getting by' and 'getting ahead.'

Urban sustainability will not be achieved if 'communities of disconnection' continue to coexist, with increasing disparities of access to critical resources and lack of integration of the social perspective in policy development. As the federal government-sponsored Policy Research Initiative has noted, '[u]nder a social capital perspective, emphasis is placed on finding the most effective ways in which citizens, service delivery agencies, institutions, and organisations interact and create linkages for developing sustainable changes in the living conditions and well-being of community members' (2005, 17). On the basis of my own research in this and other communities in Canada, this perspective is critical to third-generation sustainability responses – in particular, spatial justice. Clearly, the dumpster divers obtained far greater benefits for themselves individually and collectively by virtue of membership in the social network built and led by its founding executive director, its resultant social capital benefits through direct access to vertical social capital, such as Encorp, and changes in provincial legislation. For marginalized sectors in a community or even a marginalized community in and of itself, a social capital perspective must have a particular focus on agency at both the individual and collective levels. Third-generation sustainability responses recognize that the operation of norms and networks at the local level make an empirically demonstrable difference to economic and social outcomes (Onyx and Bullen 2000) and are a precondition for political stability and effective government (Putnam 1993; Cox 1995).

Conclusion

The implementation of sustainable community development is often dependent upon the right place, space, and time, and governments are now responding with place-based policy-making, a key component of third-generation sustainability responses, as well as taking broader systems perspectives. A systems perspective in this particular case study would be for the City of Vancouver and the GVRD, in partnership with Encorp, to implement a comprehensive, integrated approach to waste diversion that also considers aspects of spatial justice, by mainstreaming the binner economy into a comprehensive and inclusive urban strategy for waste management. This is an unparalleled opportunity to showcase integrated decision-making for sustainable community development. It also shows how the costs and benefits of such an integrated system potentially could ameliorate multiple bottom-line government social and economic objectives across government delivery services in the Downtown Eastside community. For example, the Crossroads and Lanes Clean-Up campaign could be incorporated into the city's municipal services planning and, ideally, in the long run, the Binners' Association could provide frontline help to people living on the street. This might occur through first-aid training, by working with social services to identify the community's needs, and by training members of the community to provide services directly to fellow community residents. By actively integrating the binner sub-economy into mainstream waste-management strategies, environmental, social, and economic transactions costs will be reduced and sustainable community development will be enhanced. As David Driscoll, executive director of the VanCity Community Foundation, comments, '[l]ook at what it cost us compared to what they have put back into the community' (Caledon Institute of Social Policy 1996, 8).

Such an approach will require unprecedented cooperation at multiple scales and among multiple sectors: among government departments, between the municipality and the regional district, and in strategic partnerships with private sector bin owners and product manufacturers. Public policy integration and implementation could also contemplate the aesthetic and spiritual needs of the community and help in its restoration. In this way, Vancouver also might come to be seen as a leader in holistic urban sustainable development, rather than just as one of the best cities in the world in which to live – for some. As Kingwell (2008, 64) notes, '[m]odern distributive models of justice rightly place emphasis on the fate of the least well off: in a non-distributive idea of justice. We can also update and expand this idea: a city, like a people, shall be judged by how its treats its most vulnerable members.'

NOTES

1 I am indebted to the work of two research assistants from Royal Roads University, Ms Jodi Mucha and Mr. Jesse Brown, and funding from the Social Sciences and Humanities Research Council.
2 See, for example, the case studies at Community Research Connections, Royal Roads University. http://www.crcresearch.org/case-studies.

3 Ken Lyotier, personal communication with author, 2003.
4 One of Ken Lyotier's key leadership skills is his extraordinary aptitude in bridging social capital. He gained further recognition from city officials when he was selected as the last British Columbian to bring the Olympic torch into the closing ceremonies of the Vancouver 2010 Winter Olympics.
5 Lyotier, personal communication with author, 2003.

REFERENCES

Bhaskar, R. 1994. *Plato, Etc.: The Problems of Philosophy and Their Resolution.* New York: Verso.

Borgatti, S., and P. Foster. 2003. 'The Network Paradigm in Organizational Research: A Review and Typology.' *Journal of Management* 29, no. 6: 991–1013.

Bourdieu, P. 1986. 'The Forms of Capital.' In *Handbook of Theory and Research for the Sociology of Education,* ed. J. Richardson. New York: Greenwood Press.

Burt, R. 2003. *Structural Holes: The Social Structure of Competition.* Cambridge, MA: Harvard University Press.

Buxton, J. 2003. *Vancouver Drug Use Epidemiology.* Vancouver: Canadian Community Epidemiology on Drug Use.

Caledon Institute of Social Policy. 1996. *Caledon Profiles: Real Leaders* 1 (May).

Cox, E. 1995. 'A Truly Civil Society.' 1995 Boyer Lectures. Sydney: ABC Publishing.

CS/RESORS Consulting Ltd. 1989. *A Study of the Vancouver ReConnect Program and Vancouver Street Youth.* Vancouver: RESORS Consulting.

Dale, A. 2001. *At the Edge: Sustainable Development in the 21st Century.* Vancouver: UBC Press.

Dale, A., C. Ling, and L. Newman. 2008. 'Does Place Matter? Sustainable Community Development in Three Canadian Communities.' *Ethics, Place, and Environment* 11, no. 3: 267–81.

Dale, A., and L. Newman. 2005. 'The Role of Agency in Sustainable Local Community Development.' *Local Environment* 10, no. 5: 477–86.

–. 2010. 'Social Capital: A Necessary and Sufficient Condition for Sustainable Community Development.' *Community Development Journal* 45, no. 1: 5–21.

Dale, A., and J. Onyx. 2005. *A Dynamic Balance: Social Capital and Sustainable Development.* Vancouver: UBC Press.

Dale, A., and J. Sparkes. 2008. 'Protecting Ecosystems: Network Structure and Social Capital Mobilization.' *Community Development Journal* 43, no. 2: 143–56.

–. 2011. 'The "Agency" of Sustainable Community Development.' *Community Development* 46, no. 4: 476–92.

Denscombe, M. 1998. *The Good Research Guide: For Small-scale Social Research Projects*. Buckingham, UK: Open University Press.

Dikec, M. 2007. *Badlands of the Republic: Space, Politics and Urban Policy*. Oxford: Blackwell.

Eberle, M., D. Kraus, L. Serge, and D. Hulchanski. 2001. *A Profile, Policy Review and Analysis of Homelessness in British Columbia*, vol. 2. Victoria, BC: Ministry of Social Development and Economic Security, and BC Housing.

Feagin, J., A. Orum, and G. Sjoberg, eds. 1991. *A Case for the Case Study*. Chapel Hill: University of North Carolina Press.

Foucault, M. [1967] 1986. 'Of Other Spaces.' *Diacritics* 16: 22–7. Reproduced at http://foucault.info/documents/heteroTopia/foucault.heteroTopia.en.html.

Greater Vancouver Regional District. 2002. *Research Project on Homelessness in Greater Vancouver*, vol. 1. Vancouver: GVRD.

Kingwell, M. 2008. 'Justice Denied: Is Toronto Being Overtaken by Buskers, Fauxhemians, and the "Knowledge Economy"?' *Walrus Magazine*, January–February. http://www.walrusmagazine.com/articles/2008.02-urban-affairs-toronto-culture-mark-kingwell/ (accessed 19 June 2009).

Krishna, A. 2001. 'Moving from the Stock of Social Capital to the Flow of Benefits: The Role of Agency.' *World Development* 29, no. 6: 925–43.

Mercer. 2010. 'Quality of Living Survey.' http://www.mercer.com/articles/quality-of-living-survey-report-2010#top5, (accessed 20 September 2010).

Narayan, D. 1999. *Bonds and Bridges: Social Capital and Poverty*. Washington, DC: World Bank.

Newman, L., and A. Dale. 2005. 'The Role of Agency in Sustainable Local Community Development.' *Local Environment* 10, no. 5: 477–86.

Onyx, J., and P. Bullen. 2000. 'Measuring Social Capital in Five Communities.' *Journal of Applied Behavioural Science* 36, no. 1: 23–42.

Policy Research Initiative. 2005. *Social Capital in Action: Thematic Policy Studies*. Ottawa: Queen's Printer.

Pirie, G. 1983. 'On Spatial Justice.' *Environment and Planning A* 15, no. 4: 465–73.

Portes, A. 1998. 'Social Capital: Its Origins and Applications in Modern Sociology.' *Annual Review of Sociology* 24: 1–24.

Putnam, R. 1993. 'The Prosperous Community: Social Capital and Public Life.' *American Prospect* 13: 35–43.

–. 2000. *Bowling Alone: The Collapse and Revival of American Community.* New York: Simon and Schuster.

Robinson, J.B., and J. Tinker. 1997. 'Reconciling Ecological, Economic and Social Imperatives: A New Conceptual Framework.' In *Surviving Globalism: Social and Environmental Dimensions*, ed. T. Schrecker. London: Macmillan.

Schuler, D. 1996. *New Community Networks: Wired for Change.* New York: Addison-Wesley.

Soja, E. 2010. *Seeking Spatial Justice.* Minneapolis: University of Minnesota Press.

Tolomiczenko, G., and P. Goering. 1998. 'Pathways into Homelessness: Broadening the Perspective.' *Psychiatry Rounds* 2, no. 8: 1–5.

Woolcock, M. 2001. 'The Place of Social Capital in Understanding Social and Economic Outcomes.' *Canadian Journal of Policy Research* 2, no. 1: 11–17.

Woolcock, M., and D. Narayan. 2000. 'Social Capital: Implications for Development Theory, Research and Policy.' *World Bank Research Observer* 15, no. 2: 225–49.

PART III

Reconnecting Place and Space in the Rural-Urban Divide

7 Chickens in the City: The Urban Agriculture Movement

NICK WEIGELDT

Food sustains us all, with its benefits extending beyond merely physiological to many other aspects of life: it provides comfort, offers entrepreneurial opportunities, has many social functions that bring people together, and is a way to improve local and global ecosystems. Just as global forces bring the world closer to home offering foods from the other side of the world, a countermovement is afoot to relocalize eating patterns and become more sustainable at the individual, community, and city-region levels. With the increasing size of urbanized areas, this countermovement is working to bring agriculture back into the urban environment on a localized basis. Many planning challenges will have to be overcome to make cities truly sustainable entities, and food is one driving force behind wider sustainability issues that may assist this in coming about. New ways of thinking are emerging in relation to cities, planning, and food, bringing with them new policies, programs, champions, and opportunities.

One of these opportunities has been the reintroduction of food-producing animals (for their eggs, milk, or meat) into urban spaces after centuries of city dwellers coexisting with these sources of nourishment. Eggs produced in the backyard by free-range chickens, as an example, are inherently more sustainable than those produced at a factory farm hundreds of kilometres away. Animals offer a way for marginal farm or urban land to be used productively, giving communities greater food security, sources of income, and social and economic stability; these are all hallmarks of sustainable development. This chapter begins by exploring the points of connection between urban sustainability and the reintroduction of food-producing animals to cities. I use food production, with a special emphasis on animals, as an illustrative example of how these concepts might be applied in urban areas, while detailing the challenges, opportunities, and rewards of becoming more food sustainable in the context of third-generation responses.

Urban Agriculture in the Context of Sustainability

As a process, sustainable development may be put into practice anywhere, and indeed must be made operational at all geographic and societal levels – from urban neighbourhoods to individual countries, to the biosphere – to be fully realized. Berke and Conroy (2000, 23) identify six basic principles of sustainable development that 'retain [this] explicit connection to the location, shape, scale, and quality of human settlements,' within which the process of sustainable development must operate. These include the following:

- land use and development that should *protect, enhance, and be in harmony with natural systems*;
- *liveable built environments* designed for their inhabitants' uses, offering cohesion, community, and access between land uses (see also McDonald, Chapter 10 in this volume);
- a *place-based economy* that functions within natural systems limits;
- *equitable access* by all people to important social and economic resources;
- *payment by polluters* for their adverse effects on the environment; and,
- *responsible regionalism*.

Collectively these principles offer a good foundation upon which to base policy, land use, and practical solutions to achieving sustainability. Although they inherently relate to planning issues, each individually offers more identifiable, specific guidelines and principles that can be measured to further advance the previous definitions of sustainable development as a means to move towards this goal. Balancing these six principles in the process of putting sustainable development into operation requires a new planning agenda that works within 'multiple emergent realities' (Dale 2001, 37) of post-modern democratic societies. They must also be brought to the forefront of planning and policymaking levels in both the political and social contexts within which they exist, and reconciled to begin to address third-generation responses to sustainability. Robinson (Chapter 4 in this volume) argues that, in this context, they form the basis for integrated decision-making at the urban level. This is not an easy task to accomplish and, because sustainability issues span across broad horizontal swaths of societies, it will require sweeping changes to institutional structure and fundamental shifts in paradigms or, minimally, 'a loosening of the resistance to entertain what is currently defined as alternative thinking' (Dale 2001, 116). This involves the reconciliation of a city's ecological, social, and economic imperatives (see Dale, in the Introduction to this volume).

Coordinating this reconciliation with regard to urban food production and within the context of specific communities, decision-making processes, and urban policies and bylaws has become 'the grand task ahead' (McClintock 2010, 204) for cities as they respond with place-based solutions to urban agriculture, attempting to meet head on the challenges posed by third-generation responses to sustainability. This reconciliation ranges from the social implications of healthier urban residents and the potential for greater inter-resident interaction, to the economic opportunities for entrepreneurs and food producers, to the myriad ecological benefits derived from producing food without relying on long fossil-fuel-based transportation chains or production methods (ibid). Urban agriculture is a key feature of such third-generation responses by its recognition of the need to realize local food security while, at the same time, having access to a greater diversity of food sources globally in order to sustain community resilience in the face of external crisis.

Urban agriculture encompasses 'a variety of production systems, ranging from subsistence production and processing at the household level to fully commercialized agriculture' (van Veenhuizen 2006, 2). Local food system movements in recent years, however, have especially articulated sustainability directives that call for decentralization, democratization, and self-sufficiency of food chains. This ecological rationality helps realign the gaps and inequities and remove the stovepipes that currently exist in mainstream food systems 'between nature, quality, region and local, producers and consumers' (Feagan 2007, 25–6), while building on the sense of space and place and helping build community from the ground-level up (Nordahl 2009). McClintock (2010) argues that urban agriculture, worldwide, has often emerged as a proactive local response to global forces such as capitalism, health, and ecological concerns.

Local food systems attempt to achieve a deeper sense of connection between producers, consumers, and the place in which the food is produced (Nordahl 2009). The national or global market is no longer considered the important element to capture; rather, food is directly oriented and marketed to nearby urban centres (UNDP 1996, 5). Best practices in sustainable development are more likely to emerge as a result of more affordable fresh food consumption, many fewer miles travelled, and more suitable climate- and terrain-specific crops grown – all resulting in the mitigation of serious environmental impacts and concerns. Local economies are also kept prosperous, with money remaining in the community and passing more affordably from local consumer to local producer, while economic diversity develops and business opportunities emerge that are consistent with the communities they service (Pothukuchi and Kaufman 1999; Campbell 2004; Nordahl 2009). In addition, lower-income populations may benefit from growing their own food, selling the excess, and buying fresher, less-processed, healthier food items. (Similar parallels in local economic efforts are explored by Dale, Chapter 6 in this volume.) Socially, partnerships and relationships may be formed within the community (Hendrickson et al. 2008), leading to a stronger positive network of embedded relations whereby people actively watch for their neighbours – an often key element of place (Newman and Waldron, Chapter 5; and Dale, Chapter 6 in this volume).

Despite its potential to advance progress towards urban sustainability, urban agriculture is underrealized. In his analysis of twenty-four Canadian cities' sustainability plans, Portney observes that, while being broadly environmental, not one listed any form of agriculture or food-related indicator by which urban sustainability could be measured or implemented (2002, 367). Berke and Conroy (2000) also note the absence of these indicators. This may be a surprise considering that, as early as 1987, the Brundtland Commission recommended that governments should consider supporting urban agriculture as an important part of urban development in order 'to improve the nutritional and health standards of the poor, help their family budgets, enable them to earn some additional income and provide employment. Urban agriculture can also provide fresher and cheaper produce, more green space, the clearing of garbage dumps, and recycling of household waste' (WCED 1987, 254).

While the benefits of urban agriculture are recognized, this awareness appears not to have infiltrated the minds and practice of urban planners and the policy tools they employ to guide current and future growth of communities (Campbell 2004). Only in 2007 did the

American Planning Association, for example, adopt a Policy Guide to Community and Regional Food Planning. This guide addresses many points as they relate to the role food plays in achieving social equity, and generally supports the integration of food systems into urban areas through developed land policies and economic development programs and regulations. There are several reasons urban areas, and thus planners, still do not view agriculture and food systems planning as part of the urban system. Urban planning systems traditionally have been limited to land use, transportation systems, zoning regulations, and site plans. For many residents, food is simply an everyday resource taken for granted because of its ubiquity in the urban realm. Those unable to afford or access it equitably to the same level are generally not seen unless these groups are actively sought out as part of public consultation processes or other means. Dale (Chapter 6 in this volume) explores these social equity issues in more detail. However, it has been recommended (Campbell 2004; Pothukuchi 2004) that planners not only become educated about their communities' food issues, but that the basic points of community food security actually mirror planning concerns: the needs of low-income residents, the importance and identification of community assets, and urban sustainability. It is here that urban agriculture can play a significant role.

Another key reason community food security is not high up on many urban planning and policy agendas is the historical urban-rural divide. Food and its production is viewed as a rural issue, with rural agriculture today receiving much government support, including subsidies, particularly in Europe and North America (UNDP 1996, 44). This is in stark contrast to the urban histories of many, if not most, cities today. Until the twentieth century, growing food was always regarded as an accepted urban land use as cities generally emerged where farmers congregated in areas of fertile farmland to settle. The subsequent presence of large populations also meant a perpetual market for this food (Halweil 2004, 89). In the past century, however, technology has played a key role in distancing food production from cities and the people who consume it. Transportation, refrigeration, and agricultural improvements, for example, have allowed people to consume fresh food without any real regard to the distance it has travelled. Strict zoning and bylaw regulations governing land use in most jurisdictions have also severely restricted the ability of people to both grow and raise their own food. The restriction of grocery and food stores near many residential areas combined with the added production and transportation costs for food has also limited access by, and marginalized, many often poorer populations.

These regulatory barriers and the inherent globalization of modern agricultural production provide no incentives for creating related work for people or for retaining a regional resource base. A return to inherently more sustainable local food systems, however, would provide a basis for these considerations. Vandana Shiva, in *Earth Democracy* (2006, 10), notes, as one of its guiding principles, that 'conservation of the earth's resources and creation of sustainable and satisfying livelihoods are most caringly, creatively and efficiently and equitably achieved at the local level.' It has also been noted that market forces cannot feed urban populations alone and that government and civil society must employ intersectoral and holistic approaches, including planning, agriculture, small business, and health sectors, to do so efficiently and effectively (Burns et al. 2007). These various sectors, as well as citizens, 'must acknowledge complex webs of causation between global and national policies favouring industrialization and private equity, the elimination of food-producing habitats, transformations in food retail, consumer poverty, ignorance, and anxiety' (ibid., 126). Thus, the role for planning for food systems in supporting imperatives for third-generation sustainable responses mirrors that for planning, described above and elsewhere in this volume (see Hanna and Slocombe, Chapter 2; Robinson, Chapter 4; Dale, Chapter 6).

Planners, community stakeholders, politicians, health professionals, entrepreneurs, educators, and residents all have a role to play in helping bring local food into the public realm and consciousness to move towards urban sustainability. This process would allow food to be grown, raised, and sold in the urban centres where most consumers live, and it would encourage the development of inherently human characteristics that transcend urban and rural boundaries. The following section provides several examples of where food – specifically, animal-produced food such as eggs, milk, and meat – occurs in some form as part of the urban agenda. No one city has all of the answers, and significant challenges remain in all. But numerous examples abound in which non-traditional food production has been brought back to the city through a combination of political and legislative agendas, agency – as a consequence of social capital mobilization (see Dale, Chapter 6 in this volume) – and integrated land-use planning (Hanna and Slocombe, Chapter 2 in this volume). Many international examples of urban agriculture exist, particularly in the global South (van Veenhuizen 2006; Hovorka 2008;

McClintock 2010), where animals raised in the city provide for a considerable amount of many urban dwellers' diets. One-third of households in Harare, Zimbabwe, for example, raise poultry, pigeons, or rabbits; 80 per cent of Dhakans in Bangladesh keep animals; and in Dar es Salaam, Tanzania, urban agriculture is the second-largest employer (Matthys et al. 2006). Urban agricultural movements may be relatively small scale, but as McClintock (2010, 203) notes, these 'movements – occurring as an inchoate patchwork of local sites – evolve into a semi-coordinated force, spurred on by increasing public visibility and eventually, regional or national level support.' Many of these local examples, when pieced together, can provide some 'food for thought' for cities such as Toronto that currently allow relatively little urban agriculture.

Chickens and other forms of poultry are among the easiest and most common food-producing animals to keep in cities. The sustainable aspects of chickens are many: eggs produced by hens can provide households with a fresh source of protein daily, and the chickens themselves may also be raised as a food source. Hong Kong, one of the world's largest and densest cities, for example, produces upwards of two-thirds of its residents' consumed poultry (van Wijngaarden 2001, 105). In addition, poultry, since they will eat almost anything, are a natural way to dispose of food scraps and control backyard bugs and pests. In addition to providing fertile compost for vegetable and flower gardens, urban chickens can also make easy-to-care-for, enjoyable pets. Although present in many developing countries' cities, in North America urban chickens are much less common; many local ordinances and bylaws, however, permit egg-producing hens, as discussed below.

Zoning Challenges and Local Food Production

Originally created to distance residential areas from noxious industrial zones, zoning bylaws and ordinances have been used to regulate everything deemed 'undesirable,' relegating them elsewhere or banning them outright within city limits. One urban land use deemed by most cities in the developed world as undesirable is the keeping of livestock. Rosner (2006, 130–1) cites a plethora of serious infectious disease epidemics in American cities in the mid- to late-nineteenth century believed to result from livestock, including dysentery, cholera, and tuberculosis. Crowding, poor sanitation, and a lack of adequate housing and health care access certainly were the main culprits, but the increasing numbers of animals living in cities also contributed to the unsanitary conditions.

Neighbourhood streets were often strewn to considerable depths with horse manure and urine, household and vegetable refuse, and 'thousands of dead horses, goats, pigs, and cattle [that] lay imbedded in [the] uncollected filth, often for days and weeks' (130).

By the early twentieth century, public health and sanitation reforms in North America gained prominence, as advancing medical training and knowledge connected environmental and sanitary conditions to human health. As it translated into urban public policy, public health was a primary driving force behind zoning bylaws and ordinances, tenement laws, restrictions on housing densities, and nuisance laws requiring residents to keep their properties clean (Rosner 2006, 135). This was often accomplished at the expense of forbidding city dwellers to keep subsistence livestock and poultry for personal use and consumption. In many ways, such limits are justified: improperly kept, animals can pose a health risk to humans, as evidenced by the recent epidemics of SARS and the H5/N1 influenza, or avian flu, which have had animal vectors, often through domestic birds such as ducks and chickens (Mougeot 2000, 25; Vlahov and Gibble 2006, 217). Cattle have been decimated in Britain and elsewhere by epidemics of foot/hoof-and-mouth and mad cow disease (Halweil 2004, 159). Pigs, another ungulate, have made headlines around the world as the carriers of the aptly named 'swine flu,' properly known as influenza A(H1N1), which reached global pandemic proportions after first appearing on pig farms in Mexico (World Health Organization 2009).

Understandably, as the UN notes, some 'urban agriculture activities are not as benign as others' (UNDP 1996, 125), and even regions, such as Latin America and Africa, traditionally supportive of larger livestock within urban areas are placing limitations on animals due to disease concerns. There is, however, little or no empirical evidence that animals raised in developed western cities – making a clear differentiation from those raised in intense, large-scale industrial farms found typically in rural areas in Europe and North America – pose the same risks to humans as those raised in developing countries' cities. The overall sanitary, human health, and climatic conditions are vastly different, and equating, for example, the potential risks of animal-to-human disease transfer in Vietnam or Kenya to North American or European contexts remains, at best, an unclear proposition requiring further empirical study. Only then can proper risk-benefit analyses be undertaken by cities, public health agencies, and local food and urban agriculture advocates looking to reintroduce food-producing animals back into their residents' daily lives. Should urban agriculture be allowed, then necessary restrictions and guidelines promoting human and animal health should be introduced and enforced. Raising food-producing animals in urban areas in close contact with humans poses risks, but properly kept in both developed and developing countries' cities, the risks can be minimized and are far outweighed by the benefits of the local food production. For example, Seattle Tilth, a non-profit organization whose mission touches on all aspects of civic agriculture and sustainability, estimates that a single backyard hen, properly cared for, can produce anywhere from fifteen to twenty-seven dozen eggs per year, improving a family's food security while minimizing household food costs. A city full of backyard chickens would, by extension, produce a considerable percentage of the total eggs consumed annually by the populace. To promote 'sustainable urbanism,' cities must begin to look to their pasts (Coletta 2008), when food was grown and raised locally by those in the community, rather than shipped in from far away.

As noted, many North American cities have bylaws prohibiting the keeping of animals other than those typically seen as pets – cats, dogs, rabbits – and even pets often have limits placed on their number, as well as leash and indoor restrictions. One such city is Toronto, whose Municipal Code 1184, Chapter 349 – Animals (Toronto 2006) disallows the keeping of 'either on a temporary or permanent basis, any prohibited animal in the City,' which include, among others,

- mammals;
- *Artiodactyla* (such as cattle, goats, sheep, pigs);
- *Perissodactyla* (such as horses, donkeys, jackasses, mules);
- birds;
- *Anseriformes* (such as ducks, geese, swans, screamers); and,
- *Galliformes* (such as pheasants, grouse, guineafowls, or turkeys).

Being galliformes, though receiving no special attention in the remainder of the municipal code, chickens are not permitted to be kept within city limits. Such legal restrictions in Toronto are similar to those in other large North American cities such as Ottawa and Boston (using 'no person shall keep' as extended to chickens) that disallow poultry within city limits (Boston 2007; Ottawa 2003).

Unfortunately for advocates of urban chickens in Canada, the Toronto experience is common across the country. A survey of the animal control bylaws in twenty of the largest Canadian municipalities shows that only three – Surrey and Vancouver, British Columbia, and Brampton, Ontario – allow chickens to be raised inside city limits. Even then, there are restrictions. Table 7.1 lists the specifics of the bylaws of these three cities, plus those of four smaller Canadian cities that also allow chickens inside urban limits. While an exhaustive study of every Canadian urban municipality is not within the scope of this chapter, these seven municipalities nonetheless give a snapshot of Canadian cities' bylaws governing urban poultry, and that snapshot is telling: it shows that very few Canadian urban centres allow poultry, and even then restrictions on property dimensions preclude all but owners of large suburban homes from raising chickens.

The picture is somewhat brighter in the United States, where a larger selection of cities allows chickens and other poultry to be kept for some degree of personal use and consumption. In many cases, hens are allowed, but roosters generally are not allowed for noise reasons. This has no adverse effect on hens' egg production, as store-bought eggs are unfertilized. Chicago's municipal code, for example, while banning the possession of many 'farm' animals, including chickens if intended to be slaughtered (and, ostensibly, eaten) (Chicago 2002), makes no mention of chickens raised for their eggs. Indeed, chickens are popular among many Chicagoans and are actively supported by the Chicago Food Policy Advisory Council (CFPAC 2008). In late 2007, the freedom to raise chickens within city limits was threatened when some city aldermen proposed including chickens in the bylaw that prohibits the keeping of pigeons in residential neighbourhoods. Citing noise and the attraction of rodents ('Chicagoans cry fowl,' 2007) as the reason to ban chickens from residential areas, the vote eventually was delayed and sent back to committee for further review.

Madison, Wisconsin, on the other hand, has moved in a more sustainable direction, recently bringing into effect a bylaw allowing chickens to be kept in residential areas. The zoning code was amended to allow the 'keeping of up to four chickens' in R1 single-family residential districts providing that no slaughter occurs and that chickens are kept in an enclosure at all times that is located no closer than twenty-five feet (about seven and a half metres) from a neighbouring residential structure (Madison 2004). Since then, urban chicken farming has gained in popularity in Madison with a local group, Mad City Chickens, acting as unofficial coordinators providing all forms of information for city residents ranging from coop construction to introductory 'city chickens' classes (Mad City Chickens 2004).

Table 7.1. Bylaws on Keeping Chickens, Selected Municipalities, Canada

City	Population (2006)	Bylaw	Minimum Lot Size	Maximum Number of Chickens	Other Information
Vancouver, BC	578,041	Animal Control Bylaw No. 9150, amended by No. 10066	none	none	Minimum coop size and general hen well-being regulations
Brampton, ON	433,806	Animal Control Bylaw No. 261-93, amended by No. 78-2009	none	2	
Surrey, BC	394,976	Zoning Bylaw No. 12000	0.4 ha	12 per ha	
Guelph, ON	114,943	Exotic and Non-domestic Animals Bylaw No. (1985)-11952	none	none	Chickens, ducks, geese, and pigeons allowed provided they are kept penned in areas that are dry and clean, and at least 50 feet from any school, church, or another home
Niagara Falls, ON	82,184	Animal Control Bylaw 2002-129	Detached dwelling with lot frontage of 40 feet; lot depth of 100 feet	10	
Kamloops, BC	80,376	Animal Control Bylaw No. 34-11	0.4 ha	30	
Victoria, BC	78,957	Animal Control Bylaw No. 92-189	none	none	no roosters

Sources: Various municipal bylaws; population figures from 2006 Census of Canada.

Similar examples can be found across the United States, usually with some restrictions attached to the simple keeping of poultry. Seattle allows up to three domestic fowl to be kept on urban properties (Seattle 2007), but not on those with more than three residential units. Minneapolis requires a permit and the written consent of at least 80 per cent of neighbours within one hundred feet (about thirty metres) to allow residents to keep chickens, turkeys, or ducks (Minneapolis 2008). Los Angeles simply requires that poultry not be kept for commercial purposes in its urban residential zones (Los Angeles 2008). The New York-based non-profit organization Just Food applies its sustainable local food policy mission to its City Farms program, with thirty farms across all five New York boroughs. Through the farms, Just Food runs its 'City Chicken Project,' which works within the New York City ordinances to help community groups acquire and raise hens for their eggs and distribute them fairly and justly within the community, especially to those in need.

It is community-based organizations such as Just Food and Mad City Chickens that provide much of the life, knowledge, and momentum for urban food production in those cities that allow it, especially with regards to chickens. This speaks to the strong mobilization of social capital through agency, where governance structures work vertically to allow for such opportunities (see Dale, Chapter 6 in this volume). The 'embedding of local agriculture and food production in the community' (Lyson 2004, 62) seems to be one of the most effective ways to bring food to a personal level of engagement – a holistic way of reconciling the three imperatives and achieving community sustainability. The equitable aspects of 'civic agriculture,' as Lyson defines it, allow it to reach and, perhaps most important, be controlled by, all members of the community who hold a large stake in the environmental, social, and economic aspects of their immediate locales and situations. Seattle Tilth (n.d.) also 'inspires and educates people to garden organically, conserve natural resources and support local food systems in order to cultivate a healthy urban environment and community.' Viewing chickens as one of the keys to promoting sustainable food production in the city, the organization offers residents a wealth of resources, both online and through various community workshops and clinics, about raising, caring for, and even slaughtering chickens.

By allowing chickens and other forms of livestock to be raised within urban limits and endogenously moving away from the typical 'path dependence' discussed by Dale (in the Introduction to this volume), these cities have made considerable strides towards building several of the sustainability indicators whose development is key to their long-term environmental, economic and social success. However, as with any project involving numerous stakeholders across so many spheres of public life and discourse (public policy, community and animal health, private investment, land-use planning, economic development), more could be done to make them truly sustainable as part of third-generation responses.

The Need for Planning Reform

If sustainability is to be embedded within local food systems, several changes need to take place in the urban planning system. In keeping with the six basic principles of sustainable development mentioned earlier, land use and development should protect, enhance, and be in harmony with natural systems, and liveable built environments should be designed that offer cohesion, community, and access between land uses. In addition, a place-based economy that functions within the limits of natural systems – that is, one that reconciles economic, ecological, and social imperatives) should emerge, offering equitable access by everyone to important social and economic resources. Finally, polluters must pay for their adverse effects on the environment through effective regulatory instruments, and responsible regionalism must guide development within the broader local sustainable development goals, as discussed in this volume by Hanna and Slocombe (Chapter 2) and McDonald (Chapter 10).

Although the previously mentioned cities have taken steps (possibly without knowledge) to becoming more sustainable, they could do even more by consciously applying sustainability principles to advocate the keeping of urban animals and livestock. While there are good reasons for restrictions placed on animals within city limits – health concerns, noise, odours, and waste, and concerns for the animals' well-being – additional creative solutions have been implemented in some locales that, with minor local considerations, could be implemented in every North American city.

Seattle has a relatively progressive animal zoning bylaw, allowing most farm animals (domestic fowl, cows, sheep, goats) within city limits, but only on lots of a certain minimum size. For larger farm animals, a lot must be at least 20,000 square feet (about 1,858 square metres), or almost half an acre (Seattle 2007). Additional animals may be added only with each additional 10,000 square feet of lot space. Los Angeles (2008) has similar lot size restrictions, and limits bovines and goats, for example, to areas of the city zoned 'Suburban' or 'Agricultural.' In both of these cities, larger livestock, which could provide residents substantial sources of meat and dairy products, are limited to suburban- or estate-sized lots, ostensibly owned by those with higher incomes. This places obvious barriers on inner-city residents and apartment dwellers from keeping animals. One opportunity for reconciling this in dense urban areas is provided by the Tierra de Oportunidades Farm, organized by the Nuestras Raíces community group in Holyoke, Massachusetts, a small city on the outskirts of the state capital, Springfield. This area has a large Puerto Rican population, many of whom first came to the US northeast as migrant farm workers and have remained, as a whole, relatively less affluent than the rest of the area residents. Bringing with them a legacy of communal agriculture, Nuestras Raíces founded the Tierra de Oportunidades Farm in 1992 to promote community development while serving as a 'beginning farmer training project and new business incubator, environmental conservation and stewardship project, youth development initiative and cultural development project' (Nuestras Raíces 2008). The farm features goats, chickens, pigs, rabbits, and horses on ten acres (about four hectares) near the centre of town. It has become a positive way for the community to achieve some of its food needs while contributing to the local economic and cultural needs of its users. Supported by volunteers, the city, and various grants, as well as by selling the products it produces, Nuestras Raíces' Tierra de Oportunidades Farm is an example of a community-led urban agriculture project allowed within local bylaws and one that fits into the municipality's policies.

The examples of community and local-food organizations in Seattle and Los Angeles offer opportunities for learning; they also champion the kinds of changes that would bring local food production and its benefits to the residents most in need of greater food security and community economic development in other cities. With such opportunities come social capital, environmental, and communal benefits, within structured and supported initiatives, as part of agency.

In addition to limits on lot sizes, the other major hindrance to local food production as a tool for personal and community economic development is the restrictions often placed on the selling of the goods resulting from agricultural and animal rearing. Chicago's municipal code (2008), for example, does not allow the sale of perishable meat products unless stamped by the US Department of Agriculture as meeting an official grading standard. This adds an additional bureaucratic hurdle to small-scale meat production, one that most would-be sellers are unlikely to have the time or money to clear. Los Angeles has similar restrictions: in all residential zones where livestock, from chickens to goats, are allowed, the rearing of these animals must 'not [be] for commercial purposes' (Los Angeles 2008). Chickens, rabbits, and chinchillas may be kept for commercial purposes only on lots of more than five acres (about two hectares) in size, which, for all intents and purposes, is not an urban lot.

Portland, Oregon, has some of the most permissive bylaws or ordinances in North America regarding the keeping of animals, perhaps not surprising since the city has long been lauded as one of the most environmentally progressive in the United States and has a strong citizen focus on sustainability issues. The City Code and Charter states that, with an acquired permit, 'livestock' (meaning any farm animal, including cows, goats, and chickens) are permitted within city limits provided they remain further than fifty feet (about fifteen metres) away from any building used as a residence or a commercial building where food is prepared (Portland 2008). Although the city does place minimum limits on lot sizes on which animals can be kept, it does not use minimum lot sizes as the primary determining factor.

Thus, while livestock – especially chickens, but also extending to goats, cows, and sheep – are allowed by law in many cities in North America, local ordinances and bylaws on the matter vary widely. To embark on sustainable courses of action, cities with strict laws against food-producing animals within their limits have much to learn from others. Toronto, for example, does not allow food-producing animals as accessory uses in residential areas. It could, however, follow the path of a much denser city such as New York, which allows unlimited chickens to be kept on a property provided that noise and odours are kept to a minimum.

Although urban agriculture will prove to be a significant land-use and policy challenge for planners and politicians alike, the groundwork has already been laid. In Toronto, the Official Plan (2007) is littered with references to making the city 'food secure,' and advocates that agricultural land within the city be protected. It also goes as far as to suggest that hydro corridors support agricultural practices as secondary uses (4–9). In addition, both the Toronto Food Policy Council, an independent food policy development subcommittee of the Toronto Board of Health, and FoodShare Toronto, a non-profit community-based organization dedicated to addressing food and hunger issues from field to table, have been active for several years pushing for sustainable, healthy, accessible, and secure food sources. Both agencies likely would be proponents of an increased urban agricultural yield that includes animal-produced foods.

Should bylaws be relaxed and livestock – the most obvious initial choice being chickens – be reintroduced to urban spaces, the next step might be to take an inventory of open spaces, public lands, including those more-or-less ready to yield agricultural benefits, and private properties to determine possible yields within the city. One example is the Riverdale Farm, a City of Toronto-owned, publicly accessible farm on the site of Toronto's first zoo on the eastern edge of downtown. This information would then be applied to broad and comprehensive food security and sustainability plans that look at all factors of sustainable development, including social, economic, and environmental benefits, as well as the governance issues and opportunities that might arise.

Urban planners have a unique and important role to play in this process. In addition to placing themselves in situations where their broad educational and professional approach to all three factors leading to sustainability – economy, ecology, and society – are considered, planners must also include the governance and political structures that can guide sustainable development. As also illustrated in other chapters of this volume (see, for example, Hanna and Slocombe), sustainable planning must be clear in its vision and holistic in its objectives, and must address principles on the path to sustainable development creatively and with broad citizen input (Berke and Conroy 2000, 30; Parkinson and Roseland 2002, 426). Parkinson and Roseland, in their analysis of Canadian municipal sustainability plans, note that almost all projects on this path involve some degree of collaboration (2002, 422). This occurs either within civic governments or between civic governments and outside groups, businesses, educational institutions, and citizens. Though a challenging task, these 'silos' (see Dale 2001), each with its own structures and social and corporate dynamics, must be opened up and their interdependencies and potential synergies identified and managed in order to strive effectively for sustainability.

Local food, urban agriculture, and backyard chicken advocates and cities' public health agencies have, at their cores, similar goals for healthy and active citizens engaged in sustainable environments. Translating those goals into realistic and holistic policies concerning the keeping of chickens and other food-producing animals within city limits while minimizing the potential effects of disease on human and animal health as much as possible remains the planning and political challenge moving forward. Inherent in the discussion will be planning for the future well-being of both the public and the environment. This includes what course of action – that is, whether or not to allow food-producing animals within the city – presents itself best at adhering to the precautionary principle in the event that the threat of serious environmental and human degradation outweighs scientific uncertainty (Santillo, Johnston, and Stringer 1999, 43). Urban planners must seek to navigate, manage, and resolve the inevitable conflict surrounding the uncertainty over health, environmental, and food systems that will occur in promoting final visionary solutions for the most applicable sustainable future (Campbell 1996, 305). Failure to do so will result in decisions that represent the lowest common denominator of competing interests and that do not address fully all necessary factors as part of the sustainable development process (Dale 2001, 103).

Conclusion

Urban sustainability, as showcased here and in other chapters in this volume, is not an easy concept to achieve. It requires not only the coordination, but also the same forward momentum and similar end goals, of residents and politicians, businesses and planners, community organizations and health officials, environmentalists and bureaucrats. It is a multifaceted process, one that can and must start with all sectors of city life, of which food and food security are among the most important. Food systems offer planners and other observers both an indicator of the relative strength and security of a community and a platform whereby insecure and unsustainable economic situations may start to be rectified. Parallels between third-generation sustainability responses and food emerge here in much the same way that a recipe is much more than the sum of its ingredients. So too is sustainability more than simply the sum of social, ecological, and economic imperatives.

Food security is one of the single most important sustainability challenges and, as a basic need, stretches across all facets of sustainable development. By planning for and within local and urban community food systems, the three imperatives of sustainability may not only be met; they may be bridged and given a broader role than simply improving the individual aspects of urban life they affect. In short, they can make cities more liveable, inclusive places. New planning, health, and governance paradigms that change the way people think about sustainability are necessary if cities are to be truly sustainable in the support of urban agriculture and its benefits.

The reintroduction of food-producing animals into the urban landscape would represent a profoundly new (or renewed) way of thinking in the industrialized world, at least for many cities. But cities will have to be prepared to think in such terms to remain resilient as global environmental, social, and economic problems worsen and crises manifest themselves locally. Matthys et al. (2006) see this paradigm shift not as a linear process, but one that will come about in leaps and bounds through 'surprise and change rather than average solutions and standard approaches.' In the meantime, it will be prudent for cities, their residents and their planners to become educated and to plan and prepare for the move to urban agriculture and local food production through steps such as those outlined in this chapter. With each successive step forward, cities will move closer to the end goal of urban sustainability.

REFERENCES

American Planning Association. 2007. *Policy Guide to Community and Regional Food Planning*. Chicago: APA. http://www.planning.org/policyguides/pdf/food.pdf.

Berke, P.R., and M.M. Conroy. 2000. 'Are We Planning for Sustainable Development? An Evaluation of 30 Comprehensive Plans.' *Journal of the American Planning Association* 66, no. 1: 21–33.

Boston. 2007. *City of Boston Municipal Code Chapter XVI: Prohibitions, Penalties, and Permits 16–1.8*. http://www.amlegal.com/boston_ma/.

Brampton. 2009. *Animal Control By-law No. 261–93, amended by No. 78–2009*. Brampton, ON. http://www.brampton.ca/en/City-Hall/Bylaws/Documents/animal-control.pdf (accessed 20 August 2010).

Burns, C., et al. 2007. 'The Health Equity Dimensions of Urban Food Systems.' *Journal of Urban Health* 84, no. 1: 118–29.

Campbell, M.C. 2004. 'Building a Common Table: The Role for Planning in Community Food Systems.' *Journal of Planning Education and Research* 23, no. 4: 341–55.

Campbell, S. 1996. 'Green Cities, Growing Cities, Just Cities? Urban Planning and the Contradictions of Sustainable Development.' *Journal of the American Planning Association* 62, no. 3: 18–32.

Chicago. 2008. *City of Chicago, Municipal Code Chapter 7–12: Animal Care and Control 7–12–300*. http://www.amlegal.com/nxt/gateway.dll/Illinois/chicago_il/municipalcodeofchicago?f=templates$fn=default.htm$3.0$vid=amlegal:chicago_il.

Chicago Food Policy Advisory Council. 2008. *2008 Policy Report*. Chicago: CFPAC. http://www.chicagofoodpolicy.org/2008%20CFPAC%20Report.pdf.

'Chicagoans cry fowl over proposed backyard chicken ban.' 2007. *CBC News.ca.*, 12 December. http://www.cbc.ca/consumer/story/2007/12/12/chicago-chickens.html.

Coletta, C. 2008. 'Smart City: Sustainable Urbanism.' Podcast radio program, 3 January. http://smartcityradio.fluidhosting.com/2008/01-January/010308_SmartCity.mp3.

Dale, A. 2001. *At the Edge: Sustainable Development in the 21st Century*. Vancouver: UBC Press.

Feagan, R. 2007. 'The Place of Food: Mapping Out the "local" in Local Food Systems.' *Progress in Human Geography* 31, no. 1: 23–42.

Guelph. 1985. *Exotic and Non-domestic Animals By-law No (1985)-11952*. Guelph, ON. http://guelph.ca/cityhall.cfm?smocid=1444 (accessed 7 September 2010).

Halweil, B. 2004. *Eat Here: Reclaiming Homegrown Pleasures in a Global Supermarket*. New York: W.W. Norton.

Hendrickson, J., et al. 2008. 'Interactions in Integrated US Agricultural Systems: The Past, Present and Future.' *Renewable Agriculture and Food Systems* 23, no. 4: 314–24.

Hovorka, A. 2008. 'Transspecies Urban Theory: Chickens in an African City.' *Cultural Geographies* 15. no. 1: 95–117.

Kamloops. 2010). *Animal Control By-law No. 34–11*. Kamloops, BC. https://kamloops.civicweb.net/Documents/DocumentList.aspx?ID=8206 (accessed 20 August 2010).

Los Angeles. 2008. *Los Angeles Municipal Code, Chapter 1: General Provisions and Zoning*. http://www.municode.com/Resources/gateway.asp?pid=11490&sid=23 (accessed 18 February 2008).

Lyson, T. 2004. *Civic Agriculture: Reconnecting Farm, Food, and Community.* Medford, MA: Tufts University Press.

Mad City Chickens. 2004. 'Mad City Chickens.' http://www.madcitychickens. com/ (accessed 18 February 2008).

Madison. 2004. *Code of Ordinances: Chapter 28, Zoning Code, (2)(b)8.j.* Madison, WI. http://www.municode.com/resources/gateway.asp?pid= 50000& sid=49 (accessed 18 February 2008).

Matthys, F., H. Schiere, E. Thys, and B. Rischkowsky. 2006. 'Livestock Keeping in Urbanised Areas: Does History Repeat Itself?' In *Cities Farming for the Future: Urban Agriculture for Green and Productive Cities*, ed. R. van Veenhuizen. Ottawa: International Development Research Centre. http://www.idrc.ca/ en/ev-100638–201–1-DO_TOPIC.html (accessed 28 February 2008).

McClintock, N. 2010. 'Why Farm the City? Theorizing Urban Agriculture through a Lens of Metabolic Rift.' *Cambridge Journal of Regions, Economy and Society* 3, no. 2: 191–207.

Minneapolis. 2008. *City of Minneapolis Code of Ordinances: Title 4, Chapter 4: Fowl, Pigeons and Other Small Animals.* http://www.municode.com/Re sources/gateway.asp?pid=11490&sid=23 (accessed 18 February 2008).

Mougeot, L.J.A. 2000. 'Urban Agriculture: Definition, Presence, Potentials and Risks.' In *Growing Cities, Growing Food: Urban Agriculture on the Policy Agenda*, CFP Report 31, ed. N. Bakker et al. Ottawa: International Development Research Centre.

Niagara Falls. 2002. *Animal Control By-law 2002–129.* Niagara Falls, ON. http://www.niagarafalls.ca/city_hall/departments/clerks/bylaws/pdf/ Animal_control.pdf (accessed 20 August 2010).

Nordahl, D. 2009. *Public Produce: The New Urban Agriculture.* Washington, DC: Island Press.

Nuestras Raíces. 2008. 'Tierra de Oportunidades Farm.' http://www. nuestras-raices.org/-nuestra1/en/tierra-de-oportunidades-farm (accessed 5 April 2008).

Ottawa. 2003. *By-law no. 2003–77: Respecting Animal Care and Control.* http:// www.ottawa.ca/residents/bylaw/a_z/acc_en.html (accessed 10 June 2009).

Parkinson, S., and M. Roseland. 2002. 'Leaders of the Pack: An Analysis of the Canadian "Sustainable Communities 2000 Municipal Competition".' *Local Environment* 7, no. 4: 411–29.

Portland. 2008. *City Code & Charter, Chapter 13.05: Specified Animal Regulations.* Portland, OR. http://www.portlandonline.com/auditor/index. cfm?c=28228 (accessed 18 February 2008).

Portney, K.E. 2002. 'Taking Sustainable Cities Seriously: A Comparative Analysis of Twenty-four US Cities.' *Local Environment* 7, no. 4: 363–80.

Pothukuchi, K. 2004. 'Community Food Assessment: A First Step in Planning for Community Food Security.' *Journal of Planning Education and Research* 23, no. 4: 356–77.

Pothukuchi, K., and J.L. Kaufman. 1999. 'Placing the Food System on the Urban Agenda: The Role of Municipal Institutions in Food Systems Planning.' *Agriculture and Human Values* 16, no. 2: 213–24.

Rosner, D. 2006. 'Public Health in U.S. Cities: A Historical Perspective.' In *Cities and the Health of the Public,* ed. N. Freudenberg, S. Galea, and D. Vlahov. Nashville, TN: Vanderbilt University Press.

Santillo, D., P. Johnston, and R. Stringer. 1999. 'The Precautionary Principle in Practice: A Mandate for Anticipatory Preventative Action.' In *Protecting Public Health and the Environment: Implementing the Precautionary Principle,* ed. C. Raffensperger and J. Tickner. Washington, DC: Island Press.

Seattle. 2007. *City of Seattle Municipal Code: 23.42.052: Keeping of Animals.* http://clerk.ci.seattle.wa.us/~scripts/nph-brs.exe?d=CODE&s1=23.42.052. snum.&Sect5=CODE1&Sect6=HITOFF&l=20&p=1&u=/~public/code1. htm&r=1&f=G (accessed 18 February 2008).

Seattle Tilth. n.d. 'Seattle Tilth.' http://www.seattletilth.org/ (accessed 21 February 2008).

Shiva, Vandana. 2006.. *Earth Democracy.* London: Zed Books.

Surrey. 2010. *Zoning By-law No. 12000.* Surrey, BC. http://surrey.ihostez.com/ Documents/DocumentList.aspx?ID=22775 (accessed 20 August 2010).

Toronto. 2006. *Toronto Municipal Code 1184 Chapter 349 – Animals.* http://www. toronto.ca/legdocs/municode/1184_349.pdf (accessed 18 February 2008).

–. 2007. *Official Plan.* http://www.toronto.ca/planning/official_plan/pdf_ chapter1–5/chapters1_5_aug2007.pdf.

UNDP (United Nations Development Programme). 1996. *Urban Agriculture: Food, Jobs and Sustainable Cities.* New York: UNDP.

van Veenhuizen, R., ed. 2006. *Cities Farming for the Future: Urban Agriculture for Green and Productive Cities.* Ottawa: International Development Research Centre.

van Wijngaarden, T. 2001. 'An Example of Eco-City Development: Urban Agriculture.' In *How Green Is the City?* ed. D. Devuyst, L. Hens, and W. de Lannoy. New York: Columbia University Press.

Vancouver. 2010. *Animal Control By-law No. 9150, amended by 10066.* http:// vancouver.ca/bylaw_wa/ConsolidatedReport.aspx?bylawid=9150&txtSear ch=chicken (accessed 20 August 2010).

Victoria. 1992. *Animal Control Bylaw No. 92–189*. Victoria, BC. http://www.vic toria.ca/common/pdfs/bylaw_92–189.pdf (accessed 20 Augsut 2010).

Vlahov, D., and E. Gibble. 2006. 'Cities and Infectious Diseases: Controls and Challenges.' In *Cities and the Health of the Public*, ed. N. Freudenberg, S. Galea, and D. Vlahov. Nashville, TN: Vanderbilt University Press.

WCED (World Commission on Environment and Development). 1987. *Our Common Future: Report of the World Commission on Environment and Development*, chaired by Gro Harlem Brundtland. Oxford: Oxford University Press.

World Health Organization. 2009. 'Influenza A(H1N1).' Geneva. http://www. who.int/csr/disease/swineflu/en/ (accessed 14 June 2009).

8 Finding Opportunities for Urban Sustainability in Cottage Life

NIK LUKA

This chapter is based on an unlikely premise. It argues that the exodus that we see in summertime from Canadian cities and suburbs towards waterfront cottages and cabins may offer opportunities for urban sustainability. Drawing on intensive empirical work done in Ontario's rapidly changing second-home contexts, I probe how cottage country settings can help people to think about living more sustainably in urban areas. The reductionist association of cottage life with nature is a potent mythology; the notion of the cabin in the woods might nevertheless help us to embrace and integrate natural processes more fully throughout the metropolitan regions in which most Canadians live. Given that so many people literally and figuratively buy into this mythology, the case study presented here considers these second-home areas as highlighting opportunities that are both exciting and very real for reconciling and reconnecting nature (space) with culture (place) in the quest for third-generation responses to urban sustainability.

The widespread social practice of cottage life is rife with contradictions, not the least of which is the very travel behaviour it entails. As in many parts of Canada, tens of thousands of people regularly head away from the urbanized heartland of Ontario where they live and work to a destination they call the 'cottage' or 'camp,' which may be a small, rustic cabin or an elaborate waterfront villa. These second dwellings – often called cabins or chalets elsewhere in Canada – have long been a defining aspect of life in this country (Wolfe 1951; Luka 2006, 2008b). Only a fraction of Canadians actually takes part in this social practice of 'going to the cottage,' and yet it has a powerful folkloric presence, playing important symbolic roles in the mosaic of Canadian identities. It resembles an age-old seasonal migration among northern indigenous cultures, such as the summer migration of certain Inuit populations to fishing and hunting camps. It also has clear contemporary analogues seen in the north-central United States, Norway, Sweden, Finland, Russia, and other parts of the world.

What do these far-flung superfluous dwellings have to do with urban sustainability, other than something that simple logic suggests we should avoid? The generative link is illustrated in the argument advanced by William Cronon in his provocative and highly influential essay 'The Trouble with Wilderness' (1996). He argues that the popular North American concept of the 'wilderness' is fraught with hypocrisy and a perverse desire to dissociate nature and culture: 'wilderness embodies a dualistic vision in which the human is entirely outside the natural . . . To the extent that we celebrate wilderness as the measure with which we judge civilization, we reproduce the dualism that sets humanity and nature at opposite poles. We thereby leave ourselves little hope of discovering what an ethical, sustainable, honorable human place in nature might actually look like' (80–1).

Building on Cronon's argument, the case is made here that cottage life in Ontario demonstrates a problem we need to address: commonly held notions of what constitutes 'nature' problematically hide their unnaturalness behind masks that are alluring, precisely because they seem so very 'natural.' Cottage living seems to be uncritically embraced by many of its practitioners as a natural foil to the unnatural everyday spaces of more densely built-up metropolitan areas (see also Newman and Waldron, Chapter 5; and McDonald, Chapter 10 in this volume). The cottage is thus used to reconcile an ideological attachment to the idea of 'nature' while avoiding committing to its processes, which may be perceived as distastefully complex, diverse, and fraught with uncertainty.[1]

Based on detailed primary research into the motivations of cottage users, I explore how cottage country is treated as an 'other' to the city – a context that its users treated as a place of sojourn, made meaningful in significant part by allowing them to get back to nature. This is a notion that is apparently considered difficult or impossible in urban settings. 'Nature' is thus analogous to 'wilderness' – something thought of as 'out there,' away from the city, and categorically not 'in here,' in the city (Cronon 1996). In this ironic worldview, nature is something foreign to be kept at bay, somewhere else, and the cottage represents a setting in which reluctant city dwellers can sojourn amid nature without getting too close for comfort. It may even be that cottage life exculpates people from enfolding natural process into their everyday (urban) lives.

Here is the critical connection: the irony embodied in certain attitudes people have towards second-home settings can be subverted for urban sustainability. The second-home phenomenon can represent a useful portal to urban sustainability. This chapter is therefore not an indictment of cottage life; rather, it suggests how we can find opportunities for urban sustainability in this widespread social practice. The logic of this argument has three basic components:

1 The importance of nature for many second-home users despite (and sometimes due to) the inherent tension between urban life and cottaging.
2 How this represents a great potential energy for positive change through its recurrent combination with deep attachment that anchors users to their second-home settings – reconnection to place as part of third-generation responses.
3 An unusual openness and desire on the part of many second-home users for significant change in the way cottages, cabins, and camps fit into their landscapes.

I discuss these, and offer thoughts on strategic action at the appropriate scales and in practical ways. To enable this discussion, I first provide key contextual material, briefly describing the historical extent and current magnitude of second-home activity in Canada, and summarizing issues that have come to prominence in recent years.

Defining Cottage Life

Going to a summerhouse is not uncommon in cold climates, where people tend to want to make the most of the warm season. Second-home settings are found throughout the northeastern United States, central Europe (where, for instance, the Swiss have their chalets or *Ferienwohnungen*), Norway and Sweden (where people respectively go the *hytte* or the *sommarstuga*), Russia with its *dachas*, and New Zealand (where many households maintain a *bach*). All represent a well-established practice of maintaining a supplementary dwelling of some sort, generally but not exclusively in non-urban areas and predominantly but not only on the part of households based in towns or large cities. My focus here, however, is on central Ontario – specifically, the geographical area loosely termed 'cottage country' to the north and east of Toronto and defined by its perennial links to this metropolitan region. In effect, these second-home landscapes are functionally part of the Greater Toronto Area (GTA) and tied into it by commuting patterns that take place on a weekly or monthly timeframe, rather than daily.

The term 'cottage' is the commonest term used in central Ontario and, therefore, I use it here. This is meant neither to deny that second-home cabins or camps are found in other parts of Canada, nor to imply that these analogues are less interesting or meaningful to their users (see Luka 2008b). The central Ontario case is presented instead as a chronotope, or time-space proxy, for similar contexts across Canada and around the world.[2] Indeed, the *Nelson Canadian Dictionary of the English Language* includes a definition of the word 'cottage' as 'a recreational property with a house, especially for summer use,' noting its use mainly in southern Ontario and the Prairie provinces. For present purposes, I define it as a residential structure, either moveable or fixed in place, occupied and used by a household that makes its primary dwelling elsewhere.[3] The term is often understood to mean that a body of water of some sort is nearby. The authoritative *Oxford English Dictionary* notes that this term is used in Canadian and American English to represent a summer residence (often on a large and sumptuous scale) at a watering place or a health or pleasure resort. Its first acknowledged occurrence was in 1882, in reference to seaside resorts in Maine, but the notion is no less historically true for Canada, with its three oceans, tens of thousands of lakes and rivers, and countless kilometres of shoreline. A fine example is found in a sardonic piece from the 1940s written for *MacLean's* magazine entitled 'Us Amphibious Canadians' (and later published in a collection called *A Pocketful of Canada*): 'Ask any non-seashore-going Canadian where he is going when the summer migration begins, and he will answer without a moment's hesitation: "To the Lake", or "To the Beach", or "To the Bay" . . . For the plain fact is that the Canadian will not summer anywhere except beside a lake. It does not matter much how large the lake is, nor how clean, nor what sort of odours emanate from it' (Sandwell 1946, 175).

When Ontarians refer to cottage country, they are, in effect, describing part of what François Ascher (1995) has called the *metapolis*: the physically and socially heterogeneous range of unevenly built-up geographic territory across which all, or a significant majority, of the inhabitants, economic activities, and/or built environment effectively form part of the metropolitan region, defined in terms of everyday functions.[4] In Ontario, as elsewhere, many cottage settings are linked to the metropolitan core by multiple residency – the act of households residing in more than one dwelling. These second homes and their analogues are used in large part by households based in major urban areas and are, therefore, found in significant concentrations within easy overland travel distance of notable examples of metropolitan cores such as Toronto, Montreal, Winnipeg, and Vancouver. Yet, in effect, they collectively constitute a form of urban settlement, for they are often clustered densely enough as well as being functionally connected to core metropolitan areas.

Adding to the richness of this discussion are the manners in which Ontario's cottage settings are very much part of collective imaginations as places of sojourn, connected to other parts of everyday life by meaningful travel – that is, traditional processes of recurrent mobility that are inherently embodied in the cottage as a temporary dwelling (Urbain 2002; Quinn 2004; Selwood and Tonts 2004; Rolshoven, 2005, 2006). Lister's work on map-making as place-making (Chapter 3 in this volume) illustrates the idealized conceptualization of such connections to place. This is not limited to Ontario, of course, but it is intriguing to consider how this particular regional variant has arisen.

The Ontario Case

Central Ontario's cottage country sits where the arable St Lawrence Lowlands meet the Canadian Shield, with its proliferation of small- and medium-sized freshwater lakes caused by glacial gouging of the hard granite-gneissic bedrock (Figures 8.1, 8.2). The history of these settings can reveal a great deal about Canadian attitudes to the weave of natural process in everyday (urban) life. Due to the poor potential for agriculture or other productive activities, tourism of various sorts, including cottage life, historically came to play a key economic role. Indeed, as Jasen (1995), Campbell (2004), and other historians have outlined, significant physiological and psychological benefits were associated with getting away from the industrial cities of the Great Lakes basin, and those with the means did so in increasing numbers from the late nineteenth century onward. This was made possible by the construction of railway lines, by which most people reached the lakes of the Near North (Wall 1979; Jasen 1995). One advocate of summer sojourns into the Muskoka region declared that 'the prudent man flies from all artificial conditions and yields himself to the soothing influences of nature

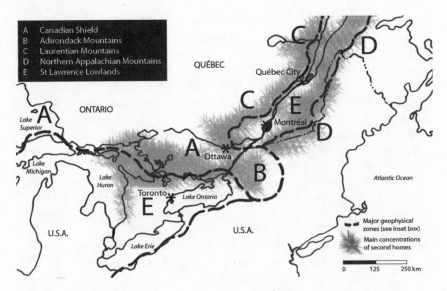

Figure 8.1. Second-home concentrations in central Canada

on the shores of the lakes and rivers in the depths of our primeval forests' (Stevenson 1886, 382). Such escapes were seen as a necessary coping strategy for regimented, overstructured, and perhaps unnatural city life. The rise of cottage life, therefore, was based on a strict dichotomy in which the dirty urban spaces of industry, production, and the working masses were seen as quite distinct from, if not irreconcilable with, the unspoiled, healthful, and regenerative spaces of the Near North (Smith 1990; Jasen 1995; Campbell 2004). This, in effect, was an expression of normative suburban impulses that shaped metropolitan regions across the Anglo-American world (Fishman 1987; Sies 1997). Observers noted that, 'by leaving an atmosphere tainted with sewer gas to inhale the tonic perfume of the pine bush,' city folk would soon find 'their cheeks flushing with freshened tints of purified blood' (Varley 1900, 29; Hague 1893, 263, respectively).

The twentieth-century rise of cottage life in Ontario was nothing short of phenomenal. By 1941, some 28,000 households owned cottages in central Ontario, and Toronto had one cottager per 60 persons – nearly six times the concentration relative to the rest of the province (Wolfe 1951). Hodge (1970, 1974) estimated that, by 1966, one Toronto-area household in seven (about 15 per cent) owned a cottage, paralleling post-war growth in the second-home phenomenon in the United

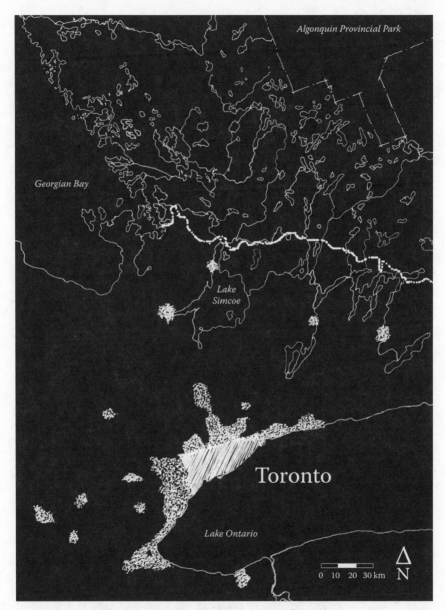

Figure 8.2. Water bodies and urban centres, central Ontario
Note: White hatching denotes the City of Toronto; the heavily dotted line indicates
where the rocky Canadian Shield emerges from beneath the arable till plains of the
St Lawrence Lowlands.

States, Australia, Norway, Sweden, and Denmark (Clout 1972, 1974; Langalden 1980; Nordin 1993; Tress 2000, 2002; Flognfeldt 2004; Frost 2004).[5] Not included in these figures were the thousands of people who rented accommodations, as was commonly the practice through the 1970s, or stayed with friends and families. As leisure time became more plentiful than in the past, a retreat from the city to a waterfront cottage setting came in the post-war years to be seen as a fundamental and sought-after pastime in the Toronto-centred metropolitan region. With echoes and variants across the country, it developed into a widely shared vision of the good life for Canadians in general. Yet the cultural effects of this surge may have exceeded their extent in real terms; no more than 20 per cent of Ontario residents have ever owned a second-home property. This without doubt is owing to the rise of visual media that portrayed cottage life as the place of choice for weekends and holidays for Toronto folk (see, for example, Rybczynski 1991; Jasen 1995). Moreover, the spread of second homes through the twentieth century was one material way in which Toronto overwhelmingly came to dominate the territory within three hundred kilometres of its centre.

In physical terms the typical central Ontario cottage property includes a wood-frame structure amid the woods near the water's edge (see Figure 8.3). Typologically, the physical environments of these

Figure 8.3. The classic image of the central Ontario cottage property, Crystal Lake. Nik Luka

Figure 8.4. Waterfront settlement pattern on Lake Muskoka: A single-tier necklace of private properties

water-oriented, second-home settings are well developed and thus lend themselves to generalized comments about central Ontario cottage country as both urban form and cultural landscape. Typically, one finds a distinctive spatial pattern of lakes and rivers that are public, but largely inaccessible because they are hemmed in by private properties forming a single-tier necklace (Figure 8.4).[6] The cottage properties themselves are eclectic in their architectural detail, but marked by a remarkably consistent organization of built form, with a driveway leading to a back door, along with a cleared space in front (that is, on the water side), often consisting of a manicured lawn, patio space, and footpaths leading to a dock used for swimming and mooring watercraft such as a canoe, the occasional sailboat, and the much more ubiquitous motorboat (Figure 8.5). The pattern varies, as do the users; some are more naturalized, others are more geared to leisure and sport.

Cottage life flourished in central Ontario even with the energy crisis and stagflation of the early 1970s – although the proportion of households owning a second home dropped from 7.4 per cent in 1973

Figure 8.5. Highly modified waterfront landscape, complete with manicured front lawns, in the typical spatial pattern of cleared space between the 'cottage' dwelling and the shoreline (Stony Lake). Nik Luka

to 5.9 per cent in 1991, it rose again to 7.9 per cent by 2006. Partially as an effect of growth pressures and transformations in the land market, but also owing to an aging population gradually taking its retirement, a rising number of cottagers – still considered for official purposes as seasonal residents – have chosen to live, since the 1980s, by the lake on a year-round basis (Halseth and Rosenberg 1995; Dahms 1996; Halseth 1998, 2004). This is a pattern not unlike that of the exurban 'senior-polis' described by Jauhianen (2009). One result is a highly dispersed landscape of year-round dwellings that are difficult to service by local municipalities (Halseth and Rosenberg 1990, 1995; Joseph and Smit 1985). The conversion of seasonal dwellings into permanent housing occupied twelve months of the year has made cottage country now more than ever an urbanizing edge and a suburban frontier of sorts: in 2004, the average waterfront cottage price in Ontario exceeded the average house cost in Toronto for the first time.[7] This renewed demand for waterfront cottages, combined with year-long appropriations, has brought significant transformations to bear on cottage landscapes, and major tensions have arisen. Prominent among these, especially in the past ten years, is growing concern over the ecological carrying capacity of waterfront settings. While this is sometimes a thinly veiled disdain for the intensification of use and the sheer increase in users, legitimate concerns are voiced over water quality, ecosystem health, and the conservation of the striking aesthetic and experiential qualities of Ontario's lakes and forests. Many second-home settings have become hotly contested spaces in which the priorities and expectations of locals, cottagers, cottagers-cum-locals, and other users collide (Halseth 1998).

Contemporary patterns of change have been concurrent with continued population increases in the GTA. This is now the most populous Census Metropolitan Area in Canada, with a population of 5.7 million in 2010 (Statistics Canada 2011) and with a typical annual increase ranging from 80,000 to 130,000 people (Bourne et al. 2003). Given that the total population of central Ontario is expected to rise by three million over the next thirty years (COSGP 2003), the late 1990s were justly marked by widespread concern and considerable public debate over sprawl in the region. This led in 2005 to the creation of a metropolitan Greenbelt using two major geophysical features – the Oak Ridges Moraine and the Niagara Escarpment – as the official limits of the continuously built-up metropolis. Hanna and Slocombe (in this volume) discuss the integration of rural and urban uses and the challenges associated with planning for the Oak Ridges Moraine. An irony of the Greenbelt as created is, of course, its disregard for whatever lies beyond, which is left largely unprotected from the pressures of population increase.

There are important considerations in terms of the diversity of individuals who practise cottage life – or, more precisely, the lack thereof. For obvious reasons, second-home ownership is limited to households with considerably high earning power. Hodge (1970, 1974) found that cottage users tended to have incomes well above the Ontario average and that they were typically owner-occupiers of large detached houses in Toronto. Their families were also somewhat larger than the provincial average. Halseth (1998, 228) has drawn attention to the stark contrast between the waterfront and the back country populations, a result of well-to-do city-based households having colonized the lakes while local residents with lower levels of formal education and household income than their seasonal neighbours reside inland. Cottage life has also historically been marked by ethnocultural homogeneity. The respondents reported in this study almost all appeared to be European in origin; aside from the category of Canadian, the only ethnic backgrounds singly named by 10 per cent or more of respondents were the thistle, shamrock, and rose as entwined in Anglo-Canadian yore – that is, Scottish, Irish, and English origins.

Even more troubling, an ethnoreligious geography historically has marked cottage country. By the 1920s and 1930s, Protestants were numerous on the big Muskoka lakes, and some evidence suggests that access by others was controlled. In their social histories of anti-Semitism in Toronto, both Betcherman (1975) and Levitt and Shaffir (1987) reported that they recalled resorts in Muskoka explicitly barred Jewish guests, even boasting through advertisements that they were for Gentiles only. Wolfe (1962) characterized the early boom in tourism as the ascendancy of the society resort, in which social divisions along economic, regional, ethnic, and religious lines may have had their strongest historic manifestation. By the mid-twentieth century, however, Jewish cottagers had come to be numerous at Lake Simcoe (Wolfe 1951). Protective covenants are also known to have barred access by eastern Europeans and other minority groups to parts of Toronto and Hamilton; evidence suggests that cottage country landowners and realtors may have similarly acted as gatekeepers. This lends an unsettling dimension to the narrative of these second-home settings as natural places, and such considerations must be kept in mind when discussing the narratives of cottage life in central Ontario and elsewhere in Canada.

Facing New Challenges and Finding Opportunities for Urban Sustainability

A critical question that arises in the second-home landscapes of central Ontario concerns the overarching challenge of urban sustainability. How can we better knit settlement patterns into natural process, or find the common middle ground to which Cronon (1996) has referred? How can we operationalize the ideas of integrative, proactive planning while avoiding rural tensions? These questions can be addressed with specific reference to the waterfront settings of cottage life. However, it is more pertinent to consider how these second-home settings can help their inhabitants think about how to dwell within nature and, in turn, enable us collectively to make sustainability more of a reality in contemporary city regions. Important work needs to be done in cultural terms on how people think about space and develop a connection to place – not merely the instrumental and technological work of manipulating physical environments, as this fundamentally influences everyday social practice. This work involves two key themes. First, many people seem more willing and able to adapt to living lightly in their cottage setting, which is seen as more natural and somehow worth treating more carefully than a city or suburban life space. They are less bound by societal norms in the leisure landscapes of cottage life and potentially experience a deeper connection, which sets the tone for more malleable ways of life. Second, cottage settings can become part of a learning ecology in that useful modifications can be made in these contexts that people might not consider appropriate in their everyday (sub)urban settings, where they are otherwise based. These changes in how people use space, in turn, can be transferred gradually into more urban contexts. In other words, people can dabble with different ways of doing things (wiser lifestyle choices vis-à-vis urban sustainability) in their cottage milieu and bring those changes to bear elsewhere – that is, in urban environments.

My arguments are elaborated in several interconnected ways. This starts with evidence that perceptions of nature, although often socially constructed and distorted in various ways, figure prominently in how many second-home users in Ontario make sense of the landscapes of cottage country – in other words, that people are usefully aware of nature's importance in their own understandings of, and connection to, place. I propose that these perceptions inform an active willingness on the part of these individuals to modify their behaviour in the interest of sustainability. It is in this belief that we have here opportunity for positive change. If cottage users have an increased sensitivity, if not always a sensibility, with respect to natural processes – specifically concerning the impacts of their own actions on the larger social, ecological, and economic spaces with which they engage–then it stands to reason that the tensions embodied in seemingly widely shared ideas of cottage country as a natural place can be linked with getting people to really think about how well their cottage as a physical thing and as a place of human behaviour literally fits into ecosystem processes.

The material I present here was collected using a dual primary research strategy: an online questionnaire and a battery of in-depth, face-to-face, semi-structured interviews undertaken with cottage users in central Ontario in 2003. These two methods were coupled to allow themes arising through the online questionnaire to be probed and veri-fied on an ongoing basis through the in-depth interviews. For the on-line instrument, which was hosted on a University of Toronto Web site, responses were indirectly solicited by several non-randomized means, and the sample should not be considered representative.[8] The final sample retained for analysis comprised a total of two hundred indi-viduals.[9] Some key descriptive points on the sample group bear noting, as follows:

- most were found to be owner-occupiers of two properties (a city dwelling and a cottage);
- the sample was evenly split by gender;
- more than half of the respondents were between the ages of forty-one and sixty – the baby boom cohort – while another one in four was between sixty-one and eighty;
- three in four respondents had children;
- most respondents were well educated, with more than half possess-ing a bachelor's or higher degree; and
- most respondents had high earning power, with two in five having a gross household income of $100,000 or more.

By these indicators, the sample respondents differ from the average resident of the GTA and, while this sample cannot be considered repre-sentative, the following exploration of results is meant to highlight important hypotheses and premises – food for thought – that could be confirmed through more comprehensive primary research.[10] More-over, while the people who practise cottage life may be the elite of the Canadian population according to critical indicators of power such as earnings and education, it is also the case that such groups are often early adopters of progressive ways of life. The challenges are to rec-ognize, unpack, and find ways to reconceptualize these popular per-ceptions. To this end, several themes are outlined in the following paragraphs.

The Indissociability of Commitment to Place and Interest in Nature

Canadian cottage folklore and popular publications suggest that second-home settings have a permanence, making them almost transcendental 'power points' in people's lives. The survey respondents expressed a profound commitment to their own cottage milieu as a place to stay, and did not see it at all as saleable commodity – although they often described their (sub)urban dwellings as goods that could be exchanged for others as needs dictated.[11] In effect, use value exceeded exchange value for just over half (56.5 per cent) of owner-occupiers in terms of wanting to keep the cottage within the family by passing it down to children or other relatives. Although selling the cottage was preferred by one-third (30.5 per cent) and 13 per cent were unsure, there is clearly a long-term commitment to place, as other observers of second homes have discussed (see, for example, Jaakson 1986; Kaltenborn 1997b, 1998; de la Soudière 1998; Dubost 1998). Respondents' comments were replete with indications of how beloved the cottage was, and in ways that could not be assigned a market value. As one woman stated, 'this place is so entrenched in my psyche that I cannot conceive of not having it as part of my life.' Aspects of the continuity and change over time marking user attachment are discussed elsewhere (Luka 2008a,b) and they are congruent in many ways with the more general considerations outlined in Lister's work on mapping processes (Chapter 3 in this volume). It should be noted, however, that cottage settings are identified as anchors through the lives of their users and as gathering places for families across generations:

> I love my waterfront property; it has been a core part of my life, and for three generations of my family. If for one reason or another I was forced to sell one of my properties, it would be my primary residence, not my cottage, so strong are my feelings. (Male respondent in his thirties, Kasshabog Lake)

To test this commitment to place, respondents were presented with a scenario in which their personal mobility was curtailed due to unforeseen circumstances. What effect would this have on their view of the cottage setting as a more-or-less permanent anchor in their lives? More than half the respondents (51.5 per cent) responded that, even if they could no longer operate a motor vehicle, they would continue to spend time at their cottage property by making special arrangements – for example, by engaging someone else to provide transportation. Only 14 per cent said with certainty that this would curtail use of their cottage country property, while another 18.5 per cent were unsure. Four in five owner-occupier respondents expressed no intention of selling

Table 8.1. Responses to Statements Asserting How Cottage Settings Represent Home Places

Statement	Mean	Mode
(5-point scale where a high score represents full agreement)		
When I am here, I have all the privacy and tranquillity I could desire.	4.18	5
I feel very safe and secure when I am in this area.	4.21	4
This place reflects the sort of person I am.	3.89	4
When I am away from here for too long, I find that I miss it.	4.32	4
This place is where I can really be myself.	4.27	4
This is a gathering place for my family and friends.	4.24	4
This place is unique.	4.22	4
When I am here, I really feel at home.	4.19	4

their property within the next two to three years. Further evidence of how cottage settings are anchors in the lives of their users can be seen in how these places satisfy the conditions of the meaning of home, as demonstrated in the literature on housing and place attachment; Table 8.1 summarizes key findings in this respect.[12]

Clearly, folkloric ideas of permanence are relevant; the second-home settings denoted by the term cottage country are deeply cherished by their users, who are firmly committed to their cottage setting and to the permanency of cottage life. This positive link between user and place among respondents and their future generations leads one to suggest the notion of 'potential energy' for sustainability initiatives. This physics analogy is quite deliberate – one could argue that the potential energy of attachment to place can be converted to useful kinetic energy through ecological design. The argument is supported above all by evidence of care and concern over perceived transformations in the cottage setting. This is first apparent in the fact that four out of five respondents declared having seen changes in their cottage settings since they began spending time there.[13] Often these were supported by detailed descriptions:

> I miss the peace, quiet and wild beauty of the past, as more and more land is developed and suburbanized. It dumbfounds me that some people want to come here and cut down all the trees ('They could fall on someone') and

grass ('It harbours West Nile mosquitoes') . . . I'm concerned that I don't hear the dawn chorus of birds anymore, or see the great variety of birds, as in years past. I wonder about the old fish species, like pickerel, that don't seem to be in the lake anymore. I miss being able to wander the woodland paths at will, since they're now so often posted as private property and/or for hunting. (Female respondent in her forties, Clearwater Lake)

Two-thirds of respondents had significant concerns about the transformations they perceived to be under way in their cottage context. As would be expected in any study of home environments, there were comments about changes that had adversely affected the quality of their personal experience, but genuine concern was more consistently expressed over threats to the distinctiveness of the cultural landscapes and ecosystem health of second-home settings:

I see too much development, too many variances to zoning, and too much suburbanization. The character of the landscape is being lost beneath lawns and suburban landscaping . . . I am an ecologist. I love Muskoka for its landscape and for its natural diversity. I don't want to spend my down time beside a suburban swimming pool. (Female respondent in her thirties, Muldrew Lake)

Of course, most individuals can be expected to respond negatively in such situations. Whether they were marshalling arguments that ecosystem health was being threatened as a vehicle for other, perhaps less noble, concerns such as decreasing property values or an influx of less desirable users, or their worries were about substantive matters in their own right, respondents provided compelling thoughts on why they found it difficult to accept change:

[I am] concerned that the traditional Muskoka cottage area will start to be like any city suburb . . . It's hard to close the doors to others, but to have the doors wide open will change the area forever. It's a tough issue . . . We have immediate neighbours who have moved up permanently and it is changing our surroundings. They want better roads, better lighting, etc. We want narrow dirt roads with trees hanging over them and no lighting! . . . We enjoy the peace and quiet, seeing the stars, walking on deserted roads, and the sense of safety. If these things were to change significantly there would not be a lot of point to making the trip each weekend. (Female respondent in her fifties, Kahshe Lake)

As the comment indicates, some individuals questioned the merit of continuing to spend time in cottage settings – indeed, about one in three respondents agreed that their plans to stay might be affected if further changes were to take place. Dushenko (Chapter 9 in this volume) observes similar concerns at the heart of rural tensions in a case study on Vancouver Island. At the same time, however, a positive message echoes commitment to place, as one-third of respondents unequivocally declared their intent to stay regardless of what changes are brought to pass. How can these convictions be reconciled, especially given that most respondents live in the core of the Toronto metropolitan region? The following paragraphs explore how this commitment to place tends to be linked to a dissociation of nature and the city in the minds of respondents.

Cottage Country as an 'Other' to Urban Life – and the Role of Nature

The first indicator of the duality of urban/cottage life is the simplest aspect of multiple residency: the fact that one must travel regularly between two settings. Three in four of the study respondents met this criterion, and the geographic scale was significant – only one in ten travelled a hundred kilometres or less between the two dwellings; for two out of three, the distance varied between a hundred and three hundred kilometres. Most of the households (71.2 per cent) were, as expected, in the GTA, the primary life-space for cottagers in central Ontario; the two areas are a functional fit, as earlier studies of the same geographical context have found (Wolfe 1951; Mai 1971; Hodge 1974). More than half (53.5 per cent) of respondents travelled between their cottage properties and their primary dwellings at least sixteen times yearly, confirming the hypothesis that these individuals quite regularly traverse a very large life-space – at least once each month on average. July and August were the peak months; only half the respondents use their second-home dwellings in the coldest months from December to March. While this exaggerated mobility may raise red flags with respect to urban sustainability, it should be kept in mind that, until the post-war years, most people travelled to cottage country by train, and mass transit of the sort found in continental Europe is a very real future possibility in central Ontario. One such model is Switzerland, where many trunk rail corridors run piggyback trains, an overland equivalent of the car ferries found in British Columbia, the Great Lakes, and the Atlantic provinces.

Users consider their cottage setting to be quite distinct from the metropolitan region, despite the clear functional connections, which they themselves maintain. A vital role is played by the desire to somehow be in a more natural setting. While only one among many motivations – such as the wish to separate work and leisure, the enjoyment of conspicuous consumption, and the desire to go somewhere different – this particular factor is importantly distinctive. The basic act of getting back to nature is undeniably grounded in physical well-being: the ability to escape from a hot, smoggy, crowded urban area in summer. There also appears, however, to be a powerful yet generic set of symbolic associations linking central Ontario cottage country to ideas about nature and wilderness – ideas often described in scholarly debate as the social construction(s) of nature.[14] This resonates with Kaltenborn's (1997a,b, 1998, 2002) findings in Norway, where people-place bonds in second-home settings are predicated on generic conceptions of nature and the landscape. Certainly this sense of otherness with respect to cities figures prominently in studies of second-home use in different cultural contexts.[15]

What sort of 'other' is the cottage setting in the eyes of its users, and what is its cultural significance? It is not widely considered to be a wilderness setting, as Cronon (1996) has shown to be so centrally important in the American psyche. Hardly one in twenty respondents agreed with the statement, 'This place is part of the wilderness,' as illustrated in the following example:

> Just go back two hundred metres and you're in wilderness, and the farther in that direction you go, the more wilderness it becomes . . . things there are basically in natural state, and that is my definition of wilderness for this area. At about two hundred kilometres from a very large mega-urban development, that's as [much] wilderness as you're going to get. (Male respondent in his sixties, Severn River)

It is intriguing to consider (instead of 'wilderness') the term *countryside*, which denotes landscapes perceived to be *settled*; it came into common usage in early eighteenth-century England to describe the perceived amenity value of productive yet scenic rural landscapes (Bunce 1994). It subsequently spawned a curious idealization of nature and country life based on a combination of romanticism and agrarianism, as shown in studies by Feldman (1990, 1996), Hummon (1990), Lorzing (2001), and Williams (1973, 1980). This idealization also has traction beyond the Anglo-American context – see Mak (2000 [1996]) in reference to the long-settled rural landscape of the Netherlands. Four of five respondents concurred that their second-home settings were part of the rural countryside, suggesting that they are understood such that their cottage represented a viable weave of nature and culture in place. Others stressed that there were subtle differences between cottage country and the rural countryside, usually associating the latter with active agricultural land through which one passes en route to the former.

Abundantly clear among respondents was the conviction that cottage settings had particular value as contexts in which they were able to interact fruitfully with nature, notwithstanding their dissociation of cottage country from the wilderness. Some sort of engagement with 'nature' is a vital dimension of the cottage experience. While respondents saw cottage settings as substantively unlike those of (sub)urban life, where nature is perceived as non-existent, the survey results did not indicate a high level of what might be termed 'ecological literacy' among cottagers. Much of the respondent discourse in fact tended to affirm the findings of Bixler and Floyd (1997) that nature is scary, disgusting, and uncomfortable, and to which one must not get 'too close for comfort' (see also Bogner and Wiseman 1997; Castree and Braun1998; Vaccarino [2000] 2008). Most cottagers do not appear to seek a direct engagement with natural processes but, rather, a symbolic and/or aesthetic interaction. Although emphatic that their cottage settings were places of high environmental quality, as the respondents defined it, three-quarters seemed to abstract natural processes, in that 'nature' simply means the presence of dense, unmanicured mature forest cover or other greenery, curious 'wild' animals, and the proximity of natural water bodies. This dimension of getting back to nature through cottage life meshes well with one appraisal of the Anglo-American countryside ideal. As Bunce (1994, 29) observes, '[t]he absorption of nature worship into a more general sentiment for rural scenery can be attributed in large measure to the belief that rural life is more natural than urban ... At heart it is an idea which romanticises pre-industrial culture, casting the traditional rural lifestyle and communities of the past in nostalgic contrast to the dynamic and individualistic culture of the present.'

Despite their nostalgic and romantic associations, there is a positive component to the points just mentioned. The expression of a collective difficulty in reconciling natural process with everyday life settings (the city or the suburb) represents an important bridge, even if it serves to help people exculpate themselves from enfolding natural process into their everyday (urban) lives. Second-home landscapes exacerbate the difficulty people seem to have in seeing the city as a setting where nature can exist in any meaningful way, but they also clearly represent an important way in which urban-dwellers negotiate a problematic tension between urban life and their longing for something more natural, however defined. The cottage setting can thus be seen as embodying a kind of urban settlement that its users, and perhaps others, see as somehow more natural than conventional (sub)urban settlement patterns. In their positive association with socially constructed ideas of nature, central Ontario's cottage country settings are also sophisticated, albeit relatively generic, representations of good places in which to spend time and connect with nature. Thus, although cottage country is very much as an 'other' to the city, its role as a place to connect with nature is vitally meaningful to users. It is in this aspect that the tension between urban life and cottage life seems to generate great potential energy for positive change, as users make positive associations between settlement patterns and natural process in second-home settings. Growth in the active awareness of such a potential linkage would nonetheless be remarkable given its minor presence in popular perceptions of urban and suburban areas.

An Openness to Behavioural Change: Room for Knowledge and Action

The palpable concern over the ecological integrity of nature, as perceived in the cottage setting, points to the potential willingness to make concessions considered too involved or altogether radical in the everyday urban context.[16] There is a sense among cottage users that they are eminently qualified to comment on how human activity influences the sustainability of their own setting, which amounts to a nascent form of stewardship. Consider the following example:

> We live year-round at our cottage, and have tried to faithfully comply with all the rules and regulations, plus being very aware of the environment–using no fertilisers, bleach, and other harmful chemicals. It's a cottage built in the early 1950s that blends into the background. Would people that move into new homes take as much care? Would the new homes blend into the background? That, to me, is a great concern. (Female respondent in her sixties, Six Mile Lake)

Raw though it may sometimes be, this sort of self-organizing stewardship – as a by-product of the strongly expressed commitment to place revealed above – is part of the potential energy on which efforts to achieve urban sustainability depend. This form of benevolent protectionism must be distinguished, however, from the unbridled knee-jerk phenomenon of 'NIMBYism' if it is to be put to good use.[17] One way forward is seen in instances where respondents alluded directly to the notion of the cottager as a good steward of both the land and of the place:

> Just because we have a demand does not mean we have to meet that demand to the detriment of the environment. We should not view ourselves as landowners but caretakers. Any new development should only occur if it can be demonstrated that the environment can support the change. Even with that caveat there should be limitations as all development, however well intentioned, will ultimately have an effect. (Male respondent in his forties, Crane Lake)

An important aspect of cottaging in central Ontario is owner-building, a second point supporting the premise for behavioural change. Owner-building quite literally refers to the process by which users construct their own houses by investing their own sweat equity instead of hiring specialized contractors. It can be seen as a historical antecedent – as shown by Rapoport (1969) and Harris (1996) – to the contemporary do-it-yourself movement. The main difference is that owner-building tends to involve the complete task of erecting one's own dwelling.[18] This is generally only possible in the absence of well-organized and strictly enforced building regulations, as was the case in most Ontario cottage settings before the 1960s (Wolfe 1951, 1977; Gravel 1968). Indeed, until recent years, speculative building by land developers was rare. Individuals tend to buy vacant land on which they build their own structure or, increasingly, have one custom-built by contractors. Among study participants, patterns of owner-building were found to be commonplace. Although local carpenters had been hired in some cases to build the cottage structure, almost half (46.0 per cent) of respondents, or their parents or grandparents, had built their own cottage; fully half (49.5 per cent) foresaw undertaking major renovations or other improvements to the cottage structure themselves. In many instances, this was indissociable from the respondent's attachment to the place itself:

This is not that shabbily built that you'd want to tear it down . . . My son-in-law asked me, would you buy a lot and build again? Ah, yeah, I'd like to do that, but I don't know–there are so many slivers in my hands from this place, you know, you've given a lot of yourself, so to lose this place . . . you'd have to be careful that you don't lose what's really valuable to you, not in the money sense, but in terms of feelings. (Male respondent in his sixties, Crystal Lake)

Owner-building in the central Ontario context affirms the findings of Chaplin (1999) among British second-home owners in rural France and of Kaltenborn (1997a,b, 2002) in the Norwegian context. In effect, user commitment to the second home involves a mingling of production and consumption practices, including a sense of purpose from being actively involved in the building, maintenance, and longer-term planning of housing space *qua* dwelling (see also Heidegger 1958, 1993). Indeed, even in more recent years, when speculative cottage building by land developers and custom building by contractors are more commonplace, this same sense is evident:

We bought the cottage that was here; we were in it for five years . . . we tried to decide what to do with it–whether we wanted to rip it down, fix it, raze it, whatever. We knew we needed to do something to it structurally; it needed things, and in the end, our builder, you know, said to us, really, we were smarter if we just tore it down and started again, and that's what we did . . . We knew exactly what we wanted. We knew how we wanted it on the lot. My husband designed it, and then of course we went to an architect to make sure that the roof would stay up. (Female respondent in her fifties, Thunder Bay Beach)

These direct modes of engagement with space and place are important because they embody the principle that everyone is a designer, an important aspect of ecological design as defined by van der Ryn and Cowan (1996). This principle is expressed in cottage settings by literally being built into cottages, cabins, and camps across Canada. The key to unlocking this potential seems to be the relative openness of a critical mass of users to architectural and behavioural experimentation as an extension of the propensity for owner-building.

If a considerable proportion of the cottager population demonstrates a reasonable awareness that the second-home setting represents a balance of nature and culture, concern over perceived transformations could help to encourage a readiness for change. For instance:

> Additional cottages on Lake of Bays would ruin (what for us is) the essence: a peaceful, quiet, spiritual, country environment . . . There is the very real risk that development will undermine the essence of cottage country . . . Traditional cottagers balanced their urban and country needs and wants. I fear that permanent cottagers will impose their urban selves here, and push for changes away from what I called the essence. Even so, maybe the inevitable push and resistance will lead to something mutually satisfying. (Male respondent in his sixties, Lake of Bays)

Under these perceived threats, many second-home users are likely to be interested in guidance, knowledge, action, and intervention. This could translate into social capital and eventual agency in mobilization processes similar to those discussed elsewhere in this volume (see Newman and Waldron, Chapter 5; Dale, Chapter 6; and Dushenko, Chapter 9). Changes now under way – not merely the transformation of the settlement system and way of life historically associated with cottage settings, but often changes in ecosystem processes – are seen as unacceptable. While these objections may be cited to buttress the argument against change of any sort, genuine concern is apparent and extends to a sense that not enough is being done. The sheer size of new cottage dwellings was often used as a proxy (or perhaps a scapegoat) in this respect:

> Our concerns are always about the effects on groundwater when huge structures are constructed. Smaller, normal cottages are no problem but that's not what is being built today . . . Groundwater is the source of all of our well water. Public beaches along the bay were closed last summer for the first time due to pollution! We monitor water twice a week and so far, our beach has been safe, but it's a constant concern now. (Female respondent in her fifties, Nottawasaga Bay)

Intermingled with general expressions of concern over emerging problems were specific 'horror stories' such as the following:

> The road created to develop the west shore of Kennisis was purpose-built in an inappropriate location by the contractor who wanted to save time and money, ruining Soap Pond and threatening loon nesting areas, as well

as other wildlife. While this particular contractor has been caught and must make reparations, we need to stop these people before they can do the damage. (Female respondent in her thirties, Kennisis Lake)

Cottage users seem ready to undertake concerted action – the social mobilization Dale describes in Chapter 6 in this volume. This can be informed by professional intervention at scales and in ways not normally considered viable in the market-driven urban contexts of North America. Most study participants expressed the conviction that intervention was desirable, if not badly needed. This was sometimes expressed in pejorative us-versus-them terms, and yet there was a clear expression of the need for individual and collective action on everyone's part, as demonstrated by the following:

[I have seen] a decline in water quality and more development impacting on natural landscape features and environmentally sensitive areas . . . Development should only proceed after environmental concerns are examined and addressed. The carrying capacity of areas should be determined by local councils to prevent degradation of water, vegetation, and wildlife resources . . . Zoning and environmental assessments should be strictly enforced and upheld and perhaps in many areas strengthened before irreparable damage or overdevelopment occurs. (Female respondent in her fifties, Georgian Bay)

Respondents clearly asserted, nonetheless, that existing regulations were inadequate, or at least poorly enforced. While accusations that local authorities are not capable or empowered to deal with concerns forms an undercurrent in any local municipality (see also Dushenko, Chapter 9 in this volume), there was a marked consistency of views among these respondents from central Ontario. The message is clear: an inadequate regulatory framework combined with a dearth of good practice amounts to death by a thousand cuts. Some respondents spoke diplomatically; others were blunter:

Careful, thoughtful development can be okay, but intensive overdevelopment without regard for the preservation of the ecology and landscape will ultimately only ruin the experience for everyone . . . [and yet] variances to zoning bylaws seem to be the norm, [with] very little planning backbone at the municipal or provincial levels. (Female respondent in her thirties, Muldrew Lake)

We're not impressed with what passes as planning in the Township. I think the local planning department has its head up its ass. A common refrain for many years, yes, but most municipalities don't see that they are allowing to be destroyed the very thing that makes the area attractive. In the end, it will come back to haunt them financially and environmentally! (Male respondent in his thirties, Bruce Lake)

Several respondents offered compelling ideas on how to deal more pro-actively with the situation. Among the specific suggestions were many calls for building-size restrictions, although these did not always articulate the elusive goodness underpinning these calls:

My concern is about the sustainability of the environment with the greater use and abuse [of cottage country] . . . [and with] the dismantling of existing cottages in order to build monster homes in the absence of building restrictions to keep this in reasonable check . . . Municipalities should place more restrictions on size of buildings allowed, and have better planning for increased population with regard to available resources. (Female respondent in her sixties, Lake Muskoka)

Many of these comments suggest that the ecosystem health of an area is often conflated with the aesthetic and functional aspects of second-home settlement patterns. Although it can be problematic, this conflation also holds promise in terms of an awareness of how human culture and natural process can and should coexist. There appears to be an emerging sensitivity to the importance of living more lightly on the land and, indeed, on the waterfront. In many cases, respondents stressed that precisely because second-home settings were so delightfully not comparable to the city or the suburbs, they merited extra effort:

[I am] strongly opposed to second-tier cottages or cottages encroaching on environmentally protected areas, and strongly opposed to large clearing of trees, changing shorelines, washing vegetation to bare rock along the shoreline, or planting lawns or gardens in front of cottages; I have seen each of these done. [I am] opposed to monstrous three- and four-storey winterized cottages by the very wealthy. (Male respondent in his fifties, Lake Rosseau)

Clearly, there is a growing hunger for significant change in the way cottages, cabins, and camps are made to fit into the natural landscape.

This represents a great opportunity for bottom-up micro-scale intervention that could then spread incrementally through the agency of the user-as-designer, and it would be a fine example of the judicious use and development of social capital. An especially good idea in this respect also reflects a more positive attitude about newcomers to cottage life:

> I have noticed that the new cottage owners have paid quite a bit for their places and seem inclined to use them every weekend, and that they can afford bigger gas-guzzling boats and many more seadoos. I also have seen a lot of development of the shorelines where it is not permitted with no one being made to stop, and a lot of the cottages that sat in disrepair are now being fixed up for future sale. I would like every new cottage owner to receive an environmental impact booklet from the government, as a lot of new owners do things in the first few years they wouldn't dream of doing later when they find out the damage they have caused. (Male respondent, age unknown, Eel's Lake)

Given the range of comments presented above, the challenge appears to be to put more tools within easy reach of users. Approaches and strategies that are viral – that induce positive change on a parcel-by-parcel, household-by-household basis – therefore hold the most promise, as is often the case with effective public policy. Further examples of how to harness the potential energy for sustainable change might include incentive programs and demonstration projects–an ecologically benign cottage compound as a resort destination, for instance.[19] The details are of lesser importance for present purposes. What matters is that users are ready for positive change, and it behooves us to help them exercise their own agency in this respect given the significant gains in social capital that could occur.

Conclusion

Several matters now prominent in debates over urban sustainability converge in Ontario's waterfront second-home settings: 1) concerns over sprawl; 2) a growing interest in the future of metropolitan landscapes, especially in terms of concern for their long-term ecological, social, and economic viability; and 3) the urgent need to develop strategic interventions. Cottage life represents a potentially useful portal for urban sustainability by offering opportunities for people to learn how to make sustainable lifestyle choices. One must, of course, eschew the mythical notion that a cabin in the woods is inherently more natural, however defined, but the very naïveté of this idea can also be strategically enfolded into efforts to embrace and integrate natural process more fully throughout the metropolitan regions in which most Canadians live. If so many people literally and figuratively buy into this myth, policy-makers and advocates of change would do well to tap into it. A winning combination would be to understand the importance of nature among second-home users – despite, or because of, the tension inherent between urban life and cottage life – and how this represents a great potential energy for positive change given the firmness with which users are anchored to their second-home settings. Such an approach would act synergistically to reveal the hunger on the part of the typical second-home user for agency and for significant change in the way their cottages, cabins, and camps are encouraged or permitted to fit into the natural landscape.

The arguments and ideas presented here are linked to the central preoccupations of urban sustainability through the notion of ecological design. As defined by Sim van der Ryn and Stuart Cowan, this is any work of design that minimizes environmentally harmful impacts by integrating itself with natural processes. It serves as a hinge connecting nature and culture as 'a form of engagement and partnership with nature that is not bound to a particular design profession'; instead, ecological integrity is maintained through responsive and responsible *design* (1996, 18). It is useful to consider the five interwoven principles suggested by van der Ryn and Cowan vis-à-vis this goal:

1 let solutions grow from place as responses to the existing weave of nature and culture;
2 inform design through ecological accounting, so that minimal adverse environmental impact is a key performance dimension for all urban growth and development;
3 design with nature by engaging processes that regenerate rather than deplete natural capital where possible;
4 recognize that everyone is a designer – that is, all users; and,
5 make nature visible in all its processes and cycles so as to continuously inform us of our place within nature.

These principles are favoured for the development of substantive, meaningful, and strategic responses to the problems of sprawl – which can be understood as settlement patterns that do little to respond to their natural and cultural context. The more paradigmatic term 'dumb design' is anything that 'fails to consider the health of human communities or of ecosystems' because it literally does not speak to place (van der Ryn and Cowan 1996, 10; see also Luka and Lister 2000). Parallels can be seen with three of the major criteria identified by Robinson (Chapter 4 in this volume) as part of third-generation responses – namely, that 1) sustainability principles must be integral to planning, design, and building rather than being tacked on at the end; 2) meaningful citizen engagement is necessary through all phases of project conceptualization, planning, design, building, and operation; and 3) cookie-cutter approaches to sustainability are bound to be less successful than place-based ones.

Positive action can occur in moving strategically and acting at the appropriate scales and in practical ways. The second-home areas scattered to the north and east of central Toronto are full of opportunities that are both exciting and very real for reconciling and reconnecting nature with culture, and can stand as proxies for similar second-home areas across Canada. Getting people to embrace change in these settings may not be as difficult as in more conventional urban contexts. Cottage users appear to be ready and willing to accept certain tradeoffs that might be rejected in other contexts. By extension, practitioners and policy-makers should consider cottage settings key sites for demonstration projects and more comprehensive, conservation-driven, ecological-design strategies. Proactive planning and design could capitalize on the images and meanings associated with cottage country to establish stronger links between the human-cultural and natural components and processes even within metropolitan regions as the principal places of human settlement.

The potential energy for ecological design, referred to earlier, has already been embodied across Canada in non-profit organizations such as the Living by Water project[20] and the Federation of Ontario Cottager Associations.[21] Both of these have been instrumental in building momentum for positive change and in building agency through the mobilization of social capital. Positive results are exemplified by a comprehensive handbook published in Alberta and Ontario (Kipp and Callaway 2002) and by a similar publication in French (Hade 2003). More broadly speaking, important policy changes are underway across Canada. Recent planning reforms in Ontario, for instance, require all municipalities to address issues of sustainability in terms of planning and design in the next five years (Robinson, Chapter 4 in this volume), including the requirement that integrated community plans be developed through engagement with community stakeholders (Hanna and Slocombe, Chapter 2 in this volume). The importance of drawing on the knowledge and concerns of people such as the respondents whose comments are cited throughout this chapter is just one example in this latter respect.

There are ongoing debates over the fiscal burden increasingly borne by waterfront landowners following provincial property tax reform (specifically, the 1998 introduction of Current Value Assessment).[22] Since local municipalities in second-home receiving areas are generally organized in townships as the primary administrative unit, water-oriented user interests might not always be well represented. This is especially noticeable as cottagers' concerns tend to be seasonal, while municipal politicians and staff are responsible for planning and administrative issues across large territories. As a result, municipalities are, by necessity, preoccupied with matters most pertinent to the year-round residential population. There are also possibilities for significant repercussions on a more abstract level. Using ecological design ideas in cottage settings could offer a tremendous potential for diffusion of these very ideas into the fold of everyday life in more conventional urban settings. Great strides could be made toward dealing with seemingly intractable problems of urban growth and change by capitalizing people's willingness to embrace change in a second-home context. In this is a compelling way in which we can rise to the challenge articulated by Cronon (1996, 90): only by ceasing to think of nature as (just) *out there* and instead by seeing it as (also) *in here* will we be able to live rightly in the world.

NOTES

1 Empirical studies of Americans and Canadians reveal that residents of cities and their metropolitan suburbs indeed tend to perceive nature as 'scary, disgusting, and uncomfortable' (see, for example, Bixler and Floyd 1997). The core characteristics of self-sustaining ecosystem processes are especially well explained by Nina-Marie Lister (1998) as complexity, diversity, and uncertainty. In a curious parallel that is also a strange contradiction, empirical work has shown that Canadians and Americans who prefer living in suburban settings have a high propensity to describe city life in similarly frightening and repugnant terms; see Feldman (1990); Hummon (1990); and Brais and Luka (2002).

2 The term chronotope, introduced by social theorist and semiotician Mikhail Bakhtin (1978), is described by Côté (2007, 55) as 'the embodiment of a specific symbolic form that characterizes a particular socio-historical context or experience'–a space-time manifestation and representation that actively contributes to the transformation of the lived reality in question.

3 Hall and Müller (2004, 5) identify three types of second homes: stationary, semi-mobile, and mobile. The cottage properties to which this study refers are strictly of the stationary type, as they are built-form (although often quite modest, sometimes merely 'shacks').

4 Ascher (1995, 34) defines the 'metapolis' as *'l'ensemble des espaces dont tout ou partie des habitants, des activités économiques ou des territoires sont intégrés dans le fonctionnement quotidien (ordinaire) d'une métropole.'*

5 Most of these cottage properties were located to the north and east of the city, but within easy travel time in the areas that were historically the most accessible from the Toronto urban area, whether by train or by other types of motor vehicle. See Wolfe (1951); Wall (1979); Halseth (1998); and Luka (2008a,b) for further detail.

6 Wolfe (1977) compares this pattern to a *Strassendorf*, a typical central European village form in which houses are arranged in a string, usually along a road. Ironically, the extensive tracts of land behind the single row of private lots almost invariably belong to the Crown, and thus are also open for full public access; under Ontario law, for instance, Crown land is generally accessible to citizens of Canada who wish to travel through it for recreational purposes, and camping is allowed free on any one site for up to twenty-one days per year except where posted.

7 Statistics Canada's 2004 Survey of Household Spending (Statistics Canada 2004, CANSIM table 203–0003) revealed that about 7.9 per cent of Ontario households (357,350 of 4,554,250) owned a second home. In late 2004, the average Toronto house cost was $325,000, while the average waterfront cottage price was $349,000 (Wong 2004).

8 The URL was posted along with a message on the Web site of the Federation of Ontario Cottager Associations, which had agreed to support the study in principle as a silent third party. A major Toronto-area newspaper published a detailed article on the research in early July 2003, including an invitation to readers to take part in the online questionnaire by providing the URL (Hanes 2003). Finally, brochures and flyers were distributed across cottage country, both through commercial establishments (restaurants, marinas, and grocery stores) and in a snowball-sample technique whereby interviewees were asked to pass along the URL to friends, family, and neighbours who had cottaging experience.

9 A total sample size of 289 was reduced to 200 through the culling of responses deemed incomplete for the purposes of analysis and those originating in areas unambiguously beyond the central Ontario region – that is, east of Bancroft through the Frontenac axis of the Canadian Shield, between Kingston and Ottawa; points north of the French River; and points on Lake Erie or Lake Huron, as well as a handful of responses from Lake Simcoe and Lake Couchiching, on the basis that significant portions of these are considered to be already part of the Greater Toronto Area according to several definitions.

10 For context, average household income in the City of Toronto in 2001 was $69,125 according to the census; only 18.0 per cent of households earned $100,000 or more (Toronto 2003). Across the Census Metropolitan Area, only 30.6 per cent of the population ages 20 to 64 in 2001 held at least a bachelor's degree (Statistics Canada 2003, CANSIM II table 051-0014).

11 This assertion is based on studies of residential mobility, notably Michelson (1977); Shlay (1985); Feldman (1990, 1996); Winstanley, Thorns, and Perkins (1993); Clark and Dieleman (1996); and Strassman (2001).

12 See, notably, Korosec-Serfaty (1984); Dovey (1985); Sixsmith (1986); Feldman (1990, 1996); Hummon (1990); Després (1991, 1993); Cooper Marcus (1995); Somerville (1997); and Springer (2000).

13 This included a span of ten years or more for seven of ten respondents, and for at least thirty years in two of every five cases.

14 On this important area of critical debate, see Williams (1973, 1980); Bunce (1994); Greider and Garkovich (1994); Cronon (1996); Smith (1996); Castree and Braun (1998); Katz (1998); Keil and Graham (1998); Littlejohn (2002); Blum et al. (2004); and Castree (2004).

15 See, for instance, Jaakson (1986); Cloarec (1998); de la Soudière (1998); Kaltenborn (1998); Urbain (2002); Quinn (2004); Selwood and Tonts (2004); Rolshoven (2005); Aubin-Des Roches (2006); and Williams and van Patten (2006).

16 Ecological integrity is defined here based on the work of Karr (1992): the sum of physical, chemical, and biological integrity, the latter understood as the capacity to support and maintain balanced, integrated, adaptive biological systems with a full range of elements and processes that would occur in the undisturbed natural habitat of a region.

17 'NIMBYism' is important to understand here as a reaction to perceived changes that seem to threaten home landscapes.

18 Rapoport (1969) examines vernacular housing in various cultural contexts, a prominent thread being that owners (and sometimes other users) were historically the very individuals who built their own dwellings, while

Harris (1996) is especially intriguing because he focuses on how unskilled workers in Toronto's early industrial suburbs used their own labour to build very modest structures. See also Moholy-Nagy (1976 [1957]); Supic (1980); Brand (1994); and Schoenauer (2000).

19 Another example would be something akin to the floating mobile architecture of Germany's *Internationale Bauaustellung Fürst-Pücker-Land* (high-performance waterborne ecohousing) in the Lusatian (Lausitz) lakelands, now being created through post-mining landscape recovery processes; see Meditsch and Feiler (2008).

20 See http://www.livingbywater.ca/.

21 See http:www.foca.on.ca.

22 Current Value Assessment (CVA) has tended to adjust the municipally assessed value of cottage properties upward. It has also involved the averaging of property values in relatively small areas based on recent market activity, but where properties turn over relatively rarely – as is known to be the case in central Ontario cottage country – CVA may be overly susceptible to outlier effects.

REFERENCES

Ascher, F. 1995. *Métapolis ou l'avenir des villes*. Paris: Éditions O. Jacob.

Aubin-Des Roches, C. 2006. 'Retrouver la ville à la campagne: la villégiature à Montréal au tournant du XXe siècle.' *Urban History Review* 34, no. 2: 17–29.

Bakhtin, M.M. 1978. *Esthétique et théorie du roman*, trans. D. Olivier. Paris: Gallimard.

Betcherman, L.-R. 1975. *The Swastika and the Maple Leaf*. Toronto: Fitzhenry and Whiteside.

Bixler, R.D., and M.F. Floyd. 1997. 'Nature Is Scary, Disgusting, and Uncomfortable.' *Environment and Behavior* 29, no. 4: 443–67.

Blum, A., V. Cadieux, N. Luka, and L. Taylor. 2004. ' "Deeply Connected" to the "Natural Landscape": Exploring the Places and Cultural Landscapes of Exurbia.' In *The Structure and Dynamics of Rural Territories: Geographical Perspectives*, ed. D. Ramsey and C. Bryant. Brandon, MB: Brandon University.

Bogner, F.X., and M. Wiseman. 1997. 'Environmental Perception of Rural and Urban Pupils.' *Journal of Environmental Psychology* 17, no. 2: 111–22.

Bourne, L.S., et al. 2003. 'Contested Ground: The Dynamics of Peri-Urban Growth in the Toronto Region.' *Canadian Journal of Regional Science* 26, no. 23: 251–70.

Brais, N., and N. Luka. 2002. 'De la ville à la banlieue, de la banlieue à la ville: des représentations spatiales en évolution.' In *La banlieue revisitée*, ed. A. Fortin, C. Després, and G. Vachon. Quebec City: Éditions Nota Bene.

Brand, S. 1994. *How Buildings Learn: What Happens after They're Built*. New York: Penguin.

Bunce, M.F. 1994. *The Countryside Ideal: Anglo-American Images of Landscape*. London; New York: Routledge.

Campbell, C.E. 2004. *Shaped by the West Wind: Nature and History in Georgian Bay*. Vancouver: UBC Press.

Castree, N. 2004. 'Nature Is Dead! Long Live Nature!' *Environment and Planning A*, 36, no. 4: 191–4.

Castree, N., and B. Braun. 1998. 'The Construction of Nature and the Nature of Construction: Analytical and Political Tools for Building Survivable Futures.' In *Remaking Reality: Nature at the Millennium*, ed. B. Braun and N. Castree. London: Routledge.

Chaplin, D. 1999. 'Consuming Work/Productive Leisure: The Consumption Patterns of Second Home Environments.' *Leisure Studies* 18, no. 1: 41–55.

Clark, W.A.V., and F.M. Dieleman. 1996. *Households and Housing: Choice and Outcomes in the Housing Market*. New Brunswick, NJ: Rutgers University, Center for Urban Policy Research Press.

Cloarec, J. 1998. 'Pied-à-terre . . . pieds dans l'eau!' In *L'autre maison: la 'résidence secondaire,' refuge des générations*, ed. F. Dubost. Paris: Éditions Autrement.

Clout, H.D. 1972. 'Second Homes in the United States.' *Tijdschrift voor Economische en Sociale Geografie* 63, no. 6: 393–401.

–. 1974. 'The Growth of Second-Home Ownership: An Example of Seasonal Suburbanization.' In *Suburban Growth: Geographical Processes at the Edge of the Western City*, ed. J.H. Johnson. London: Wiley.

Cooper Marcus, C. 1995. *House as a Mirror of Self: Exploring the Deeper Meaning of Home*. Berkeley, CA: Conari Press.

COSGP (Central Ontario Smart Growth Panel). 2003. *Shape the Future: Central Ontario Smart Growth Panel Final Report*. Toronto: Queen's Printer for Ontario.

Côté, J.-F. 2007. 'Comparing the Cultures of Cities: Epistemological Perspectives on the Concept of Metropolis from the Cultural Sciences.' In *Urban Enigmas: Montreal, Toronto, and the Problem of Comparing Cities*, ed. J. Sloan. Montreal; Kingston, ON: McGill-Queen's University Press.

Cronon, W. 1996. 'The Trouble with Wilderness; Or, Getting Back to the Wrong Nature.' In *Uncommon Ground: Rethinking the Human Place in Nature*, ed. W. Cronon. New York: W.W. Norton.

Dahms, F. 1996. 'The Greying of South Georgian Bay.' *Canadian Geographer* 40, no. 2: 148–63.

de la Soudière, M. 1998. 'L'appel des lieux: une géographie sentimentale.' In *L'autre maison: la 'résidence secondaire,' refuge des générations*, ed. F. Dubost. Paris: Éditions Autrement.

Després, C. 1991. 'The Meaning of Home: Literature Review and Directions for Future Research and Theoretical Development.' *Journal of Architectural and Planning Research* 8, no. 2: 96–115.

–. 1993. 'A Hybrid Strategy in a Study of Shared Housing.' In *The Meaning and Use of Housing*, ed. E.G. Arias. Aldershot, UK: Avebury.

Dovey, K. 1985. 'Home and Homelessness.' In *Home Environments*, ed. I. Altman and C. Werner. New York: Plenum.

Dubost, F. 1998. 'De la maison de campagne à la résidence secondaire.' In *L'autre maison: la 'résidence secondaire,' refuge des générations*, ed. F. Dubost. Paris: Éditions Autrement.

Feldman, R.M. 1990. 'Settlement – Identity: Psychological Bonds with Home Places in a Mobile Society.' *Environment and Behavior* 22, no. 2: 183–229.

–. 1996. 'Constancy and Change in Attachments to Types of Settlements.' *Environment and Behavior* 28, no. 4: 419–45.

Fishman, R. 1987. *Bourgeois Utopias: The Rise and Fall of Suburbia*. New York: Basic Books.

Flognfeldt, T. 2004. 'Second Homes as a Part of a New Rural Lifestyle in Norway.' In *Tourism, Mobility and Second Homes: Between Elite Landscape and Common Ground*, ed. C.M. Hall and D.K. Müller. Clevedon, UK: Channel View Publications.

Frost, W. 2004. 'A Hidden Giant: Second Homes and Coastal Tourism in Southeastern Australia.' In *Tourism, Mobility and Second Homes: Between Elite Landscape and Common Ground*, ed. C.M. Hall and D.K. Müller. Clevedon, UK: Channel View Publications.

Gravel, P. 1968. 'The Distribution and Impact of Cottagers in Toronto's Urban Field.' Seminar paper 4. Toronto: University of Toronto, Centre for Urban and Community Studies.

Greider, T., and L. Garkovich. 1994. 'Landscapes: The Social Construction of Nature and the Environment.' *Rural Sociology* 59, no. 1: 1–24.

Hade, A. 2003. *Nos lacs: les connaître pour mieux les protéger*. Montreal: Éditions Fides.

Hague, J. 1893. 'Aspects of Lake Ontario.' *Canadian Magazine* 1, 263.

Hall, C.M., and D.K. Müller. 2004. 'Introduction: Second Homes, Curse or Blessing? Revisited.' In *Tourism, Mobility and Second Homes: Between Elite Landscape and Common Ground*, ed. C.M. Hall and D.K. Müller. Clevedon, UK: Channel View Publications.

Halseth, G. 1998. *Cottage Country in Transition: A Social Geography of Change and Contention in the Rural-Recreational Countryside*. Montreal; Kingston, ON: McGill-Queen's University Press.

–. 2004. 'The "Cottage" Privilege: Increasingly Elite Landscapes of Second Homes in Canada.' In *Tourism, Mobility and Second Homes: Between Elite Landscape and Common Ground*, ed. C.M. Hall and D.K. Müller. Clevedon, UK: Channel View Publications.

Halseth G., and M.W. Rosenberg. 1990. 'Conversion of Recreational Residences: A Case Study of Its Measurement and Management.' *Canadian Journal of Regional Science* 13, no. 1: 99–115.

–. 1995. 'Cottagers in an Urban Field.' *Professional Geographer* 47, no. 2: 148–59.

Hanes, T. 2003. 'Cottage country: survey examines leisure property growth.' *Toronto Star*, 12 July.

Harris, R. 1996. *Unplanned Suburbs: Toronto's American Tragedy, 1900 to 1950*. Baltimore: Johns Hopkins University Press.

Heidegger, M. 1958. *Ideas*. London: Allen and Unwin.

–. 1993. *Basic Writings: From Being and Time (1927) to The Task of Thinking (1964)*. San Francisco: HarperCollins.

Hodge, G. 1970. *Cottaging in the Toronto Urban Field: A Probe of Structure and Behaviour*. Centre for Urban and Community Studies Report 29. Toronto: University of Toronto, Centre for Urban and Community Studies.

–. 1974. 'The City in the Periphery.' In *Urban Futures for Central Canada: Perspectives on Forecasting Urban Growth and Form*, ed. L.S. Bourne, R.D. MacKinnon, J. Siegel, and J.W. Simmons. Toronto: University of Toronto Press.

Hummon, D.M. 1990. *Commonplaces: Community Ideology and Identity in American Culture*. Albany: State University of New York Press.

Jaakson, R. 1986. 'Second-Home Domestic Tourism.' *Annals of Tourism Research* 13, no. 3: 367–91.

Jasen, P. 1995. *Wild Things: Nature, Culture, and Tourism in Ontario, 1790–1914*. Toronto: University of Toronto Press.

Jauhianen, J.S. 2009. 'Will the Retiring Baby Boomers Return to Rural Periphery?' *Journal of Rural Studies* 25, no. 1: 25–34.

Joseph, A.E., and B. Smit. 1985. 'Rural Residential Development and Municipal Service Provision: A Canadian Case Study.' *Journal of Rural Studies* 1, no. 4: 321–37.

Kaltenborn, B.P. 1997a. 'Nature of Place Attachment: A Study among Recreation Home Owners in Southern Norway.' *Leisure Sciences* 19, no. 4: 175–89.

–. 1997b. 'Recreation Homes in Natural Settings: Factors Affecting Place Attachment.' *Norsk Geografisk Tidsskrift* 51: 187–98.

–. 1998. 'The Alternative Home: Motives of Recreation Home Use.' *Norsk Geografisk Tidsskrift* 52: 121–34.

–. 2002. 'Å bo i naturen – meningen med hyttelivet.' *UTMARK Tidsskriftet for utmarksforskning* 3.

Karr, J.R. 1992. 'Ecological Integrity: Protecting Earth's Life Support Systems.' In *Ecosystem Health: New Goals for Environmental Management*, ed. R. Costanza, B.G. Norton, and B. Hakell. Washington, DC: Island Press.

Katz, C. 1998. 'Whose Nature, Whose Culture? Private Productions of Space and the "Preservation" of Nature.' In *Remaking Reality: Nature at the Millennium*, ed. B. Braun and N. Castree. London: Routledge.

Keil, R., and J. Graham. 1998. 'Reasserting Nature: Constructing Urban Environments after Fordism.' In *Remaking Reality: Nature at the Millennium*, ed. B. Braun and N. Castree. London: Routledge.

Kipp, S., and C. Callaway. 2002. *On the Living Edge: Your Guide for Waterfront Living (Alberta edition)*. Edmonton: Federation of Alberta Naturalists.

Korosec-Serfaty, P. 1984. 'The Home from Attic to Cellar.' *Journal of Environmental Psychology* 4, no. 2: 303–21.

Langdalen, E. 1980. 'Second Homes in Norway: A Controversial Planning Problem.' *Norsk Geografisk Tidsskrift* 34: 139–44.

Levitt, C.H., and W. Shaffir. 1987. *The Riot at Christie Pits*. Toronto: Lester and Orpen Dennys.

Lister, N.-M. 1998. 'A Systems Approach to Biodiversity Conservation.' *Environmental Monitoring and Assessment* 49, nos. 2–3: 123–55.

Littlejohn, B. 2002. 'Wilderness and the Canadian Psyche.' In *Endangered Spaces: The Future for Canada's Wilderness*, ed. M. Hummel. Toronto: Key Porter.

Lorzing, H. 2001. *The Nature of Landscape: A Personal Quest*. Rotterdam: Uitgiverij 010.

Luka, N. 2006. 'Placing the "Natural" Edges of a Metropolitan Region through Multiple Residency: Landscape and Urban Form in Toronto's "Cottage Country".' PhD diss., Department of Geography / School of Graduate Studies, University of Toronto.

–. 2008a. 'Le "cottage" comme pratique intergénérationnelle: narrations de la vie familiale dans les résidences secondaires du centre de l'Ontario.' *Enfances, Familles, Générations* 8. http://www.erudit.org/revue/efg/2008/v/n8/018493ar.html.

–. 2008b. 'Waterfront Second Homes in the Central Canada Woodlands: Images, Social Practice, and Attachment to Multiple Residency.' *Ethnologia Europaea (Journal of European Ethnology)* 37, nos. 1–2: 70–87.

Luka, N., and N.-M. Lister. 2000. 'Our Place: Community Ecodesign for the Great White North Means Re-integrating Local Culture and Nature.' *Alternatives* 26, no. 3: 25–30.

Mai, U. 1971. 'Der Fremdenverkehram Südrand des Kanadischen Schildes: Eine Vergleichende Untersuchung des Muskoka District und der Frontenac Axis unter Besonderer Berücksichtigung des Standortproblems.'PhD diss., Philipps-Universität.

Mak, G. 2000 [1996]. *Jorwerd: The Death of the Village in 20th century Europe* [*Hoe God verdween uit Jorwerd*], trans. A. Kelland. London: Harvill Press.

Meditsch, A., and M. Feiler, eds. 2008. *Mobile schwimmende Architektur: Dokumentation des internationalen Wettbewerbs / Floating Mobile Architecture: Documentation of the International Design Competition*. Grossrächen, Germany: Internationale Bauaustellung Fürst-Pücker-Land GmbH.

Michelson, W. 1977. *Environmental Choice, Human Behaviour, and Residential Satisfaction*. New York: Oxford University Press.

Moholy-Nagy, S. 1976 [1957]. *Native Genius in Anonymous Architecture*. New York: Schocken Books.

Nordin, U. 1993. 'Second homes.' In *National Atlas of Sweden: Cultural Life, Recreation and Tourism*, ed. H. Aldskogius. Stockholm: Royal Swedish Academy of Science.

Quinn, B. 2004. 'Dwelling through Multiple Places: A Case Study of Second Home Ownership in Ireland.' In *Tourism, Mobility and Second Homes: Between Elite Landscape and Common Ground*, ed. C.M. Hall and D.K. Müller. Clevedon, UK: Channel View Publications.

Rapoport, A. 1969. *House Form and Culture*. Englewood Cliffs, NJ: Prentice-Hall.

Rolshoven, J. 2005. 'Going South! Lokalität und Mobilität in einer touristischen Übergangsregion.' In *Ort–Arbeit–Körper: Ethnografie Europäischer Modernen (34. Kongress der Deutschen Gesellschaft für Volkskunde, Berlin 2003)*, ed. B. Binder, S. Göttsch, W. Kaschuba, and K. Vanja. Münster, Germany: Waxmann.

–. 2006. 'Woanders daheim: Kulturwissenschaftliche Ansätze zur multilokalen Lebensweise in der Spätmoderne.' *Zeitschrift für Volkskunde* 102, no. 2: 179–94.

Rybczynski, W. 1991. *Waiting for the Weekend*. New York: Penguin.

Sandwell, B.K. 1946. 'Us Amphibious Canadians.' In *A Pocketful of Canada*, ed. J.D. Robins. Toronto: Collins.

Schoenauer, N. 2000. *6,000 Years of Housing*, rev. and expanded ed. New York: W.W. Norton.

Selwood, J., and M. Tonts. 2004. 'Recreational Second Homes in the South West of Western Australia.' In *Tourism, Mobility and Second Homes: Between Elite Landscape and Common Ground*, ed. C.M. Hall and D.K. Müller. Clevedon, UK: Channel View Publications.

Shlay, A.B. 1985. 'Castles in the Sky: Measuring Housing and Neighborhood Ideology.' *Environment and Behavior* 17, no. 5: 593–626.

Sies, M.C. 1997. 'Paradise Retained: An Analysis of Persistence in Planned, Executive Suburbs, 1880–1980.' *Planning Perspectives* 12, no. 2: 165–91.

Sixsmith, J. 1986. 'The Meaning of Home: An Exploratory Study of Environmental Experience.' *Journal of Environmental Psychology* 6, no. 4: 281–98.

Smith, A. 1990. 'Farms, Forests and Cities: The Image of the Land and the Rise of the Metropolis in Ontario.' In *Old Ontario: Essays in Honour of J.M.S. Careless*, ed. D. Keane and C. Reade. Toronto: Dundurn Press.

Smith, N. 1996. 'The Production of Nature.' In *Future Natural: Nature, Science, Culture*, ed. G. Robertson et al. London: Routledge.

Somerville, P. 1997. 'The Social Construction of Home.' *Journal of Architectural and Planning Research* 14, no. 3: 226–45.

Springer, S. 2000. 'Homelessness: A Proposal for a Global Definition and Classification.' *Habitat International* 24, no. 4: 475–84.

Statistics Canada. 2003. *Population of Census Metropolitan Areas*. Cat. 91-213-XIB. Ottawa: Statistics Canada.

–. 2004. *Survey of Household Spending, Household Spending on Shelter, by Province and Territory, Annual (1997–2003)*. Ottawa: Statistics Canada.

–. 2011. *Population of Census Metropolitan Areas*, table 051-0046. Ottawa: Statistics Canada.

Stevenson, A. 1886. 'Camping in the Muskoka Region.' *The Week*, 13 May.

Strassman, P. 2001. 'Residential Mobility: Contrasting Approaches in Europe and the United States.' *Housing Studies* 16, no. 1: 7–20.

Supic, P. 1980. 'Vernacular Architecture: A Lesson of the Past for the Future.' In *The Impact of Climate on Planning and Building*, ed. A. Bitan. Lausanne: Elsevier Sequoia SA.

Toronto. 2003. *Profile Toronto: Population Growth and Aging*. Toronto: City of Toronto, Urban Development Services, Policy & Research Section.

Tress, G. 2000. 'Die Ferienhauslandschaft: Motivationen, Umweltauswirkungen und Leitbilder im Ferienhaustourismus in Dänemark.' PhD diss., Department of Geography and International Development Studies, University of Roskilde.

–. 2002. 'Development of Second-home Tourism in Denmark.' *Scandinavian Journal of Hospitality and Tourism* 2, no. 2: 109–22.

Urbain, J.-D. 2002. *Paradis verts: désirs de campagne et passions résidentielles*. [Lausanne]: Payot.

Vaccarino, R. [2000] 2008. 'Nature Used and Abused: Politics and Rhetoric in American Preservation and Conservation.' In *Nature, Landscape, and Building for Sustainability*, ed. W.S. Saunders. Minneapolis: University of Minnesota Press.

van der Ryn, S., and S. Cowan. 1996. *Ecological Design*. Washington, DC: Island Press.

Varley, W.B. 1900. 'Tourist Attractions in Ontario.' *Canadian Magazine* 15, 29.

Wall, G. 1979. 'An Historical Perspective on Water-based Recreation.' In *Water-based Recreation Problems and Progress*, ed. J. Marsh. Peterborough, ON: Trent University, Department of Geography.

Williams, D.R., and S.R. Van Patten. 2006. 'Home and Away? Creating Identities and Sustaining Places in a Multicentered World.' In *Multiple Dwelling and Tourism: Negotiating Place, Home, and Identity*, ed. N. McIntyre, D. Williams, and K. McHugh. Cambridge, MA: CABI Publishing.

Williams, R. 1973. *The Country and the City*. New York: Oxford University Press.

–. 1980. 'Ideas of Nature.' In *Problems in Materialism and Culture: Selected Essays*. London: Verso.

Winstanley, A., D.C. Thorns, and H.C. Perkins. 1993. 'Moving House, Creating Home: Exploring Residential Mobility.' *Housing Studies* 17, no. 6: 813–32.

Wolfe, R.I. 1951. 'Summer Cottagers in Ontario.' *Economic Geography* 27, no. 1: 10–32.

–. 1962. 'The Summer Resorts of Ontario in the Nineteenth Century.' *Ontario History* 54, no. 3: 149–61.

–. 1977. 'Summer Cottages in Ontario: Purpose-built for an Inessential Purpose.' In *Second Homes: Curse or Blessing?* ed. J.T. Coppock. Oxford: Pergamon.

Wong, T. 2004. 'Renovation nation: price of cottage serenity keeps rising.' *Toronto Star*, 23 May.

9 Urban-Rural Tensions, Place, and Community Sustainability

WILLIAM T. DUSHENKO

Urban sprawl, as described by Thomas (2001), refers to the outward expansion of urban centres as a result of land use development. This phenomenon has been observed at a number of different spatial and temporal scales and is not confined strictly to the encroachment of large populated cities on surrounding suburban, rural, and natural landscapes (see Newman and Waldron, in this volume). As small municipal districts in rural areas strive to meet the economic and social needs presented by often unmitigated or unplanned growth, there has also been an increased push towards the annexing of land in surrounding electoral area communities. Thomas (ibid) describes this expansion as being of three general types, occurring 1) at the periphery of the municipality's jurisdiction, without spillover impacts on adjacent communities; 2) beyond their periphery, with impacts on adjacent communities; or, 3) beyond their periphery and having impacts on adjacent communities, with consequent effects on the urban centre in a type of 'feedback loop.'

Social tension can occur at the rural interface, particularly where issues of annexation are concerned (Edwards 2008), and much of this is grounded within the contexts of 'space' and 'sense of place.' In its most physical or base form, 'space,' as defined in *Merriam-Webster's Dictionary of English Usage*, is a boundless three-dimensional extent in which all objects and events occur and have relative position and direction. Within a more social context, 'space' is the conceptual framework in which we view, experience, and make sense of the world and its relationships. It is from this meaning that a sense of place arises. 'Place' might be best defined as elements of physicality, activity, and meaning, which add up to a feeling that a community is a special place with a unique history and/or cultural identity that are distinct from anywhere else, and meriting 'preservation' (Stokes, Watson, and Mastran 1997; Shamsuddina and Ujang 2008; see also Lister, in this volume). This perception of preservation or the long-term continuity of place as a social construct is central to community sustainability, whether occurring in the urban or the rural context.

Callaghan and Colton (2008, 934; following from Prugh 1999) partially describe connection to place in their analysis of elements of community sustainability or resiliency. They discuss the informational component of natural capital in which the world we live in, its environmental spaces, and their inhabitants 'teach us about itself and ourselves from the varied perspectives of aesthetics, spirituality, heritage, culture and science.' Brehm (2007) similarly emphasizes the natural environment as an important, albeit complex dimension to community attachment and sense of place, in addition to the social environment. It is these 'learnings' from natural and other forms of capital (social, cultural, and economic) that can provide the basis for a shared sense of place and community identity. As Sampson and Goodrich (2009, 902) note further, place becomes vitally important due to its centrality within the social world and, 'as setting, has the potential to contribute to the manner in which individuals develop and maintain a sense of place, belonging and identity . . . Places may be large as a city, or as small as a favourite chair . . . and expressed in the material form.' Lister (in this volume) also explores these meanings visually through the process of collaborative map-making.

In this chapter I explore a municipal district and the annexation of surrounding unincorporated communities on southern Vancouver Island, British Columbia, and the tensions that arise at their interface. The perceived threat of annexation is often observed to expose and heighten community identity and connection to place among its members. This conscious, place-based process of reconnection or reconciliation with space, resulting in the mobilization of social capital, is an important component of community or urban sustainability. One perspective is that of landowners, particularly developers, in surrounding communities, who welcome municipal or urban annexation, in the belief it will result in benefits from increased community servicing and infrastructure, increased property values, and greater long-term sustainability (Edwards, 2008). Another perspective is that of local residents who oppose annexation over concerns about the socio-economic, cultural, and environmental impacts on their lifestyles and their arguably strong connection to a sense of place.

To be consistent with the definition of (urban) sustainability Dale provides in the Introduction to this volume – that is, guaranteeing the local population, or the community, a non-decreasing level of well-being in the long term without compromising the possibilities of development of surrounding areas or reducing the harmful effects of development on the biosphere – each community should have the right to self-determination and to choose those who will govern it. But can such communities coexist and preserve a sense of place and associated identity in the face of annexation and other forms of municipal restructuring and planning? To do so requires equally responsive governance and integrated decision-making structures. This chapter also explores possible alternative governance models for ensuring community sustainability and preserving a contextual sense of place from space that might otherwise be compromised by annexation and sprawl. The case study underscores the importance of respecting the identity of communities in this context as part of spatial justice (more specifically, sustainability for all), and their equal engagement in the decision process as part of both planning and governance. Providing a deeper understanding of space in the social context by exploring the process by which a sense of place identity arises from and asserts itself in such spaces; recognizing spatial justice; and realizing these as part of engaged and integrated decision-making are all important elements of third-generation responses to sustainable development.

District of Sooke

The harbourside district of Sooke, on southwestern Vancouver Island, was incorporated as a municipality in December 1999. Historically, the area was used as a summer fishing village by the T'sou-ke people,[1] who availed themselves of the area's abundant clam beds and salmon runs. The first European settler on Vancouver Island was Captain Walter Colqohoun Grant of the Royal Scots Greys, who, in 1849, established a homestead at Sooke (Peers 2002). Additional European settlers arrived in the mid-1800s, establishing sawmills and engaging in ship-building activities in the harbour area. Forestry quickly became an important resource-based industry for economic development, particularly in the latter portion of the 1800s. This was accompanied by fish trapping and processing in the early 1900s, which continued on into the 1960s. The decline of fish stocks towards the latter part of the last century curtailed much of the commercial industry (Urban Aspects Consulting Group et al. 2001).

Current-day Sooke covers an area of just over fifty-eight square kilometres with a population of more than nine thousand, based on the
1996 census, or an average density of approximately one person per
two and a half hectares. The population has been expanding at a rate of
1 per cent per year over the past few years, with an envisioned population of more than fifteen thousand by 2026.[2] The Sooke community supports a combination of rural and semi-rural lifestyles along with more
suburban development, and consists predominantly of single detached
housing (72 per cent). To the southeast, Sooke is separated by other
rural municipalities from the increasingly urbanized centre of Victoria. The City of Victoria is confined to its current urban boundary by a
number of other independent jurisdictions, and any continued growth
is manifest as increased density as opposed to sprawl. By contrast,
Sooke is surrounded by pristine natural environment, including rivers, streams, wetlands, marine shores, and wooded areas. This attracts
residents and visitors to the district, providing increased opportunities for growth and expansion (Urban Aspects Consulting Group et al.
2001).

Governance and Development in the District of Sooke

The District of Sooke has an elected mayor and six councillors, who
oversee the planning, management, services, operations, and other affairs of the municipality. As a step towards providing services and infrastructure more typical of a growing semi-urban community, in June
2006, Sooke constructed a community sewer system. With increased
population pressure, the district and its municipal government have
also been challenged in more recent years to diversify the economic
base in a sustainable manner, from primarily resource extraction activities to tourism, light industry, wood processing, and service industries
(Urban Aspects Consulting Group et al. 2001). Callaghan and Colton
(2008) refer to this element of community sustainability or resiliency as
'commercial capital' – commercial engagement or the for-profit provision of services and products – and note that such activities must be
developed consistent with a community's fabric to be truly sustainable.
Rangwala (2010) refers to this component of community resiliency or
sustainability as 'placed-based economy.' The goals of Sooke's urban
growth management strategy include the following:

- identifying, through the establishment of an Urban Growth Area
  Boundary, a contiguous area of manageable size where detailed

planning can establish the location and parameters for extensive, higher-density growth well in advance of growth taking place, thereby reducing growth pressure and development conflict from remaining areas of the community; this is intended to reduce or eliminate suburban sprawl and strip development;
- identifying nodes within the Urban Growth Area Boundary around which more intensive development can take place – for example, mixed use development, including multiple-family and commercial development; and
- creating a visually attractive, walkable, economically sustainable, more densely developed Town Centre containing a compatible blend of commercial, civic, recreational, and residential uses (Urban Aspects Consulting Group et al. 2001).

These goals illustrate the connection between place ('visually attractive, walkable') and space (the Urban Growth Area Boundary) in terms of how urban growth and development will be played out over the coming decades. Sooke's Urban Area Growth Boundary illustrates the concept of 'urban containment,' whereby regenerative development is concentrated within already urbanized areas, most often in larger central cities. As Nelson et al. (2004, 421) explain, '[u]rban containment . . . shift[s] metropolitan development demand away from rural and exurban areas outside of containment boundaries to suburban and urban areas inside them.' In light of their distinctiveness, both the District of Sooke and the Juan de Fuca Electoral Area, collectively known as the Western Communities, still serve as bedroom communities for a number of residents working in Victoria, a thirty- to forty-five-minute commute to the northeast. Despite this perceived 'duality,' as illustrated by the parallel 'transition' between city and cottage life (Luka, in this volume), a strong connection to rural place is still extant among community residents.

The Juan de Fuca Electoral Area

Following Sooke's incorporation in 1999, the remaining outlying rural regions in the Sooke Electoral Area were combined with the Langford Electoral Area to become the new Juan de Fuca Electoral Area (EA) within the Capital Regional District (CRD). Other local European-established communities are Otter Point,[3] Port Renfrew,[4] Malahat,[5] East Sooke,[6] Shirley,[7] Jordan River,[8] and Willis Point.[9] Each has its own unique origins and history within the larger region.

The EA, comprising Electoral District H (Part 1 and 2) of the CRD, occupies a total land base of over 1,500 square kilometres (64 per cent of the total area of the CRD), with a total population of approximately 4,480 (BC Statistics 2009a,b). This is less than half the current population of Sooke and only 1.3 per cent of the total population of the CRD. The average density in the EA is correspondingly less than that in Sooke, with an average of approximately one person per 40 hectares. Average population growth in the EA has been conservatively estimated at approximately 2.7 per cent per year (Otter Point 2006), more than twice that of Sooke. Although this growth rate suggests that the total population of the EA may reach nearly 7,600 by 2026, it would still be only half of that estimated for Sooke. Population growth is also quite variable for individual communities, ranging from virtually 0 for Port Renfrew over the past thirty years (Port Renfrew 2003) to 24 per cent for Otter Point in the past five years (Otter Point 2006).

The rich geographic, diverse, and historical tapestry that makes up the communities of the EA collectively suggests a strong sense of place supported by a decidedly more rugged, rural lifestyle than is the case in Sooke. It consists almost exclusively of very low density, single-family rural homes or exurban development with minimal services (wells or lake water and septic systems). This lifestyle, and the strong social capital and connectivity it can support, is best summarized by observations on the spectrum between urban and rural communities by Kozeny (2005, 75):

> rural (communities) usually enjoy cleaner air, and less noise pollution (except when tractors or chainsaws are fired up, or when construction projects are underway). The deep country quiet is especially inspiring at night in the winter, and in the summer the nocturnal sounds of insects, (wolves), and hoot owls can keep a city visitor awake for many hours – while the city's background noise of passing trucks and car alarms often has a similar effect on visitors from the farm. And with low levels of light pollution, on a clear night the rural skies are amazing to behold . . . Being more spread out and farther from things in general, people living in rural communities tend to interact more with their fellow community members than do their urban counterparts.

Mahon, Fahy, and Ó Cinnéide (2009) empirically reinforce many of these notions in their examination of the sociological and geographic origins of quality of life and the makings of place-based community as experienced by similar rural fringe communities outside Galway,

Ireland. Shared values about space were evident given the broad agreement found on quality-of-life dimensions. The most frequently reported physical dimensions of quality of life in household surveys included the peace and quiet of the rural village setting and the existence of natural settings and scenic views. Frequently reported social dimensions included good neighbours, community spirit, and personal safety and trust, which also suggest the existence of social networks (capital), at least at the informal level. The authors also noted that conditioned proximity to amenities (provided by the city) was also important, which, although still within the context of sustainability, were not consistent with typical notions of rural life.

One can see parallels in the Vancouver Island case, where some residents in the community of Sooke and the EA commute to work in the larger urban centre of Victoria, and many likely also rely on the amenities available there. In their commentary on authenticity, character, and sense of place within the context of urban planning and conservation, Jivén and Larkham (2003) conclude that an individual and community's values and attitudes may change or evolve over time, with some elements – in this case, amenities – valued now, but not in the future, or the reverse. This does not diminish, however, the 'authenticity' of sense of place held by a community where this element carries positive 'experiential value' – that is, people's experience of this value.

Governance and Development in the EA

Governance and planning services for the EA are provided by the Capital Regional District. This is accomplished through an elected regional director who oversees land-use control, including development, official community plans, land-use planning, and other community services such as economic development.[10] Some advocacy, service, and/or education activities are also given agency through a mix of government-instituted and community-based groups.

Official Community Plans (OCPs) for all communities in the EA have been in development over the past few years and are at various stages of being enacted as bylaws under the CRD. Overall, the plans for each community vary in their approach to further (economic) development and sustainability. The OCPs strongly reflect a commonly held sense of place by the members of each community and their desire to see their unique vision for their community's sustainability carried into the future.

The small, but resolute, residential community of Willis Point, for example, advocates a status quo approach that its current size be maintained, with any future development being 'extremely modest' and 'a logical extension of the existing (park-like) character of the community' (Willis Point 2002). Residents in Malahat envision limited commercial development, confined mostly along the Trans-Canada Highway and to home-based businesses, to minimize traffic through the area (Malahat 2004). In Shirley and Jordan River, residential and commercial development is encouraged in designated areas, permitting residents to both live and work in their community (Shirley/Jordan River 2006). Otter Point desires all future residential growth to be clustered into 'designated settlement containment areas' with restricted industrial, commercial and high-density (apartment) development, the maintenance of 'agricultural, forestry and other residential uses on larger lot sizes' and promotion of other economic activities such as fishing (crab and shrimp), and tourism (for example, adventure vacationing) (Otter Point 2006). This attempt to consolidate growth into already developed areas is not unlike the concept of 'urban containment' (Nelson et al. 2004) discussed earlier, albeit at an even smaller and more exurban development scale than Sooke. In East Sooke, the community promotes the clustering of growth in specified settlement areas. This includes local encouragement of existing and promotion of new businesses (home-based, agricultural, tourism or neighbourhood commercial activities), and special needs, rental, and affordable housing. Given the three regional parks bordering East Sooke (East Sooke, Roche Cove, and Matheson Lake Regional Parks), the community prohibits any large-scale industrial development (East Sooke 2006).

Although each community in the EA shares a similar sense of place in terms of its rich rural character and history, it is also clear that each is quite different in terms of its desire for future economic growth and development of its space. Such disparate views of what constitutes community sustainability illustrate the emerging realization of just how strongly contextual this concept is in terms of place and space, especially with respect to the scale of economic development and the notion of 'limits.' Considerations of spatial justice may also be quite complex. Hansen et al. (2005), in their study of the effects of exurban development, also note that even this type of development may not necessarily be sustainable in that it can carry ecological consequences, having disproportionately large effects on the diversity of natural species.

Community Sustainability and Municipal Restructuring

Over the years, in addition to economic development, population growth in Sooke and the EA has placed increased pressure on governments for the provision of new and more complex services and decision-making. This supports the contention of the provincial Ministry of Municipal Affairs (British Columbia 2000) that population growth pressure is the most common reason for interest by local governments and communities in restructuring. The ministry further notes that the term 'municipal restructuring' can cover a wide range of socio-geographic changes to communities, from municipal incorporation to major extensions of municipal boundaries to amalgamation of rural areas. Along with the provision of services and local control and decision-making, the most frequent arguments for municipal restructuring in British Columbia include effective political representation and accountability, fair revenue sharing, social cohesion through community interests, and more effective growth management with fewer cross-jurisdictional problems.

It should be noted that such well-intentioned notions by a higher and more regionalized level of government, without considering the cultural context of the communities it governs, may often result in misplaced focus on a particular purpose (for example, political desires), rather than any explicit consideration of community identity or spatial justice. In his discussion on urban renaissance and urban policy in the United Kingdom, Raco (2003, 235) notes that 'empowered and mobilized communities can and should play an enhanced role in the development and implementation of urban policy agendas . . . with the state's role moving from that of a provider of (welfare) services to that of a facilitator.' I explore this notion in the current case study from the perspective of community restructuring.

The first attempt at municipal restructuring in the area came in 1991, when the rural communities in the former Sooke Electoral Area (including Sooke and the current EA) were presented with a referendum to amalgamate with the unincorporated community of Sooke to form a district municipality. The referendum was defeated by the surrounding communities. A major concern expressed by the outlying rural communities was how the restructuring would affect their rural lifestyles – in essence, their sense of place and associated attachment. This illustrates the most typical reasons often-marginalized rural communities fear and oppose municipal restructuring: the loss of political control and access, increased costs of municipal status (taxes), contentment with the current rural level of regional district services, and loss of self-determination through community planning – all resulting in a subsequent loss of the rural environment or atmosphere (British Columbia 2000). These concerns parallel the challenges of equitable access Dale notes (Chapter 6 in this volume) for marginalized communities in large urban centres. Raco (2003) also observes that moving from a reactive to a more proactive form of engagement is likely the greatest challenge for affected communities. Through this approach, the opportunity for developing participation, rights, and responsibilities can be developed, which help in recognizing and sustaining a community's unique identity and its members' sense of place.

Despite the failed amalgamation attempt, Sooke continued to move ahead with its own municipal restructuring. It sought and obtained municipal incorporation by referendum in 1999 with a locally elected and independent council. In this way, Sooke determined that its interests – the level of local services and control of local planning, property taxes, and decision–making – and growth would be managed in a more coordinated way than as part of the original Sooke EA under the governance of the CRD. Incorporation to protect similar interests has also been observed historically in other Canadian communities, generally in response to governance structures around a largely agricultural population in rural townships that disregarded their needs and wants (see Stott 2007).

Although these arguments are not likely authentically place based, they are in line with those favouring municipal restructuring as described by the Ministry of Municipal Affairs. Meligrana (2000), in his development of a process model in local government restructuring, describes incorporation of local governments as the first stage that a city-region will undergo in a five-step reformation process towards urbanization. The potential opportunities for sustainable planning here through the principles of process-oriented sustainability, including considerations of place, discussed by Robinson and Dale (Chapter 1 in this volume) are many.

The 'Urban-Rural Fringe'

With Sooke's incorporation, the remaining communities of the original Sooke EA (East Sooke, Otter Point, Shirley, Jordan River, Port Renfrew) and portions of the former Langford EA (Malahat and Willis Point) were amalgamated into the new Juan de Fuca EA. From the perspective of an outside observer, the end result of Sooke's restructuring process was the creation of a small municipality with a large, partially associated 'rural fringe' represented by the outlying areas of the EA. This geographic setting is similar to the rural fringe communities outside Galway on the west coast of Ireland examined by Mahon, Fahy, and Ó Cinnéide (2009).

'Urban fringe' was first coined in the 1930s by T.L. Smith (as cited in Pryor 1968) in a study on Louisiana to describe 'the built-up area just outside the corporate limits of the city (or urban centre).' It is often used interchangeably with 'rural fringe' – as in urban-rural fringe – in many treatises on the subject (see Gallent et al. 2004; Sullivan, Anderson, and Lovell 2004). Some of this confusion arises from the perception of the 'urban centre,' which Pryor (1968) noted can range in scale from a small village (such as Sooke) to a larger metropolitan area (such as Victoria). Each exhibits its own unique characteristics regarding growth rate, functioning, and the hierarchical relationship that exists between the centre and its outlying areas. In first presenting the concept of the 'urban-rural' fringe, Pryor differentiated this region into two interrelated zones. The first is the 'urban fringe' – those areas in contact and contiguous with the urban centre and exhibiting similar characteristics (such as higher land-use conversion and population density increases). In contrast is the 'rural fringe,' a contiguous subzone of the urban fringe, but exhibiting characteristics similar to those of rural areas (such as lower land-use conversion rate, lower population density). In the smaller 'suburban' scale of this case study, 'rural fringe' is the most apt definition of the zone of socio-demographic and landscape transition between the town centre of Sooke District and the surrounding rural hinterland and countryside represented by the communities of the EA.

Hite (1998) also introduced an interesting economic component to land use within fringes by proposing that economic 'returns to land from (higher-yielding) traditional and customary urban land uses' (such as commerce and industry) are roughly in balance with those of lower-yielding rural land uses (such as farming, forestry, and other primary resource extraction and value-added industries). Although identifying the specific location of any fringe may be difficult, Hite concedes that, during periods of major economic change, the fringe and land uses within this zone may become highly fluid. Add to this the fact that most fringe areas, regardless of how one defines them, are poorly planned and managed (Gallent et al. 2004), it comes as no surprise that, in the face of increasing population growth, land-use and associated socio-political conflicts may arise in areas such as the EA without due consideration of a community's sense of place.

Municipal Restructuring and Rural Tensions at the Fringe

The EA communities most closely associated with the rural fringe of Sooke are those immediately adjacent to the municipality – namely, Otter Point, East Sooke, and, to a lesser extent, Shirley. Although these outlying communities fall under a separate local CRD governance structure and tax base, services – such as street lighting, routine road maintenance, water and sewage, and retail/commercial – do not exist to the same degree as in the nearby municipality. For residents seeking the more 'rugged' rural lifestyle of these communities, this becomes an accepted and often even welcome state of affairs for maintaining their sense of place (Juan de Fuca Electoral Area 2006). Developers purchasing land in these communities in the hope of creating higher-density housing and greater economic returns, however, desire the same level of services as provided by the nearby municipality of Sooke. (This desire for amenities is also observed in rural fringe communities in Ireland by Mahon et al. [2009] despite a more pastoral lifestyle.) Efforts to satisfy the desire for identical services can also affect local property taxes and the interwoven tapestry of place for these EA communities.

The fact that unmanaged pressure for growth can cause tensions within communities, as well as between the fringe and the town centre, again provides support for assertions in the literature that fringe areas are poorly planned and managed (Gallent et al. 2004). In discussing the challenges of sustainable planning for urban growth management in the CRD, Boyle, Gibson, and Curran (2004, 21) particularly note that '[British Columbia] does not have a tradition of strong regional governance and the CRD is the creature of sixteen municipalities and electoral areas.'

Given that the appointed members of this regional government body represent quite disparate interests and autonomous constituencies at times, there is limited authority for the CRD to provide clear policy direction or carry out decisions with respect to growth or planning without other unique social and provincial political factors associated with place (Boyle, Gibson, and Curran 2004). This also has the potential to affect integrated planning severely, as Hanna and Slocombe discuss (in this volume).

This lack of cohesion within the EA is clearly illustrated by the different policies for economic growth and development expressed in each community's OCP. The end result is a patchwork of poorly integrated community 'islands,' which can result in a further loss of ecological landscape (Hansen et al. 2005), uneven development, and marginalization between the regions. The special characteristics of place, including social capital, that exist in these communities, however, also indicate that the fringes of the Juan de Fuca EA are more than just a transition area between the rural town centre of Sooke and unspoiled west coast hinterland. They are hard boundaries against change imposed from 'outsiders.' Gallent et al. (2004), in examining case studies from England's urban fringes, recognize these special characteristics and note the importance of multifunctionality and integration in planning (see also Hanna and Slocombe, Chapter 2 in this volume) to manage and support this diversity and address coexisting multiple uses and conflicts that may arise as part of spatial justice.

Other place-based elements that can add to tensions as a consequence of growth and development pressures include 'free-rider' issues. Area communities may benefit from services provided by the municipality for which they do not bear the full or fair costs (British Columbia 2000; see also Edwards 2008). In the case of the EA, this may include roads and lighting in Sooke that provide throughfare and access to these communities at little or no cost to users, as well as access to other facilities such as local parks. Other advantages related to the free-rider issue include access by Juan de Fuca EA residents to larger commercial establishments (retail stores in Sooke) and other amenities in the urban centre. This occurs without the associated environmental, aesthetic, and other costs of establishing these types of centres in their own communities and the conflict with the more rugged, pristine rural lifestyle that would likely result.

On the flip side of the coin, growth inevitably could result in Sooke's having an unfair share of the local industrial or community tax base, which could also exacerbate rural tensions (British Columbia 2000). Fischel (1991) states that, if growth management strategies are to be implemented effectively, the costs of added services should be fairly borne by those who benefit from them, and those who bear special costs from regional projects should be compensated properly. Clearly, reconciliation of these competing conflicts is critical for the future sustainable development of all these communities.

Amalgamation or Annexation?

In the perceived absence of effective local planning and service arrangements, as in the case of the communities of the EA, the Ministry of Municipal Affairs (British Columbia 2000) notes that local governments such as Sooke's may consider boundary restructuring or annexation/amalgamation as a solution. The ministry is constitutionally responsible for ensuring local governments have the capacity to adapt to growth. The ministry notes, however, that the instrument of change and evolution and decision-making (via approved electoral voting) will always rest with the local constituency. Integral to this 'facultative approach'[11] to restructuring, adopted back in the mid-1980s, is a five-step process: 1) consultation with and evaluation by the provincial government (specifically, the Ministry of Municipal Affairs); 2) establishment of a restructuring committee; 3) completion of a restructuring study, overseen by the committee along with public consultation; 4) presentation of results and decision on whether to recommend a referendum to the provincial government; and, 5) conducting the referendum, cabinet approval of the final decision, and implementation of restructuring, accompanied by ministry financial assistance.

It is again important to note that, despite the assertion that decision-making will rest with the local constituency, the provincial government affords little opportunity in this process to incorporate elements of place relating to identity or community as part of urban or rural sustainability planning and governance, as discussed by Raco (2003). Clearly, the potential for conflict was present in this case study as a result of the lack of appreciation for third-generation responses to sustainable development.

In the February 2005 referendum on whether to amalgamate with the municipality of Sooke the EA – specifically, the communities of East Sooke, Otter Point, and Shirley/Jordan – again voted 78 per cent against the restructuring, echoing the same sentiments seen in the 1991 referendum. Among other concerns, the proposed amalgamation was also conceived as being misaligned with the Capital Region's twenty-five-year Regional Growth Strategy. Adopted in 2003, this strategy advocates higher density in already built-up areas, with modest and controlled development in rural areas such as the EA (Capital Regional District 2003; Tweedy 2005).

Despite the second failed amalgamation referendum, the District of Sooke continued its efforts at municipal restructuring in the spring and summer of 2005 through annexation. Part of this initiative was identified as requests from property owners (particularly developers) to have their properties included in Sooke (Sooke 2005b). The district's arguments for the boundary extensions were:

- an estimated additional $47,000 in tax revenue to the municipality;
- substantial tax revenue from the development of these properties;
- municipal improvements provided and paid for by the developers as part of the development process on these parcels; and,
- application of some of revenues towards fire protection in these annexed areas, as well as major improvements throughout Sooke, including road upgrades, park maintenance, and revitalization projects.

In addition to these revenue arguments, opportunities could be provided to the owners of annexed properties to increase the density of development through rezoning and amendment of the district's OCP (Sooke 2005a,b). Meligrana (2000) notes annexation of surrounding territory as usually the second stage of reform by municipal governments, typically occurring at the expense and identity of (marginalized) rural areas that are not as well organized politically, and without place-based considerations related to sustainability.

Many of the motives behind the District of Sooke's decision to annex are also acknowledged by Edwards (2008) in her examination of examples from the United States. These include the increased ability of a locality to preserve and enhance its economic base, the desire for orderly and/or controlled growth, political considerations, the wish to increase the tax base, reduce fragmentation, and gain governance efficiencies, and as a defensive strategy against annexation by other jurisdictions. Whether or not such motives produce the desired outcomes depends on a number of factors, including, but not limited to, land area, use, density, and unique local financial characteristics, but Edwards adds these are still contested in the urban planning literature and require further research. Closer to home, Meligrana (2007), in his analysis of 106 municipal governments in British Columbia between 1971 and 2001, concludes that annexing municipalities, in fact, did not demonstrate more growth in terms of population and new housing construction, economic development, or more compact development patterns than did non-annexing municipalities.

Despite opposition from EA communities and their agencies, the Sooke municipal council voted in August 2005 to annex these properties. In November, the decision was put to a municipal referendum following a petition by residents of Sooke, but, as before, without the input of the communities concerned in the EA.[12] More than 60 per cent of municipal residents voted in favour of both the east and west boundary extensions. Annexation of East Sooke and Otter Point, along with their accompanying tax bases, was subsequently authorized through an Order-in-Council passed by the provincial government in February 2006 (OPSRRA 2006a).

Of three types of urban containment – 'closed, isolated, and open' – identified by Nelson et al. (2004) in their research on larger US urban centres, the annexation practices of Sooke, although a considerably smaller municipality, suggest that planning for this jurisdiction falls into the 'open' category. In this scenario, growth boundaries change frequently, and regional land policies to prevent rural sprawl by reconciling with community elements of place do not exist. As a result, annexation of non-contiguous land in the surrounding EA communities of the rural communities could continue into the foreseeable future. This annexation of parcels, referred to as 'cherry picking' or 'leap frogging' by residents of Otter Point and East Sooke (OPSRRA 2006d) has refuelled concerns over the fragmentation relating to watersheds and an eroding tax base. Reynolds (as cited in Edwards 2008) observes that annexation practices can be abused where municipalities are able systematically to choose and incorporate territory through willing owners – in this case, developers – effectively subverting the opposition of other landowners – in this case, community members. This makes it difficult for future planning activities related to community fire departments and other services, not to mention issues around jurisdictional access by such services and the gradual loss of social cohesion and identity and lifestyle (place) in rural communities (Sloan 2005; Tweedy 2005; OPSRRA 2006d).

Although the District of Sooke was free to hold its own referendum under the Community Charter and the Local Government Act, residents in the surrounding EA communities concluded they were viewed by the province as tertiary stakeholders in the overall process – in essence, marginalized, compared with primary stakeholders in other incorporated areas. Annexation of parcels in the EA may continue in a similar fashion into the future as development pressure on Sooke increases and in the absence of a more viable option for governance (OP-SRRA 2006b) that would take into consideration aspects of place and community identity and integrated planning. In a satisfaction survey of EA communities (including East Sooke, Otter Point, and Shirley/Jordan River) conducted in June 2006 by the director of the CRD, up to 77 per cent of respondents disagreed that this type of annexation process should continue (Juan de Fuca Electoral Area 2006).

Place Connection and Social Capital

A key factor maintaining the rural communities of the EA in the face of the municipal restructuring process has been each community's strong social capital, sense of place, and identity. Edwards (2008, 131) emphasizes that 'self-determination is a fundamental issue surrounding annexation and generates intense emotions among residents,' as observed in this case study. This is despite, and likely partially in response to, a comparatively weak regional government structure. As Falk and Kirkpatrick (2000) theorize, social interactions draw upon resources typified by knowledge (networks, skills, precedents/procedures/rules, sites for communication, community attributes) and identity (self-confidence, values, vision, trust, commitment). These resources are used simultaneously, building social capital for action or cooperation for the benefit of community members through agency. These knowledge and identity resources are also central to maintaining a sense of place for the EA communities in this case study, as confirmed by the 2006 satisfaction survey conducted by the Juan de Fuca Electoral Area.[13] The vast majority of EA residents preferred the rural lifestyle with 'country style roads and the current level of services and taxes.' What was clear from the survey is that the current governance structure in the EA – one regional director and six land use committee representatives, with the Capital Regional Board serving as its 'council' – may not have been working as effectively as it could. Opinion was closely split between those satisfied (up to 41 per cent) and those not satisfied (up to 44 per cent) with the current governance model; up to 29 per cent were neutral on the issue. While a good majority of residents surveyed in Otter Point and Shirley/Jordan River (up to 64 per cent) would prefer not to change to a municipality with mayor and council, opinion was more split in East Sooke, with a larger proportion (43 per cent) favouring such a change than did not (41 per cent). A similar split was found for those satisfied with the current land use process in place for the EA (Juan de Fuca Electoral Area 2006).

Is maintaining the rural lifestyle of the outlying communities of the EA, with their lower density and level of services, any more or less sustainable than the higher density land use, services, and taxation pursued by the municipality of Sooke or even the increasingly urbanized centre of Victoria (see Hansen et al. 2005)? Given the ambiguity of a consistent definition of sustainability, promulgated by earlier foundational first- and second-generation approaches, such a question may remain unanswerable in the near term. What is clearly more important, as demonstrated in this case study and elsewhere, is the realization that sustainability, whether in rural or urban contexts, is strongly founded on the dynamic interaction and connection to place among small, mid-, and large-scale communities. Place-based decision-making and the inclusion of community engagement processes (Raco 2003) supported by the mobilization of social capital are essential. This must be supported by an effective governance structure and policy, as illuminated elsewhere in this book (see Dale, Chapter 6). This is essential if the changes critical to urban and rural sustainability are to be implemented in a coherent, integrated way at multiple scales.

Reconnecting Place: Models for Sustainable Community Governance

Exploring alternatives to the 'annex or not to annex' approach is key to reconciling issues around non-contiguous urban sprawl and its impact on surrounding rural and natural areas and associated lifestyles as part of spatial justice. This also illustrates one of the possible feedback mechanisms in local government systems to municipal annexation, identified by Meligrana (2000) and Edwards (2008), whereby communities seek sustainability and to maintain a sense of place through their own incorporation or other solution to avoid falling under an adjacent municipality's authority.

A number of different models exist that might allow unincorporated communities in the EA to participate in a more effective governance process. These include amalgamating with each other to form one or more stand-alone municipalities; amalgamating with other neighbouring municipalities aside from Sooke (such as Metchosin) that share a similar sense of values with respect to place; forming a rural alliance within the EA exclusively or with neighbouring municipalities with similar values; and improving the existing electoral area governance structure (OPSRRA 2006c).

The first model, amalgamation of the EA into one or more stand-alone municipalities similar to the neighbouring District of Metchosin, does not appear to be favoured by the provincial Ministry of Community Services, for a number of reasons (OPSRRA 2006b). The primary one is likely the large number of existing municipalities (thirteen, including Sooke) serving a population of 345,000 within the relatively small area of the CRD. To place this into perspective, the Greater Vancouver Region District consists of less than twice the number of municipalities (twenty-one) serving a population (more than two million) almost six times that of the CRD. This unique structure relates to the social history of individual settlements (as described earlier) resulting from a diverse natural resource base from which have arisen independent communities. This pattern has been reinforced by a phenomenon that Newman and Dale (2007, 83) describe as 'homophily,' whereby 'groups form from similar actors – in this case, communities – and then become more similar with time.' The end result is that these communities have become self-reinforced and disconnected from 'bridging ties' that would allow for more broad integration, in this case, politically. This clearly has important and larger implications for urban and rural sustainability in the CRD, including effective resource use and integrated decision-making as part of third-generation responses. The question of reconnecting place with economies of scale and limits, although outside the purview of this book, is a key question for third-generation responses.

As Edwards (2008) examines, having such a large number of municipalities in the CRD can create challenges in terms of efficiencies and expense where each is attempting to create, develop, and support its own services, planning, and governance – along with the infrastructure and associated complexity in supporting these at the provincial level. As even some of the existing municipalities within the CRD face challenges in providing services, the smaller, more widespread population base of communities within the EA, combined with a somewhat differing sense of place for each, makes this an extremely challenging endeavour. Many of the EA communities, however, wished to keep this option open as a consideration in governance studies (OPSRRA 2006b).

The second model, direct amalgamation with the rural municipality of Metchosin, has been proposed and petitioned for study by the EA communities of East Sooke and Malahat. In the 2006 satisfaction survey described earlier, 72 per cent of those surveyed in East Sooke favoured a feasibility study on the option of joining the neighbouring District of Metchosin, compared with only 43 per cent and 22 per cent, respectively, of those surveyed in Otter Point and Shirley/Jordan River (Juan de Fuca Electoral Area 2006). These responses are not unexpected given the relative differences in geographical proximity of each community to Metchosin. The stronger arguments for amalgamation by East Sooke and Malahat include shared borders, history, sense of place, and the perception that the protection of the 'world class' wilderness of this area and its economic value (in terms of tourism) would be strengthened (OPSRRA 2006b). The key challenges to amalgamation, however, include Metchosin's lack of clarity and concern about what amalgamation would entail, including additional services and (taxation) costs, and that any referendum to amalgamate would not succeed without a complete understanding of the implications by the residents of Metchosin (Metchosin 2006). This latter point was a key factor in the rejection of a similar request to amalgamate with East Sooke in April 2002 (OPSRRA 2003). Metchosin has agreed, however, to put aside scepticism and proceed with the process for a governance study, in recognition of the potential consequences of not doing so to the rural sense of place in East Sooke and neighbouring EA communities (Metchosin 2006).

The third model, a rural alliance among some or all of the communities in the EA, has many advantages, including the opportunity to establish clear borders, share services (such as policing, planning, bylaw enforcement, roads, and emergency services) with 'like-minded communities' as part of place-based considerations while guaranteeing self-determination in areas such as recreation, finances, and economic development as a way to preserve their sense of place (OPSRRA 2006d). This is certainly an alternative to self-incorporation, which residents of Otter Point highly desire (OPSRRA 2006b,c). Some of the challenges associated with this model include a governance structure that supports all member communities without impairing place-based self-determination, such as a ward system with elected council members. Whether or not the Ministry of Community Services would consider supporting such a rural alliance remains an open question, given unforeseen per capita costs, the implications from an electoral and taxation perspective, and the added pressure on communities to embrace greater density and urbanization. It would also depend on a greater understanding by the ministry on the degree of support within the EA and, possibly, Metchosin for this option (OPSRRA 2006c).

The advantages of the fourth model, modifying the existing EA governance structure, would include more political control, access, and place-based, integrated decision-making powers on the part of EA communities through members elected to governance positions. It might also be supported by the provincial government since it would not require a major overhaul of the existing system and associated expenses, and would support the government's desire to see the EA work more efficiently (OPSSRA 2006c). The challenge here is whether such a governance structure would have the support of the EA communities, given their current dissatisfaction with the current 'one-director' model. Either the rural alliance model or strengthening the current EA governance structure would allow these communities to foster a greater sense of agency and self-determination as part of reconnecting communities at an appropriate scale. It would also provide the opportunity to employ principles of integrated approaches in a regional planning context, as discussed by Hanna and Slocombe (in this volume).

How governance and municipal restructuring will play out in the Juan de Fuca Electoral Area in the coming years is speculative at best. Some of the challenges of alternative governance models, such as rural alliances, do not fit well into the ages-old conventional 'box thinking' of provincial politicians, while the possible creation of new municipalities would not be welcomed or perceived as sustainable at the regional table. The end result might be a combination of options, such as Shirley/Jordan River and Otter Point forming a rural alliance to preserve their sense of place and community identity, eventually leading to an incorporation/amalgamation model similar to that of Metchosin, as predicted by the process and pathway models of Meligrana (2000). The communities of East Sooke and Malahat conceivably could form an amalgamation or rural alliance with neighbouring Metchosin, whose residents share similar values and a strong place affinity with respect to preserving a sense of rural place in the face of increasing urban sprawl in the CRD. In the less likely event of maintaining the status quo EA governance model, it is conceivable that Sooke District's attempts to annex the EA rural-urban fringe communities, particularly Otter Point and East Sooke (and eventually Shirley/Jordan River), will continue, along with development pressure and disregard of spatial justice due to the absence of balanced attention to each community's sense of place in decision-making supported by social engagement (capital) and an effective governance structure.

Place and Community Resiliency

Regardless of the outcome, one thing is clear: population growth will continue on south Vancouver Island and in the CRD, and it is only a matter of time before it begins banging at the door of the EA. Whether any given community can maintain its resiliency in the face of impending annexation, be it in a rural or an urban context, depends on a number of factors. One part of the resiliency equation will be strong and responsive governance models that recognize the unique identity of their constituent communities and the sense of place and connection held by their members. This also means including these communities as equal and informed partners in integrated planning processes (Raco 2003) as part of third-generation responses to sustainability.

Another part of the resiliency equation quite possibly stems from capacities within the communities themselves, in a theoretical framework that Callaghan and Colton (2008) define as 'community capital.' Within this framework, community resiliency is supported by a series of common capital subsystems on which all community members rely and to which they contribute. The first of these is 'environment capital,' which, in addition to the 'information function' (knowledge and connection) described earlier, includes functions of natural regulation, space for habitation, and sustenance (production). In addition to the commercial and social capital discussed earlier, Callaghan and Colton discuss human capital (including, but not limited to, education and skills), cultural capital (heritage), and public structural capital (including institutions). The interrelationships and energy flows among these various forms of community capital and their dynamic balance, the authors contend, contribute to community resiliency. Just as second-generation responses to environmental sustainability have advocated balance among ecological, social, and economic imperatives, so the growth of one source of community capital at the expense of another creates imbalances and lowers resilience within the entire system supporting the community. Reduced resiliency means increased community vulnerability to crises, including the threat of annexation.

As each community, and the capital systems that ultimately support it, is unique, Callaghan and Colton (2008, 939) emphasize that, to be resilient, each 'must find the balance of energy flows to and from different forms of capital that works best for [it].' It is also incumbent upon community leaders to recognize and take stock of these various forms of community capital and how they vary over time, and balance their dynamic interrelationships to ensure continued community flexibility and resiliency as part of third-generation responses to urban sustainability. As Callaghan and Colton (2008) also note, this will require strong leadership, vision, and effective communication with municipalities and communities to facilitate a shift from the current and more common paradigm of crisis management and revenue growth. The framework is not merely theoretical: Callaghan and Colton provide Canadian examples of communities such as Whistler, British Columbia, and Wolfville, Nova Scotia, which are collecting baseline information – ranging from community life and economic vitality to partnerships and the environment – to begin measuring change and development in their community capital.

The recognition of community capital and its dynamic balance will be important to the resiliency of the EA communities of this case study in maintaining their sense of identity and place. This includes the continued development, reassessment, and implementation of robust official community plans that are closely aligned with the CRD's Regional Growth Strategy across a variety of dimensions. Integrated planning (see Hanna and Slocombe, Chapter 2 in this volume) can also play a key role here since not only must the plans align with regional strategies; they must also capture the land-use preferences that preserve a sense of place for each community through integrated economic, social, and environmental perspectives. The community visions articulated by the EA communities have all the elements of a second-generation response to sustainability. Their successful implementation in the future, however, will be an important aspect of a third-generation approach relating to form and function and rooted firmly in place by an effective governance structure. Although the focus here has been on the rural context, there are clearly parallels for community sustainability and identity in Canada's larger urban centres. Planning and governance structures must reflect and take into account their collective communities and the shared sense of place held by their members, as equal partners at the table as part of third-generation responses to (urban) sustainability.

NOTES

1 The name T'sou-ke refers to the stickleback fish found at the mouth of the Sooke River. See http://www.district.sooke.bc.ca/about-history.htm.
2 Sooke makes up 3.8 per cent of the population of the Capital Regional District, according to projections (Urban Aspects Consulting Group et al. 2001).

3 Otter Point originated with the establishment of the Tugwell farm during the 1860s and shares a common boundary with Sooke to the northwest.

4 Believe to have been named after the Prince of Wales, Baron of Renfrew, who visited Canada in 1860, Port Renfrew is located in the far west corner of the Capital Regional District.

5 Named after the Malahat First Nation, who consider the local mountain to be of great ceremonial significance and one of the most sacred sites on southern Vancouver Island, Malahat is located just northeast of Sooke on a road that originated as a cattle trail in the 1860s and was upgraded to a wagon road in the mid-1880s; it eventually become part of the Trans-Canada Highway in the 1960s.

6 East Sooke, established in the 1880s, shares a common boundary with Sooke to the southeast.

7 Shirley was founded in the early 1900s and shares a common boundary with Otter Point to the southeast.

8 Jordan River was established in 1908 to support the logging, hydro-electric power, and copper mining industries, and shares a common boundary with Shirley to the southeast.

9 Willis Point was founded in the 1930s as a community independent from Saanich (Sloan 2005) and is located northeast of the Malahat across the Saanich Inlet.

10 See http://www.crd.bc.ca/jdf/planning.htm.

11 Defined as a 'move away from top-down restructuring built upon BC's local tradition of changing local government structures through local assent using referenda' (British Columbia 2000, 15).

12 Property owners within the proposed boundary extension areas were encouraged to express their objections (Sooke 2005b).

13 A total of 1,031 surveys were sent to overall to the communities of East Sooke, Otter Point and Shirley/Jordan River with 298 (28 per cent) responses (Juan de Fuca Electoral Area, 2006).

REFERENCES

BC Statistics. 2009a. '2006 Census Profile Capital H (Part 1), Regional District Electoral Area.' Victoria. http://www.bcstats.gov.bc.ca/data/cen06/profiles/detailed/ 59017054.pdf (accessed June 2007).

–. 2009b. '2006 Census Profile Capital H (Part 2), Regional District Electoral Area.' http://www.bcstats.gov.bc.ca/data/cen06/profiles/detailed/59017056.pdf (accessed June 2007).

Boyle, M., R.B. Gibson, and D. Curran. 2004. 'If Not Here, Then Perhaps Not Anywhere: Urban Growth Management as a Tool for Sustainability Planning in British Columbia's Capital Regional District.' *Local Environment* 9, no. 1: 21–43.

Brehm, J.M. 2007. 'Community Attachment: The Complexity and Consequence of the Natural Environment Facet.' *Human Ecology* 35, no. 4: 477–88.

British Columbia. 2000. Ministry of Municipal Affairs. 'Managing Changes to Local Government Structure in British Columbia: A Review and Program Guide.' Victoria. October.

Callaghan, E.G., and J. Colton. 2008. 'Building Sustainable and Resilient Communities: A Balancing of Community Capital.' *Environment, Development and Sustainability* 10: 931–42.

Capital Regional District. 2003. Regional Planning Services. 'Regional Growth Strategy for the Capital Regional District.' Bylaw No. 2953, a Bylaw to Adopt a Regional Growth District Strategy for the Capital Regional District. Victoria, BC. August.

East Sooke. 2006. 'Official Community Plan for East Sooke.' Bylaw No. 1, 2006. East Sooke, BC.

Edwards, M.M. 2008. 'Understanding the Complexities of Annexation.' *Journal of Planning Literature* 23, no. 2: 119–35.

Falk, I., and S. Kilpatrick. 2000. 'What Is Social Capital? A Study of Interaction in a Rural Community.' *Sociologia Ruralis* 40, no. 1: 87–110.

Fischel, W.A. 1991. 'Good for the Town, Bad for the Nation? A Comment.' *Journal of the American Planning Association* 57, no. 3: 341–44.

Gallent, N., et al. 2004. 'England's Urban Fringes: Multi-functionality and Planning.' *Local Environment* 9, no. 3: 217–33.

Hansen, A.J., et al. 2005. 'Effects of Exurban Development on Biodiversity: Patterns, Mechanisms, and Research Needs.' *Ecological Applications* 15, no. 6: 1893–1905.

Hite, J. 1998. 'Land Use Conflicts on the Urban Fringe: Causes and Potential Resolution.' Clemson, SC: Clemson University, Strom Thurmond Institute.

Jivén, G., and P.J. Larkham. 2003. 'Sense of Place, Authenticity and Character: A Commentary.' *Journal of Urban Design* 8, no. 1: 67–81.

Juan de Fuca Electoral Area. 2006. 'Juan de Fuca Electoral Area Newsletter: Satisfaction Survey, July 2006.' Juan de Fuca Electoral Area, BC. http://www.crd.bc.ca/jdf/documents/July_news_2006.pdf#view=Fit (accessed September 2007).

Kozeny, G. 2005. 'The Urban/Rural Spectrum.' *Communities* 129 (Winter): 75–6.

Mahon, M., F. Fahy, and M. Ó Cinnéide. 2009. 'The Significance of Quality of Life and Sustainability at the Urban-Rural Fringe in the Making of Place-based Community.' *GeoJournal*, November. Online.

Malahat. 2004. 'Official Community Plan for Malahat.' Bylaw No. 1, 2004. Malahat, BC.

Meligrana, J.F. 2000. 'Toward a Process Model of Local Government Restructuring: Evidence from Canada.' *Canadian Journal of Regional Science* 23, no. 3: 509–33.

–. 2007. 'Testing the Elastic-Cities Concept within a Non-metropolitan Environment: Evidence from British Columbia, Canada, 1971 to 2001.' *Environment and Planning A* 39: 700–27.

Metchosin. 2006. 'Minutes of the Planning & Environment Committee Meeting.' 10 October. Metchosin, BC. http://www.district.metchosin.bc.ca/minutes06/10–10 per cent20PE.pdf (accessed September 2009).

Nelson, A.C., et al. 2004. 'Urban Containment and Central-City Revitalization.' *Journal of the American Planning Association* 70, no. 4: 411–25.

Newman, L., and A. Dale. 2007. 'Homophily and Agency: Creating Effective Sustainable Development Networks.' *Environment, Development and Sustainability* 9, no. 1: 79–90.

Otter Point. 2006. 'Official Community Plan for Otter Point, Bylaw No. 1.' Capital Regional District Bylaw No. 3354, a Bylaw to Establish an Official Community Plan for Otter Point. Otter Point, BC.

OPSRRA (Otter Point & Shirley Residents & Ratepayers Association). 2003. *Newsletter*. December.

–. 2006a. Information Update. March. Otter Point, BC.

–. 2006b. 'Juan de Fuca Electoral Area Governance Study.' Notes of a Meeting Held with Provincial Government Officials, Otter Point, 21 July. Otter Point, BC.

–. 2006c. Minutes of the Annual General Meeting, Otter Point, 21 February. Otter Point, BC.

–. 2006d. Notes of a Meeting Held with Provincial Government Officials, Otter Point, 10 January 10. Otter Point, BC.

Peers, E. 2002. 'Where the Rainforest Meets the Sea: The District of Sooke.' http://www.district.sooke.bc.ca/about-history.htm (accessed September 2007).

Port Renfrew. 2003. 'Comprehensive Community Development Plan for Port Renfrew Bylaw No. 1.' Capital Regional District Bylaw No. 3109. Port Renfrew, BC.

Prugh, T. 1999. *Natural Capital and Human Economic Survival*, 2nd ed. Boca Raton, FL: CRC Press.

Pryor, R.J. 1968. 'Defining the Rural-Urban Fringe.' *Social Forces* 47, no. 2: 202–15.

Raco, M. 2003. 'New Labour, Community and the Future of Britain's Urban Renaissance.' In *Urban Renaissance? New Labour, Community and Urban Policy*, ed. R. Irmie and M. Raco. Bristol, UK: Policy Press.

Rangwala, K. 2010. 'Place-based Economy.' *Economic Development Journal* 9, no. 1: 42–7.

Sampson, K.A., and C.G. Goodrich. 2009. 'Making Place: Identity Construction and Community Formation through "Sense of Place" in Westland, New Zealand.' *Society and Natural Resources* 22, no. 10: 901–15.

Shamsuddina, S., and N. Ujang. 2008. 'Making Places: The Role of Attachment in Creating the Sense of Place for Traditional Streets in Malaysia.' *Habitat International* 32, no. 3: 399–409.

Shirley/Jordan River. 2006. 'Official Community Plan for Shirley/Jordan River Bylaw No. 1.' Capital Regional District Bylaw No. 3352, a Bylaw to Establish an Official Community Plan for Shirley/Jordan River. Shirley/Jordan River, BC.

Sloan, P. 2005. 'Where the Heck Is Willis Point?' *Rural Observer* 2, no. 5: 16.

Sooke. 2005a. 'Proposed Extension of Municipalities: East Boundary (Gillespie Road), West Boundary (Kemp Lake).' *Proposed Boundary Extension Newsletter* 1, 16 August. http://www.district.sooke.bc.ca/Boundary/Newsletter-Aug1605.pdf (accessed September 2007).

–. 2005b. 'Proposed Extension of Municipalities: East Boundary (Gillespie Road) and West Boundary (Kemp Lake) – Background Information.' *Proposed Boundary Extension Newsletter* 2, 24 August. http://www.district.sooke.bc.ca/Boundary/FinalNewsletter2Aug2405.pdf (accessed September 2007).

Stokes, S.M., A.E. Watson, and S.S. Mastran. 1997. *Saving America's Countryside: A Guide to Rural Conservation*, 2nd ed. Baltimore: Johns Hopkins University Press.

Stott, G. 2007. 'Enhancing Status through Incorporation: Suburban Municipalities in Nineteenth-Century Ontario.' *Journal of Urban History* 33, no. 6: 885–910.

Sullivan, W.C., O.M. Anderson, and S.T. Lovell. 2004. 'Agricultural Buffers at the Rural-Urban Fringe: An Examination of Approval by Farmers, Residents, and Academics in the Midwestern United States.' *Landscape and Urban Planning* 69, nos. 2–3: 299–313.

Thomas, P.G. 2001. 'A Layman's Perspective on the Issue of Urban Sprawl.' Draft Report prepared for the Manitoba Capital Region. http://www.gov.mb.ca/ia/capreg/reports_docs/reports/related/urban.html (accessed September 2007).

Tweedy, B. 2005. 'To Amalgamate or Not to Amalgamate? That Is the Question – Otter Point Community News.' *Rural Observer* 2, no. 1: 11.

Urban Aspects Consulting Group Ltd., idealink Architecture Ltd., Cloghesy & Doak Ltd., and GMK 2000. 2001. 'Sooke Official Community Plan.' Sooke, BC.

Willis Point. 2002. Comprehensive Community Plan for Willis Point Bylaw No. 1, 2002. Willis Point, BC.

10 Sustainable Buildings: A Necessary Component of Sustainable Communities

RODNEY C. MCDONALD

We shape our buildings, and afterwards our buildings shape us.
– Winston Churchill (1943)

Nothing reflects human interaction with ecosystems better than the pattern, form, and function of our buildings. From the earliest constructed shelters to the tallest LEED (Leadership in Energy and Environmental Design) Platinum skyscraper, we have a long-standing history of constructing shelter to intermediate between ourselves and our environs. In Canada, efforts to design and construct buildings that have less impact on the environment have ebbed and flowed. In the early 1970s, the energy crisis led to new, concerted efforts to create more energy-efficient buildings. Yet, by the early 1980s, this focus drifted as designers and engineers turned their attention to aesthetic and structural challenges. The potential for buildings to offer contributions beyond serving the needs of their occupants, however, are many. These include meeting broader corporate social responsibility goals and reinforcing a sustainable or greener brand identity to stakeholders at the organizational level (Telus 2006), and opportunities at the community level for energy-efficient building and green building design in responding to issues such as energy demand, supply, and security, and climate change. As our collective recognition of the importance of sustainable development in the built environment continues to grow, as part of third-generation responses, we have begun to consider how, and to what extent, our buildings might better advance sustainability from the household to the community to the global scale. For these efforts to contribute to progress towards urban sustainability, however, buildings must be part of integrated approaches across different scales.

This is not unlike similar integrated approaches used for regional planning discussed by Hanna and Slocombe (in this volume), which also address community and equity issues.

This chapter explores the process of the evolution of sustainable building design by demonstrating how buildings can be used, in an integrative way, as a tool to contribute to the economic, environmental, and community imperatives of sustainability. Buildings, as features of human activity, are virtually indelible on the landscape, which can help or hinder the advancement of community-scale sustainability. Although sustainable buildings are a necessary component of sustainable communities, as Robinson (Chapter 4 in this volume) argues, they are not sufficient in and of themselves. This interconnectedness, however, is a key element of third-generation responses. Buildings, when conceived of in a broader sustainability agenda, have the potential to foster density and walkability in urban communities (see Newman and Waldron, in this volume), support a variety of transport options (bike, bus, rail, auto share), advance resource (energy, water, material) efficiency, promote renewable energy, maintain clean air and water quality, reduce greenhouse gas emissions and solid wastes, realize an attractive return on investment, stimulate a green economy and create green jobs, provide occupants with good indoor air quality and daylight, inspire other sustainable practices (see Luka, in this volume), and address infrastructure deficits.

Buildings and Community Sustainability

Much has been written and discussed about the globalization of human society. While capital in its natural, manufactured, financial, or intellectual form is transportable to almost any location around the globe, buildings are not. Once a building is built, it generally remains in its original place for the remainder of its useful life. This makes buildings local to the place they are built. At the same time, because the aforementioned types of capital and resources are easily transportable, buildings are also often global. For example, building materials, products, and technologies can travel the globe before reaching the final building site, and knowledge and experience about building practice is also shared globally through a variety of media. For large-scale building projects, it is also common for design teams to include consultants from across the globe sharing ideas and information.

It is possible to build a sustainable building in an unsustainable community, but it is not possible to realize a sustainable community without sustainable buildings. Callaghan and Colton (2008), in their discussion of community sustainability, refer to this as 'public structure capital' (see also Dushenko, Chapter 9 in this volume), and include stocks and services such as roads, water systems, parks, libraries, town centres, and the like. The sustainability of a physical human community, therefore, is shaped by the sustainability of the buildings. Sustainable buildings offer many opportunities in the social, environmental, and economic realms. Compared with conventional buildings, sustainable buildings are more energy efficient, which is an important benefit considering growing concerns about energy security, supply, and price (Canada 2006; Council of Energy Ministers 2007; WBCSD 2008). Sustainable buildings also produce fewer greenhouse gas emissions, especially important in the context of the current global focus on addressing climate change (IPCC 2007). They also use less potable water and, in some cases, reuse water and/or capture rainwater, which reduces demands on municipal water supplies and expensive wastewater and storm water infrastructure. Given the impending global water crisis (de Villiers 1999; Barlow and Clarke 2002), realizing the opportunities for sustainable buildings to reduce water use is critical.

Ideally, a sustainable building contributes to a sustainable community because the building is located so that people can easily access it by walking, cycling, or taking public transit, thereby reducing commuter costs and energy requirements. This should also reduce reliance on automobile transport and its associated effects, such as excessive energy use, greenhouse gas emissions, and costly infrastructure requirements (see also Newman and Waldron, in this volume). From the perspective of physical matter, sustainable buildings may also incorporate reused materials such as lumber or bricks recovered locally from a building that has been demolished, new materials that have recycled content (such as carpet with recycled nylon or ceramic tile with recycled glass), and materials made from resources that are rapidly renewable (plant crops such as bamboo) or were harvested in a manner that is more ecologically sustainable (for example, not by clear-cut logging). Sustainability is also enhanced if materials are sourced closer to building sites to reduce the cost and negative environmental effects of transport over long distances.[1] Recognizing and addressing how buildings are created in sustainable ways and can contribute to sustainable pattern, form, and function in urban communities in an integrated and regenerative way at different scales is a central tenet of third-generation responses. The term 'regenerative,' in the context of this chapter, refers not only to the positive effects of sustainable buildings on the environment (the ecological imperative) and on the social well-being of the community (the social imperative), but also to how, by the very nature of their form and function, such buildings can lead to reinvestment in and restoration of both financial and natural (ecological) capital and the development of social capital and spatial justice through the spaces they create within them.

Buildings and the Environment

According to Canada's Energy Use Data Handbook (Canada 2005), buildings and houses in Canada account for 31 per cent of total secondary energy use and 30 per cent of total greenhouse gas emissions, including electricity-related emissions. Similar statistics are reported by the US Green Building Council for energy use by buildings and houses in the United States (USGBC 2007). Buildings also have upstream and downstream effects on natural systems, including the generation or extraction of energy and the global climate effects of emissions; the contamination of surface water and groundwater; impervious surfaces that impede water drainage and groundwater aquifer recharge; natural resources extraction (cutting, mining, drilling); materials processing and manufacturing; and the use of landfills for construction or demolition waste. Compounding the ecological footprint is the supporting land and infrastructure, energy, and/or waste by-products that support many of these activities.

One contributing factor to these effects is the linear flow of energy, water, and materials through a building over the course of its life (see Figure 10.1). According to William McDonough, 'the industrial idiom of design, failing to honor the principles of nature, can only violate them, producing waste and harm, regardless of purported intention' (1993, 8). This design ideology, similar to the ideology of industrial economies (Pearce and Turner 1990; McDonough and Braungart 1998), treats the environment as a warehouse of resources and a sink for wastes. From this perspective, the conception of buildings, as we design them today, is that of boxes that transform resources into wastes. It is also this notion that to some extent resulted in the emergence of first- and, to a certain extent, second-generation responses to sustainability.

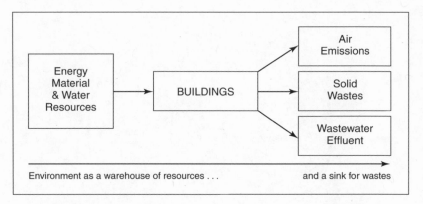

Figure 10.1. Buildings from an environmental perspective: Boxes that transform resources into wastes

Resource Efficiency, Sustainable Building, and Sustainability: A Systems Approach

The nested nature of resource efficiency, green building, and sustainability is illustrated in Figure 10.2. In this context, resource efficiency includes energy efficiency, water efficiency, and raw materials efficiency. Resource efficiency is only a foundation of sustainable building practice, in that it is impossible to have a sustainable building that is also not energy or water efficient. Sustainable building, in turn, is a foundation of sustainability, whether at the organizational, the community, or the global level.

Important linkages must be made, both conceptually and practically, between resource efficiency, sustainable building, and sustainability. For some people, these linkages may be easier to see from a systems perspective, as 'the systems view looks at the world in terms of relationships and integration' (Capra 1982, 266). A building is a system, and sustainable building practice must go beyond just working on the building system, since it is nested within and connected to systems of infrastructure, the environment, economies, communities, material supply chains, and other human systems, including industrial, corporate, and academic. The design of a building's system, then, needs to incorporate elements of these interconnected systems at the design stage where the majority of its external costs are seen. Indeed, as Dale (2006, 2) notes, 'we need to act now in the fundamental *design and re-design* of

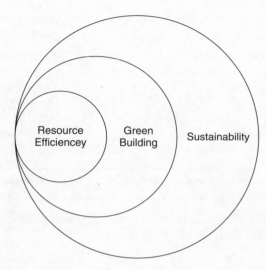

Figure 10.2. Nested domains of resource efficiency, green building, and sustainability

our systems of commerce and production such that they maintain and restore ecological systems.'

Like sustainable communities in urban centres, sustainable buildings must consider and attend to the three domains or imperatives of sustainable development: ecological, economic, and social. What is required to attend to these nested domains as part of third-generation responses is a holistic, integrative systems-based approach to transform the market to embrace sustainable building practices. A holistic approach is one that considers changes at the level of the whole, rather than focusing on one or a few of the parts (Capra 1982). For example, some may perceive that the answer to transportation problems in cities is wider roads or more fuel-efficient automobiles, while others may believe it to be bicycles and effective public transit; perhaps, however, a mix of all would provide the best solution.[2] Developing solutions that can be sustained over the long term requires a holistic mindset and approach that allow for the consideration of all options in an integrated manner, as also advocated in approaches to regional planning by Hanna and Slocombe (in this volume), and sets out a new course of principled organization to fully implement the ideals required for sustainability (Dale 2006).

Integration emphasizes both vertical and horizontal integration in systems (see also Dale, Chapter 6 in this volume), based on the concept of integrated, rather than silo-based, decision-making at both the macro and the micro scale. The macro scale is the community system, where government, business, and civil society create the conditions for sustainable buildings and where policy instruments (laws, regulations, policies, programs) and market forces help guide them into being. The micro scale refers to the building itself, where there is opportunity to procure, design, construct, inspect, operate, maintain, and deconstruct buildings and infrastructure in a way that contributes to and advances sustainability at the community scale. Like all systems, these are nested (Meadows 1999; Dale 2001) in that the buildings we build today (sustainable or not) are built within a network of systems that all have an influence on the final product. Understanding these systems, the leverage points in each, and the interconnections between systems is key to advancing sustainable building design and construction.

Whether approaching sustainable building at the macro or micro scale, it is necessary to work at multiple levels within each scale (see Figure 10.3). There are four levels at which people can approach the practice of sustainable building: products, tools, processes, and mindset. At the products level the focus is on what materials, products, or technologies should one put into a sustainable building. Many people new to sustainable building practices start at this level. They want to be told the most energy-efficient lighting or heating technologies to put into a building, or what materials and products are greenest – in other words, that have the least negative environmental impact. Government and utility incentive programs draw attention to the products level. Many of these incentive programs are product or technology specific.

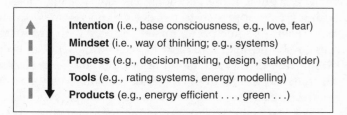

Figure 10.3. Working at multiple levels
Source: Author's adaptation from Reed, Hubbard, and Batshalom (2004).

Most major Canadian utilities have multi-million-dollar budgets for financial incentives for residential, commercial, and industrial customers to choose energy-efficient lighting, heating systems, insulation, and appliances.

The level of process identifies decision-making processes or, in the case of buildings, design processes used to establish the end result or product. While the product is tangible and tactile, as discussed earlier, building design processes are somewhat intangible and are often not well documented. In the context of sustainability and sustainable buildings, there needs to be holistic decision-making processes, rather than compartmentalized and silo-based decision-making, and integrated design.

Mindset, the way one thinks, is established by cultural norms, values, education, experience, and social influences such as family, friends, and peers. It can be based on linear or systems thinking, or conventional or integrative thinking (Martin 2007), and it often operates without being conscious of its influence on one's thoughts and belief systems. Societies and buildings are a reflection of the values and consciousness of a society at a given point in time. Societal values about the environment are changing, and awareness of the impact of human activities on the natural environment and, consequently, on human health is becoming more prevalent (James Hoggin and Associates 2006). It is a natural outcome, therefore, that buildings and building practices continue to evolve to match these changing values and consciousness as part of third-generation responses.

How most people generally approach sustainable building is illustrated by the grey arrow pointing up in Figure 10.3 – that is, starting at the bottom and working up. Designers, for example, begin by asking what products or technologies to put into a building, then realize there are tools that can guide those decisions. They may realize or learn that taking an integrated approach to the design process makes using the tools much easier. At some point, this experience with products, tools and processes should lead to a shift in one's mindset – an epiphany, a new perspective, or the proverbial light bulb going on. Another approach, of course, is to start at the top and work one's way down, as indicated by the black arrow in Figure 10.3. From my perspective, echoed by Dale (2006) and Lister (2006), this is the preferred route to sustainable building. Changing one's mindset with respect to how design affects the processes used will, in turn, change the tools one uses, and then guide the products one puts into a building.

The following three case studies explore the nature of first-, second-, and emergent third-generation sustainability responses implemented through building design and construction. The first case study – the process to convince the Canadian Commission on Building and Fire Codes (CCBFC) to update the Model National Energy Code of Canada for Buildings for energy efficiency – illustrates a first-generation response at the national scale. The second case study focuses on second-generation responses at the community scale by reviewing the development and implementation of Manitoba's green building policy as a means of advancing community sustainability. The third case study is at the organizational scale and illustrates third-generation responses of integrated, interconnected, and regenerative design. It describes a public hydroelectric utility, Manitoba Hydro, that uses sustainable building as a tool to provide a healthy and productive environment for employees, demonstrating brand commitment to energy efficiency, and contributing to the sustainability of the local community.

First-Generation Responses: The Evolution of Energy Efficiency in the Model National Energy Code of Canada for Buildings

This case focuses on using building codes as a tool to advance sustainable building practices – specifically, energy efficiency in commercial buildings. It describes the process used to update Canada's Model National Energy Code for Buildings and highlights the need for integrated decision-making when bringing together energy efficiency professionals and building code professionals. The important role of codes and standards in advancing and/or supporting sustainable building and community design was highlighted in a building industry stakeholder workshop on sustainable building hosted by the Canadian Standards Association (CSA) in 2007. Stakeholders identified these public policy instruments as barriers to sustainable building practice, noting, 'policy instruments are not written and developed with a sustainability focus' (Canadian Standards Association 2008). The CSA also stated that the same could be said of municipal planning and zoning bylaws in that there are opportunities for such bylaws to advance and/or support sustainable building and community design.

Under the Constitution Act, 1867, building regulations are a provincial responsibility. The National Building Code of Canada has four core objectives: safety, health, accessibility, and fire and structural stability (CCBFC 2005). Technical requirements in the code fall under one or a combination of the four core objectives. Historically, elements of sustainable building design such as energy efficiency, water efficiency, resource efficiency, or environmental sustainability have not been reflected in the National Building Code. It was not until 2008 that a council of provincial and territorial premiers agreed to include energy efficiency.

Energy efficiency was addressed in the late 1990s with the publication of the Model National Energy Code of Canada for Buildings and the Model National Energy Code of Canada for Houses (CCBFC 1997). Similar to the National Building Code, the Model National Energy Codes are written in code language – meaning a language and format that allows for the adoption of the code document by a province or territory via regulation. Unlike the National Building Code, however, the Energy Codes have not been adopted by every province and territory primarily because of the additional resources and expertise that would be required to enforce them. The exceptions are the provinces of British Columbia, Ontario, and Quebec, and the City of Vancouver. Work is under way, however, to update the Energy Codes, with interest from a number of the provinces and territories to adopt this through regulation.

In December 2005, Natural Resources Canada hosted a meeting of provincial and territorial energy ministers to share information on the status of establishing minimum requirements for energy efficiency in new buildings, and to gauge interest in updating the Model National Energy Codes. With provincial and territorial support, Natural Resources Canada established the Building Energy Codes Collaborative, a federal-provincial-territorial committee to generate political and financial support for the adoption of the Model National Energy Codes by the CCBFC, an independent body composed of industry, government, and non-government representatives from across Canada responsible for overseeing the development and update of the country's model national building codes. Both the CCBFC and the Canadian Codes Centre stressed to the Building Energy Codes Collaborative the importance of adding representatives from provincial and territorial code ministries to the committee. The result was that the Collaborative became a unique committee composed of representatives with disparate but complementary perspectives. On the one hand were energy representatives with an understanding of energy efficiency and the urgency of energy security and climate change issues, but little understanding of building codes and the code development process. On the other hand were building code representatives with reciprocal skills and perspectives.

Communication was initially difficult between the energy and building code representatives, with their different perspectives, their own
accustomed language, and mutual unfamiliarity with the acronyms
used in their respective fields of practice – not unlike the two 'silos'
of industry and environment experienced by the National Task Force
on Environment and Economy described by Dale in the Introduction
to this volume. In fall 2006, the Building Energy Codes Collaborative
created an opportunity for each field of experts to learn, understand,
and respect the other perspective with a view towards integration. This
was critical to the Collaborative's being able to develop and present
a business plan to the CCBFC to update the Model National Energy
Codes, making a strong case for energy efficiency and consistent with
the CCBFC's perspective. This shared understanding of the important
issues that make up sustainability, design, and building processes is
highlighted by Dale (2006), who notes that finding a common language
and bridging between disciplines and professions is critical to coopera-
tively engage in effective design and building of industrial ecological
and sustainable systems (see also the Introduction to this volume).

In June 2007, following work by federal, provincial, and territorial
representatives, at the political and administrative levels over a period
of eighteen months, Natural Resources Canada and the National Research Council announced a joint effort to update the Model National
Energy Codes by 2011. Natural Resources Canada, which houses the
Office of Energy Efficiency, is providing funding to update the codes,
while the CCBFC works to develop or update code documents, with
technical and administrative support provided by the Canadian Codes
Centre, which exists within the National Research Council's Institute
for Research in Construction. After years of subsequent work by a committee of technical experts, the new National Energy Code for Buildings
was published in November 2011 (Canada 2011).

As described earlier, effective systems thinking requires an understanding of the nested and interconnected structure of the systems, as
well as their function. In this case, understanding the code development system and the interconnection of that system to provincial regulatory systems, was key to the success of the Building Energy Codes
Collaborative. The ability to break, or at least bend, institutional path
dependence by different levels of government is key to advancing sustainable initiatives in building design and operation.

Ultimately, this case study demonstrates that concepts critical to
sustainability – integrated decision-making and understanding the
structure and function of systems – can be applied to realms that are

considered not presently to support sustainability in order to help advance sustainability in those realms. It is also important to note that, in addition to the national code development process, it is also possible for a province or territory to add objectives to a building code on minimum green or sustainable requirements, or to make allowances for green or sustainable practices. The Ontario Building Code (Ontario 2006), for example, includes three additional objectives: resource conservation, environmental integrity, and the conservation of buildings. The resource conservation objective is in response to the province's commitment to reduce peak electricity demand, reduce greenhouse gas emissions, and create a culture of conservation. British Columbia, Manitoba, and Nova Scotia have established similar energy efficiency requirements in their building codes. At the time of writing, other provinces, including Alberta, Quebec, and New Brunswick are in the process of or intend to establish requirements for energy efficiency in their respective building codes.

Second-Generation Responses: Manitoba's Green Building Policy

Governments in Canada and the United States are establishing green building policies to govern direct expenditure decisions on new government-owned or government-funded buildings. In some cases, the requirements also apply to existing government-owned buildings and/or to buildings or portions of buildings leased from the private sector. A number of governments in Canada have established green building requirements for new construction, referencing the green building rating system of LEED Canada for New Construction and Major Renovations. In some cases, such as in Manitoba, requirements also apply to additions to existing buildings and major renovations to existing buildings. Green building has been a great attempt to advance sustainability in building practices and is broader in scope than efforts to address energy-efficient building envelopes alone. There are many definitions of green building in the literature (Cole 2000; Kats et al. 2003). The US Green Building Council, a subnational-level non-government organization with a mandate to drive green building, defines such construction as 'design and construction practices that significantly reduce or eliminate the negative impact of buildings on the environment and occupants' (USGBC 2005, slide 4). Building the elements of natural capital and externalities into this definition, green building might best be defined as design and construction practices that reduce negative impacts on the environment, but that continue to rely on stored stocks of natural capital and to produce external costs, which is consistent with second-generation approaches to sustainability.

It is important to note, however, that, during a presentation at Green-build 2004[3] in Portland, Oregon, Bob Berkable, of BNIM Architects and founder of the American Institute of Architects Committee on Environment, stated that, even if every building were a LEED Platinum building, these structures would still have a negative impact on the natural environment (2004). This is because even LEED Platinum buildings still may use conventional materials and resources such as fossil fuels to heat or cool; be connected to municipal water mains and sanitary sewers; use a wide range of building materials made of raw materials extracted in unsustainable ways from the natural environment, for example, petrochemicals for piping and wiring; use finished materials manufactured using various processes that can negatively impact the natural environment and are transported long distances using fossil fuels; and use noxious substances such as glues with certain chemicals that affect the quality of the indoor environment.

Thus, while the movement toward green building as a second-generation response is a step closer to a more robust alignment of built-form and sustainability, it signals the need to further consider how the processes of designing, building, and occupying buildings might be better attuned to their environment, The case of the Manitoba Green Buildings policy sheds light on the importance of governance in sustainability efforts. Here, the intervention of the provincial government has shifted the market mindset to one in which new, more progressive practices and product considerations are possible.

In June 2006, the Manitoba provincial government announced a Green Building Policy for Government of Manitoba Funded Projects, which took effect on 1 April 2007 (Manitoba 2007). This came about as a result of a request from the provincial Treasury Board to establish requirements for new buildings funded, in whole or in part, by the Manitoba government. The policy requires the use of an integrated design process, minimum levels of energy efficiency, life-cycle costing of the building or building systems, minimum LEED Silver certification, and preference for low or zero carbon renewable energy sources. In its extension to non-government projects, the Manitoba policy is more far reaching than most government green building policies. The policy was developed by the Green Building Policy Interdepartmental Working Group, composed of representatives of a number of different provincial government departments involved in the construction, operation, and maintenance of buildings. This inclusive and integrated approach at the provincial government level helped to ensure that the perspectives of many departments were considered in the development of the policy. As Manitoba has moved forward with the policy, three departments – Infrastructure and Transportation; Innovation, Energy and Mines; and Family Services and Labour (specifically, the Office of the Fire Commissioner)[4] – have been working with Manitoba Hydro to support its implementation.

This coordinated approach promotes what I have labelled 'sustained market transformation.' Manitoba's Green Building policy is transforming the market by creating demand for green building and pulling the market to adopt current best practices. Manitoba Hydro, with a suite of financial incentives for energy efficiency, is encouraging better-than-standard practices. Upcoming building code changes, which will incorporate energy and water efficiency, will push the market to a place where many people think it should already be. These three instruments – policy, incentives, codes – can be applied in isolation, but are more effective if they are coordinated in an integrated way, such that the policy and incentives prepare the market for future code changes, which, in turn, support the policy and incentives.

Governments alone, however, cannot transform the market regardless of the number of policy instruments at their disposal; markets also pay a role from a systems perspective. Examples of market decisions or instruments emerging to support elements of sustainability and sustainable building include the following:

- institutional investors, such as pension funds, choosing to invest in green buildings, such as the sale of the TELUS building – a LEED-certified building – in Ottawa to a German pension fund (White 2008);
- energy efficient mortgages (see Roseland 2005; United States 2005) requiring homes to have some type of energy-efficiency rating or be built to some type of verifiable voluntary program; this verification assures the lender that the homeowner will indeed realize the energy savings;
- insurance products specifically for green buildings (see Fireman's Fund Insurance Company 2007), to protect both financial and environmental investments in buildings; and

- 10 per cent discounts on the mortgage loan insurance premium by Canada Mortgage and Housing Corporation (CMHC 2008) to those who purchase an energy-efficient homes or who make energy-efficient upgrades or renovations to an existing house.

Manitoba's Green Building policy is illustrative of the evolution from first- to second-generation responses to sustainability. It represents a move from a single focus on building energy use to an expansion of requirements for green buildings and to provincial government initiatives to create conditions in which the market is encouraged to deliver on the design and construction of such buildings. Despite this progress, however, much room remains between green buildings and broader urban sustainable development.

Third-Generation Responses: Integrated Design
Process in Manitoba Hydro Place

In the 1990s, Natural Resources Canada developed and administered a high-performance program for commercial and institutional buildings called the C-2000 Program for Advanced Commercial Buildings. One objective of the program was to determine the best mix of technologies to make a building sustainable. Although the program ended in 2001, one of its legacies was the realization that it is not the best mix of technologies that results in a sustainable building, but rather the design process (McDonald and Dale 2004). The conventional process to designing a building is linear: the client hires an architect to design the building, engineers take the design and figure out how to heat, cool, and light the building, and then a contractor builds the building. Although this is an oversimplification, it demonstrates that there is little opportunity for the contractor to share his or her perspective and experience during the building design stage; for the engineers to influence the architectural design of the building; for the landscape architects to integrate the building into landscape surrounding it; or for the planners to ensure the building integrates into the community around it. As a result, there are many lost opportunities during the conventional design process, particularly those that incorporate sustainability. Robinson (Chapter 4 in this volume) also notes that '[s]ustainability principles must be an integral part of the planning, design, and building processes; they cannot be added on at the end.'

In response to these shortcomings, a new Integrated Design Process was developed based on systems thinking that engages the client and the entire design team early on in a facilitated collaborative process, with a clear vision and goals, to realize high-performance, cost-effective sustainable buildings. This is in contrast to the conventional building design process or even to the green building process, which tends to be more linear and does not allow for the integration needed to achieve broader sustainability objectives. By incorporating integrated decision-making at the design stage, where 80 per cent of the building's environmental impact is determined, the final result is much more likely to be one that maintains and restores ecological and sustainable systems (Dale 2006). From a sustainability perspective, integrated design is one example of integrated decision-making; it is the building design community's example of the processes advocated by Hanna and Slocombe (in this volume) and Robinson (Chapter 4 in this volume). For example, in the field of community planning, integrated decision-making is referred to as Integrated Community Sustainability Planning (Ling, Dale, and Hanna 2007). Integrated design is particularly important for building owners, as it is a way to capture operating cost savings and erect a building with little or no capital cost premium compared to conventional construction. Elements of successful sustainable building and authentic integrated design include the following elements:

- an engaged building owner – the building owner understands the benefits of sustainable building and is engaged in the design process;
- a shared vision – one that clarifies direction and helps to motivate people to take action in the same direction; the building owner establishes a clear vision, chooses a design team that understands the vision (or develops the vision with the design team and other stakeholders), and consistently communicates it;
- clear and measurable goals – setting goals, in this case performance targets, is a key factor for success; the owner, perhaps working with an internal or external team, sets goals for items pertinent to the organization and/or project that typically include an energy efficiency target and a water efficiency target, and may include targets for items such as transit access or ecological preservation on the site;
- an engaged team – one of the principles of integrated design is that everyone on the design team is at the table from the start; the team

is also encouraged to find solutions beyond the building and the immediate site, and all major design decisions are made with the team present (if major design decisions are made back in the architects' or engineers' office, it is not integrated design);
- a skilled facilitator – the role of the facilitator is to be the keeper of the process, allowing the design professionals to focus on what they are good at (namely, designing buildings); a good facilitator will draw out the shared vision and ensure all perspectives are acknowledged;
- engaged stakeholders – if the project is community based (such as a hospital or community centre), the inclusion of local community members and stakeholders (building users) can help bring new insights and understandings; when engaging non-technical people, it is important to develop a shared non-technical language, or the stakeholders could quickly become disengaged; and
- good project management – a realistic schedule with milestones from start to finish, realistic budget, list of tasks and activities, and responsibilities assigned.

These characteristics also help to promote integrated decision-making, as they emphasize collaboration rather than confrontation, dialogue rather than debate, and the sharing of perspectives rather than the staking of positions. Consideration should be given, however, to the integration of two aspects: first, the integration of the requirements or issues that the building owner, design team, and contractor must consider when planning, designing, and constructing the building; and, second, the integration of the entire design team and the perspectives of the various members of the team. The concept of the Integrated Design Process (IDP) is gaining recognition with sustainable building practitioners as a necessity when designing a green or sustainable building. Studies and anecdotal evidence (Interface Engineering 2005) show that integrated design is the only way to achieve progressive sustainable building targets with no, or very minimal, capital cost premiums, compared to conventional design and construction practices. This is reinforced by Natural Resources Canada, which notes, 'the [Commercial Building Incentive Program] projects that report using integrated design are generally the projects that achieve the highest energy performance levels. They are also the projects that often report no incremental capital cost for the project' (quoted in McDonald and Dale 2004, 21).

Manitoba Hydro is a publicly owned Crown corporation and Manitoba's major energy utility, generating, transmitting, distributing, and selling hydroelectric power to residential, commercial, and industrial end-use consumers. One of its corporate goals is to be a national leader in implementing cost-effective energy conservation and alternative energy programs. Since the early 1990s, Manitoba Hydro has offered a wide array of award-winning, energy efficiency incentive programs for residential, commercial, and industrial consumers under its PowerSmart brand.[5] The corporation's new $278 million head office in Winnipeg is a 65,000-square-metre, twenty-two-storey building providing office space to two thousand of Manitoba Hydro's six thousand employees. At the time of writing, the building was LEED registered and is aiming for LEED Platinum certification by the Canada Green Building Council. Manitoba Hydro's head office building is one of three buildings that helped Canada win second place out of more than sixty countries in the 2008 international Sustainable Building Challenge,[6] behind only Germany, which is known for its advancements in high-performance sustainable building design.

Manitoba Hydro articulated a set of nine guiding principles for the development of its new head office building, which, in some cases, outlined performance targets. The building was to

1 be a world-class, energy-efficient structure and a global leader in sustainability and green building design;
2 be designed and constructed in accordance with sustainable development principles using Power Smart and the C-2000 sustainable building standards as established by Manitoba Hydro and Energy and Mines Canada and targeting a minimum 60 per cent saving in energy consumption and a gold-level LEED . . . certification;
3 provide greenhouse gas savings and exemplify Manitoba's commitment to the Kyoto protocol;
4 provide a healthy and effective contemporary office environment for employees;
5 be designed to be adaptable to changing technology and workplace environments to suit Manitoba Hydro's present and future business needs;
6 be cost effective in both construction and operation and represent a sound financial investment;
7 strengthen and contribute to the sustainable future of Winnipeg's downtown through new investment, increased downtown activity,

and positive integration into the existing fabric and infrastructure of transit, walkway systems, and retail space;

8 be a contemporary and distinctive 'signature' design that celebrates the importance of Manitoba Hydro to the province and that enhances the overall image of the downtown;

9 be constructed through a collaborative process that involves the development community in providing enhanced, value-added opportunities to the project, but places the overall project control of the site location and building design with Manitoba Hydro to ensure a creative, sustainable and cost-effective world-class building (Manitoba Hydro n.d.).

Manitoba Hydro designed a rigorous site selection process to ensure the company built the most appropriate building on the best available site. The available land and building parcel was assessed and evaluated using Manitoba Hydro's own evaluation criteria matrix, which included visibility, identity and image, context, proximity to conference, day care, and fitness facilities, south-facing green space, access to nearby parking, lot size, solar access, detrimental shading, east-west land, building reuse, energy management opportunities, a brownfield site proximity to transit, an enclosed public walkway, proximity to existing retail and commercial areas, green space connection, value-added cost, and overall impact. The result was its current site, which scores high points for existing infrastructure, development density, and access to transit.

Manitoba Hydro also established a vision statement for its head office building and a set of guiding principles for its development. The vision statement, which was communicated consistently and publicly, provided clear and definitive direction to the design team. 'Manitoba Hydro's new head office building . . . will be a state-of-the art energy-efficient, cost-effective structure that embodies and demonstrates Manitoba Hydro's commitment to sustainable development. While meeting the business needs of Manitoba Hydro, the office building will have a positive impact on the sustainable future of Winnipeg's downtown and be a source of pride for Manitobans' (Manitoba Hydro n.d.).

Easy access to transit has helped Manitoba Hydro employees to reduce total annual commuter energy use and associated greenhouse gas emissions. As a result, a large number of Manitoba Hydro employees use the EcoPass program, which offers an employer-subsidized price for a monthly transit pass. In addition, a new park-and-ride bus loop was built at Manitoba Hydro's former head office, which is still in use for staff in other divisions. For employees who cycle to work, a secure bike storage facility is available in the building's parkade, as well as showers and change room facilities.

Manitoba Hydro understood that the placement of the new building would have a profound, immediate, and long-lasting effect on the area surrounding it. The utility could have built a sustainable building on a suburban site, but that would likely have resulted in higher commuter energy use and costs, and greater greenhouse gas emissions from transport. The location of Manitoba Hydro's former head office was close to a suburban neighbourhood in Winnipeg and built during the housing boom following the Second World War. It influenced the patterns of residential choice for many Manitoba Hydro employees still in the employ of the company.[7] Many current employees live in the same southwest quadrant of the city where the former head office building is located. It will be interesting to see if, in the future, employees' choice of residency is similarly influenced by the location of Manitoba Hydro Place. This would clearly expand the influence of the building on local community sustainability and urban design.

At 65 per cent more energy efficient than indicated in the Model National Energy Code for Buildings, Manitoba Hydro's new headquarters is one of the most energy-efficient office buildings in Canada and, indeed, the world.[8] To achieve this high level of energy efficiency while maintaining occupants' comfort, the building has a climate-responsive design that maximizes the use of passive systems to take advantage of free natural processes, such as south-facing winter gardens, natural daylight, and a solar chimney that draws air naturally through the building; the building also minimizes the use of active systems such as dimmable, programmable fluorescent lighting. The building's location and design were selected to maximize the use of solar energy; high ceilings help maximize natural lighting, exterior walls are made of low-iron glass for maximum solar gain, and double walls buffer against the extreme climate. As well, the building features operable exterior wall vents and interior windows, automated solar shading, a geothermal heating and cooling system, an underground parkade that is heated by recovered energy from exhaust air, air that is preheated before entering the building, raised floors with a displacement ventilation system, highly energy-efficient, high-output lighting, with occupancy and light sensors on each fixture, an advanced computer-based Building Management System to coordinate the operation of energy management and building systems, and, to top it off, a green roof (Manitoba Hydro n.d.).

Manitoba Hydro Place is an excellent example not only of green building, demonstrating elements of sustainable building, but also of the importance and lasting impact of site selection on land use, urban form, and community sustainability.[9] To achieve this level of efficiency and sustainability, the building was constructed through a collaborative Integrated Design Process, which was new to some members of the design team and a success factor for sustainable buildings. The IDP team was a consortium of Manitoba Hydro's project manager, an in-house energy expert, the design architect, the architect of record, an advocate architect, an energy engineer, and other professionals who customarily provide expertise and value to the building design process. The result was so significant, and left such an impression, that some of the design team have formed a new Integrated Design Consortium to 'apply [IDP] principles to produce climate controlled, sustainable design for the ultimate benefit the health of its users and to contribute to the vibrancy of urban life' (PR Newswire 2009). A Web site was created to document the full IDP team and process, and to track the performance of the Manitoba Hydro Place project.

The consortium demonstrates the power of exposing people to new processes and how those social capital processes can shape future approaches to building and community design. Manitoba Hydro Place, therefore, is also an example of the lasting impact a project can have on the sustainability of the place where the building sits and on the people who use it, creating a ripple effect into the broader community. As this case study shows, through the deployment of an IDP, the broader principles of sustainability are beginning to be better addressed. By repositioning the building within a more holistic process that considers a wider range of required elements, the process of designing the structure was altered, producing a more robust sustainability outcome.

Reconciliation: Systems Thinking and Integrated Decision-making

By using significant resources and generating large quantities of waste, buildings have a measurable and meaningful effect on communities' ability to move towards sustainability. Sustainable buildings thus are necessary for sustainable communities, though they are certainly not sufficient on their own. Following from the definitions of green and sustainable building, restorative or regenerative building can be defined as

Table 10.1. Spectrum of building design and performance

Type of building	Code-compliant building	Energy-efficient building	Green building / Living building	Sustainable building with integrated design	Restorative building / Regenerative building
Effects on Natural Environment:	Many negative effects on the natural environment	Fewer negative effects on the natural environment from energy use	Fewer negative effects on the natural environment	No net negative effects on the natural environment (a balance)	Positive effects on the natural environment
Natural Capital Requirements:	Relies on stored stocks of natural capital	Relies on stored stocks of natural capital	Still relies on stored stock of natural capital	Relies only on current flows of natural capital	Reinvests in and restores natural capital
External Costs/ Benefits:	External costs	Reduced external costs from energy use	Some external costs remain	No external costs, all costs are internalized	External benefits

Degeneration
Disrespectful

First-generation response

Second-generation response

Third-generation response

Atomistic

Holistic

Regeneration
Respectful

Sustainable Buildings 261

design and construction practices that have a positive effect on the environment, help the natural environment improve its ability to sustain living systems, and reinvest in and restore natural capital, producing external benefits rather than external costs. The evolutionary process of moving to greater levels and deeper meanings of sustainability, based on different approaches to building design, ranging from green to sustainable/living to restorative, is demonstrated in Table 10.1.

Although communities, and society in general, have a long way to go before reaching the point of restorative building design, this chapter has endeavoured to demonstrate that moving towards sustainable buildings requires a holistic and integrative approach – at the macro scale, it means creating the conditions within the community for sustainability to be a hallmark of buildings; at the micro scale, it means starting with building design and leading to supply procurement, construction, inspection, operation, and maintenance. At the macro scale, if government policy is not aligned with market forces, the system can break down, as demonstrated by the issue of mandating green roofs for multi-unit residential buildings in British Columbia. At the micro scale, a critical determining factor of the cost effectiveness of a sustainable building at the outset is the degree of integration of the design process. A true and authentic IDP provides an opportunity to realize very high levels of performance in a new building without prohibitive increases in capital cost, compared with conventional unsustainable buildings.

Here is an opportunity for change that is nothing less than transformative. As sustainability is the human imperative of the twenty-first century, society must continue to foster and develop the seeds of transformation that will lead us to the realization of sustainable communities. Building sustainable communities requires sustainable building. Sustainable building requires new products and technologies, the use of new tools, and collaborative and integrated processes, and, most important, a shift in mindset at both the macro and micro scales. To succeed each of us must first be the change we want to see in the world, as espoused by Mahatma Gandhi, which will make it easier for us to do sustainable building, and then have a collection of sustainable buildings. A sufficient critical mass will help to support the emergence of sustainable communities. At this point of transition between second- and third-generation sustainability responses, the Integrated Design Process represents the most holistic and integrated method of producing buildings that strive to contribute to the broader sustainability agenda. The next step in advancing sustainability through built-form requires architects and engineers to collaborate strategically with landscape architects and planners to find new, integrated, and holistic methods of designing, building, and redeveloping sustainable communities. Innovative programs like LEED Neighbourhood Design have the potential to knit sustainable buildings together to produce more sustainable neighbourhoods with strong place-based elements, such as walkability, as discussed by Newman and Waldron (in this volume).

The opportunity before us will demand that communities and stakeholders work together in ways we are not accustomed to at present. This demands insightful leadership that persuades us to transcend established paradigms (Meadows 1999). As mentioned in other chapters in this volume, it also demands new governance structures (Dushenko, Chapter 9) and novel forms of agency (Dale, Chapter 6) that break long-established silos to promote integrated decision-making (Hanna and Slocombe, Chapter 2) and both vertical and horizontal collaboration – within and between governments, business, and civil society. Finally, the cases explored here can offer a further advancement of our refinement of third-generation approaches. The effective mobilization of third-generation efforts requires us to look beyond the immediate horizon of our own jurisdictional, professional, or ecosystem-derived boundaries to consider what lies beyond.

NOTES

1 Sustainable building design, in the context of sustainable community planning, is not new. In cities such as London, New York, and Toronto, buildings built as far back as the late nineteenth and early twentieth centuries embody what today we would label as sustainable building principles. These older buildings are often mixed use, within walking distance of residential areas or close to subway and/or streetcar lines, constructed of locally available materials, and designed to invite natural daylight deep within the building while relying on passive cooling during the summer. Most important, many of these buildings are durable and remain in good repair today. Although these buildings were perhaps not as energy efficient as new buildings and used some materials now deemed toxic, they also used some materials that are making a comeback due to their environmental benefits, such as linoleum flooring made from linseed oil. These late nineteenth- and early twentieth-century buildings also allowed for a long life and loose fit, one of ten measures of sustainable design articulated by the American Institute of Architects (2004). It is also

critical to the idea of ecological design, as articulated by Lister (2006), whereby adaptability is paramount. This means that, to be ecological and, indeed, sustainable, design must also accommodate future change and uncertainty. In Winnipeg, the author's birthplace, low-rise brick and timber buildings in the Exchange District, originally built in the late 1800s and early 1900s as warehouses for dry goods storage, have been converted to offices, residential condominiums, colleges, restaurants, bars and night clubs, and retail stores. Newman and Waldron also note similar regenerative trends of historic buildings (Chapter 5 in this volume) in other large urban centres such as Toronto. Many of the principles used to design these buildings are re-emerging today in the context of sustainability, including the use of natural daylight, local materials, and locating buildings close to public transit, which are features for which new building projects earn points in green building rating systems.

2 There is a growing number of tools at the disposal of a sustainable building practitioner today. These include voluntary green building rating systems, such as LEED, Green Globes Design, and BREEAM (BRE Environmental Assessment Method), computer energy-modelling programs such as Energy Plus, DOE2, and EE4, and other analysis software such as RETScreen. Tools have garnered a fair bit of attention because green building rating systems and energy modelling are relatively new and still evolving, and governments are starting to reference them in public policy, as described in the section on green building. While financial incentives for tools are not as prevalent as the financial incentives for products, an example of an incentive program for the use of an energy-modelling tool is the former Natural Resources Canada Commercial Building Incentive Program (CBIP). This program provided a financial incentive of up to $80,000 for commercial buildings designed to be at least 25 per cent more energy efficiency than Canada's Model National Energy Code for Buildings 1997, as demonstrated by an energy model.

3 Greenbuild is the US Green Building Council's annual conference and expo.

4 Infrastructure and Transportation is responsible for most of the government-owned buildings; Innovation, Energy and Mines is responsible for energy and climate change policy; and Family Services and Labour is where the Office of the Fire Commissioner, the main official responsible for the building code, resides. Manitoba Hydro offers financial incentives for energy efficiency to support the policy implementation. See http://www.firecomm.gov.mb.ca/ministers_message.html.

5 The success of Manitoba Hydro's PowerSmart programs has helped the province win top grades twice in a row in the Canadian Energy Efficiency

Alliance's bi-annual ranking of energy efficiency efforts by the Canadian federal government and provinces (Canadian Energy Efficiency Alliance 2008)

6 The Sustainable Building Challenge is a bi-annual worldwide sustainable building competition hosted by the International Initiative for a Sustainable Built Environment (www.iisbe.org) as part of the World Sustainable Building Conference.

7 To understand the lasting impact of the downtown site selection, it is important to note that Manitoba Hydro's employees tend to be long-term employees, with years of service ranging from twenty to forty.

8 For context, Natural Resources Canada used to provide a financial incentive to buildings that were designed to be 25 per cent more energy efficient, and offered a pilot program for a short while for buildings that were 50 per cent more energy efficienct.

9 Building the new head office downtown, rather than in a suburban area of the city, was one of the terms of the sale of Winnipeg Hydro by the City of Winnipeg to Manitoba Hydro in 2002.

REFERENCES

American Institute of Architects. 2004. Committee on the Environment. 'Defining Sustainable Design: AIA Committee on the Environment's Measures of Sustainability and Performance Metrics.' Washington, DC. http://www.aiatopten.org/hpb/includes_AIA/AIA_TT_Requirements_2005.pdf (accessed 22 November 2008).

Barlow, M., and T. Clarke. 2002. *Blue Gold: The Battle against Corporate Theft of the World's Water.* Toronto: McClelland & Stewart.

Berkable, B. 2004. 'Integrated Design: When Pigs Fly.' In *Greenbuild International Conference & Expo Proceedings,* CD 1, no. 100 [CD-ROM]. Jamestown, NY: Digitell Inc.

Callaghan, E.G., and J. Colton. 2008. 'Building Sustainable and Resilient Communities: A Balancing of Community Capital.' *Environment, Development and Sustainability* 10: 931–42.

Canada. 2005. Natural Resources Canada. *Energy Use Data Handbook,* various issues. Ottawa. http://oee.nrcan.gc.ca/corporate/statistics/neud/dpa/data_e/handbook05/datahandbook2005.pdf (accessed 19 November 2006).

–. 2006. Natural Resources Canada. *Canada's Energy Outlook: The Reference Case 2006.* Ottawa. http://www.nrcan-rncan.gc.ca/inter/pdf/outlook2006_e.pdf (accessed 23 November 2008).

–. 2011. Canadian Codes Centre. *2011 National Energy Code of Canada for Buildings*. Ottawa: National Research Council of Canada, Institute for Research in Construction. http://www.nationalcodes.nrc.gc.ca/eng/necb/index.shtml (accessed 12 February 2012).

Canada Mortgage and Housing Corporation. 2008. 'Energy-Efficient Housing Made More Affordable with Mortgage Loan Insurance.' Ottawa. http://www.cmhc-schl.gc.ca/en/co/moloin/moloin_008.cfm (accessed 29 November 2008).

Canadian Energy Efficiency Alliance. 2008. '2007 Report Card on Energy Efficiency.' Mississauga, ON. http://www.energyefficiency.org/eecentre/eecentre.nsf/009217a0b33cd394852569b9001701c6/76afec8fe9bc5333852574c1004d0e34?OpenDocument (accessed 23 October 2008).

Canadian Standards Association. 2008. 'Standards Solutions: Sustainable Buildings in Canada.' Workshop proceedings report, CSA Stakeholder workshop, 26–27 November 2007. Mississauga, ON: CSA.

Capra 1982. *The Turning Point: Science, Society, and the Rising Culture.* New York: Simon and Schuster.

CCBFC (Canadian Commission on Building and Fire Codes). 1997. *Model National Energy Code of Canada for Buildings*. Ottawa: National Research Council of Canada.

–. 2005. *National Building Code of Canada 2005*, vol. 1. Ottawa: National Research Council of Canada.

Cole, R.J. 2000. 'Editorial: Cost and Value in Green Building.' *Building Research & Information* 28, nos. 5–6: 304–9.

Council of Energy Ministers. 2007. *Moving Forward on Energy Efficiency in Canada: A Foundation for Action*. Ottawa: Natural Resources Canada. http://www.nrcan-rncan.gc.ca/com/resoress/publications/cemcme/cemcme-eng.pdf (accessed 24 November 2008).

Dale, A. 2001. *At the Edge: Sustainable Development in the 21st Century.* Vancouver: UBC Press.

–. 2006. 'Linking Industry and Ecology in Canada: A Question of Design.' In *Linking Industry and Ecology*, ed. R. Cote, J. Tansey, and A. Dale. Vancouver: UBC Press.

de Villiers, M. 1999. *Water*. Toronto: Stoddart.

Fireman's Fund Insurance Company. 2007. 'Green-Guard Coverages.' Novato, CA. http://www.firemansfund.com/servlet/dcms?c=business&rkey=437 (accessed 11 August 2007).

Interface Engineering. 2005. 'Engineering a Sustainable World: Design Process and Engineering Innovations for the Centre for Health & Healing at Oregon Health & Science University.' Portland, OR: Interface Engineering. http://

www.interfaceengineering.com/pdfs/case-studies/sustainable-world.pdf (accessed 22 November 2008).

Intergovernmental Panel on Climate Change. 2007. *Climate Change 2007: Synthesis Report. Contribution of Working Groups I, II and III to the Fourth Assessment Report of the Intergovernmental Panel on Climate Change*. Geneva: IPCC. http://www.ipcc.ch/ipccreports/ar4-syr.htm (accessed 24 November 2008).

Kats, G., et al. 2003. 'The Costs and Financial Benefits of Green Buildings: A Report to California's Sustainable Building Task Force.' Washington, DC: Capital E. http://www.cap- e.com/ewebeditpro/items/O59F3259.pdf (accessed 12 March 2005).

Ling, C., A. Dale, and K. Hanna. 2007. 'Integrated Community Sustainability Planning Tool.' Victoria, BC: Royal Roads University, Community Research Connections. http://crcresearch.org/files-crcresearch/File/PlanningTool(1).pdf (accessed 26 November 2008).

Lister, N.-M. 2006. 'Industrial Ecology as Ecological Design: Opportunities for Re(dis)covery.' In *Linking Industry and Ecology*, ed. R. Cote, J. Tansey, and A. Dale. Vancouver: UBC Press.

Manitoba. 2007. Manitoba Green Building Policy Interdepartmental Working Group. *Green Building Policy for Government of Manitoba Funded Projects*. Winnipeg. http://www.gov.mb.ca/mit/greenbuilding/pdf/policy.pdf (accessed 27 November 2008).

Manitoba Hydro. n.d. 'Manitoba Hydro Place Head Office.' Winnipeg. http://www.hydro.mb.ca/corporate/mhplace/index.shtml?WT.mc_id=2611 (accessed 15 November 2008).

Martin, B. 2007. 'Green roofs not covered by B.C. insurers.' *Journal of Commerce*, 14 May. http://www.journalofcommerce.com/article/20070514300 (accessed 11 August 2007).

McDonald, R., and A. Dale. 2004. 'The Economics of Green Buildings in Canada [e-Dialogue transcript].' Victoria, BC: Royal Roads University, Community Research Connections. http://crcresearch.org/files-crcresearch/File/Green_Buildings_Oct_2004.pdf (accessed 24 November 2008).

McDonough, W. 1993. 'A Centennial Sermon: Design, Ecology, and the Making of Things.' Speech delivered at the Cathedral of St John the Divine, New York, 7 February. http://www.mcdonough.com/Sermon.pdf (accessed 12 February 2012).

McDonough, W., and M. Braungart. 1998. 'The Next Industrial Revolution.' *Atlantic*, October, 82–92.

Meadows, D. 1999. 'Leverage Points: Places to Intervene in a System.' Hartland, VT: Sustainability Institute. http://www.sustainer.org/pubs/Leverage_Points.pdf (accessed 25 November 2008).

Ontario 2006. Ministry of Municipal Affairs and Housing. *Ontario Building Code*. Toronto.

Pearce, D.W., and R.K. Turner. 1990. *Economics and Natural Resources and the Environment*. Baltimore: Johns Hopkins University Press.

PR Newswire. 2009. 'Manitoba Hydro Place – A Model for Extreme Climate Responsive Design.' 30 September. http://www.prnewswire.com/news-releases/manitoba-hydro-place-a-model-for-extreme-climate-responsive-design-62904307.html (accessed 5 October 2009).

Reed, B., G. Hubbard, and B. Batshalom. 2004. 'Managing the Integrated Design Process.' PowerPoint presentation to the Greenbuild International Conference & Expo, Portland, OR, 12 November.

Roseland, M. 2005. *Toward Sustainable Communities*, rev. ed. Gabriola Island, BC: New Society Publishers.

Telus. 2006. 'Menkes Developments and TELUS break ground on TELUS tower in Toronto.' Toronto, 14 September. http://about.telus.com/cgi-bin/media_news_viewer.cgi?news_id=743&mode=2 (accessed 15 October 2010).

United States. 2005. Department of Energy. *Energy Policy Act of 2005*. Washington, DC. http://frwebgate.access.gpo.gov/cgi-bin/getdoc.cgi?dbname=109_cong_bills&docid=f:h6enr.txt.pdf (accessed 13 February 2012).

USGBC (United States Green Building Council). 2005. 'An Introduction to the U.S. Green Building Council and the LEED Green Building Rating System.' PowerPoint presentation. Washington, DC. http://www.slideshare.net/jetsongreen/about-usgbc-leed (accessed 13 February 2012).

–. 2007. 'Why Build Green?' Washington, DC. http://www.usgbc.org/DisplayPage.aspx?CMSPageID=291& (accessed 26 February 2007).

WBCSD (World Business Council for Sustainable Development). 2008. 'Energy Efficiency in Buildings: Business Realities and Opportunities: Summary Report.' Geneva. http://www.wbcsd.org/DocRoot/H94WhkJoIYq5uDts LfxR/WBCSD_EEB_final.pdf (accessed 20 November 2008).

White, A. 2008. 'German pension fund buys TELUS green building.' Toronto: Real Estate News Exchange. http://www.renx.ca/Detailed/1438.html (accessed 29 November 2008).

Reflections

ANN DALE AND WILLIAM T. DUSHENKO

All the preceding chapters in this volume illuminate various stages and modes in the evolution of third-generation responses in Canadian communities to implementing sustainable development. Canadian cities are facing complex, messy, wicked problems and the reality that their pattern of space is the product of post-industrialization, transportation systems, and design ideologies (Hough 1984) that are not amenable to third-generation responses. Other challenges include asymmetries of scale, differential access to resources (Dale, Chapter 6), and pressures of uneven, over-, and underdevelopment (Dushenko, Chapter 9), with many trying to sustain the characteristics of place and community identity they hold important. While there are many theorizations of place and space and the relationship between them, a prevailing theme throughout this book is the strong identity Canadians have with the characteristics of the place in which they live.

Although people often use place and space interchangeably, even in this volume, geographic space is generally considered the space that encircles the planet, in which biological life exists. It is often differentiated from 'outer space' and 'inner space' (interiority). 'Place' as Tuan (1997) defines it, is something that comes into existence when humans give meaning to a part of the larger, undifferentiated space. Soja (2003) talks about *synoikismos* or *synekism*, defined as the conditions that derive from dwelling together in a particular home place or space and the essential spatiality of urban phenomena. Relph, who has been writing about place and sense of place for some time, cautions that 'place is a powerful concept and an invaluable component of human experience that should not be reduced to abstract generalizations and measures of profitability . . . Above all, place should be viewed with the clear understanding that it is not possible to design everything about them' (cited in Seamon 1993, 27). Dushenko (Chapter 9) and Lister (Chapter 3) further illustrate that sense of place, with varying definitions and complexity, is strong and central to our social world. Its uniqueness and contextual aspects often equate to the emergence of a community identity that is special and distinct from elsewhere and, from the perspective of its members, requires some degree of protection to ensure its sustainable development into the future.

Nevertheless, we are now occupying so much space in the biosphere that third-generation sustainability responses must focus on deliberatively designing and, in some cases, redesigning places to sustain the things we care about. The complexities around the meaning of place, what we value, and what we wish to sustain are more visible in larger urban centres, due to their scale and population concentration. They are further complicated by the fact that what we value changes over time and, hence, there is an inherently dynamic nature to the implementation of sustainability responses on the ground. As we increase our density and scale, we have a tendency to reduce, rather than to optimize, the diversity of both the built and the non-built environment as part of the urban built environment and renewal. Sustainability responses are also complicated by inequality between neighbourhoods in large urban centres and requisite concepts of spatial justice (Soja 2010).

Islands of neighbourhoods, separated by 'have' and 'have-not' neighbourhoods, and the increasing concentration of lower-income and marginalized people in one place in urban centres do little to create the agency (Newman and Dale 2005) and social capital needed to make a difference in people's ability to thrive, rather than simply survive. Access to diverse forms of social capital has been identified as the difference between some communities 'getting by' to 'getting ahead' and its mobilization for sustainable community development (Dale and Onyx 2005). Although the transition to sustainable development has been alarmingly slow (see Kastenhofer and Rammel 2006), with large implementation gaps, others claim we have enough information and enough knowledge to act now.

Institutional transformation and governance have been identified as the critical issue in addressing these implementation gaps (Dale 2001; Dushenko, Chapter 9 in this volume). Although some may consider institutional transformation to be wishful thinking, our understanding and knowledge, despite the gaps, have deepened nevertheless since the Brundtland Commission report (WCED 1987). Just what have we learned from the case studies presented in this volume about third-generation responses 'and the necessary reconciliation between place and space?

Let us first revisit what we mean by third-generation responses. As Lister summarizes (Chapter 3), first-generation approaches in their most basic form are characterized largely by a focus on outcomes – that is, their environmental and economic performance – to ensure that the needs of the present do not compromise the needs of future generations. Although processes to address these outcomes – such as the concept of ecovillages[1] operating largely independent of local government – began to emerge in the 1960s and 1970s (see Dawson 2006), greater realization of the importance of process has also emerged as part of second-generation approaches, in the form of strategies of civic engagement, empowerment, and collaboration in decision-making and a growing understanding of the importance of social capital. Third-generation responses, although largely contextual and place based, as illustrated by the case studies in this volume, can be characterized generally by a dynamic balance between process and outcomes. These outcomes, which are constantly evolving, stem from a complex mix of processes, including the behavioural interactions of diverse agents and the public policy context – for example, the community responses to regional government policy Dushenko observes in Chapter 9 – that can serve either to constrain or to engender their implementation. Much of this success depends on the prevailing governance structures in place and on the novel and integrated processes required to support such interaction and engagement (see, for example, Hanna and Slocombe, Chapter 2).

Third-generation responses move beyond taking stock and operationalization to integrated decision-making and the transformation of governments at all levels. By accepting that solutions lie in multi-agent social innovation and interaction, the new role of government should be to foster collaboration between diverse actors and sectors. This is contrary to government's previous role in first- and second-generation responses as a disconnected external actor independently regulating public issues through silo and stovepipe-like approaches. Many notable initiatives in the past occurred largely in parallel with or independently of government. In third-generation responses, multi-level governance arrangements are essential to local implementation. Such arrangements are about changing the rules of the game, not merely reorganizing departments, as exemplified by Weigeldt's discussion in Chapter 7 on the barriers imposed by existing regulations on urban food production.

The United We Can case study (Chapter 6) demonstrates the potential efficiencies that can be gained by progressive and strategic policy development by government that engenders and mobilizes local agency and social capital, rather than working with existing models that have often unintentionally continued to marginalize sectors of the population or a community.

Third-generation responses are more than cleaning up pollution, environmental performance, or increasing energy efficiency – these typified first- and second-generation responses. Instead they are about preventing pollution in the first place through the design of new processes and products that mimic and complement ecological processes that are regenerative, rather than degenerative (see McDonald, Chapter 10). Although the focus of this book has been on both process and product/ outcomes and the critical importance of governance to third-generation implementation, place has been shown to have intrinsic value independent of human meaning, with essential ecological functions and processes that need to be sustained for all life, as well as human well-being.

Thus, in addition to the reconciliation of the three imperatives, third-generation responses reconnect with place (Dale, Ling, and Newman 2008) and space, through the design and redesign of the built environment that recognize and nurture connections to the non-built environment (see Luka, Chapter 8; McDonald, Chapter 10). In Chapter 5, Waldron and Newman discuss how walkability is one such strategy facilitating reconnection to place. Third-generation responses realize the need to discuss the meaning of reconciling diversity (Dale and Newman 2010), limits (Newman and Dale 2008), and scale (Newman and Dale 2009), and the requirement to integrate often undervalued community engagement processes with integrated, long-term planning (Hanna, Ling, and Dale 2009) to address implementation gaps.

Third-generation responses also rely on a deepening understanding of the dynamic connection between identity and place. Given this contextual nature, the framework presented in this volume can be neither prescriptive nor widely generalizable in the sense that other regions and other cities will have pursued very different approaches. What the Canadian cases presented here can offer in sharing knowledge on third-generation responses, however, is a recognition of the emerging interdependency of certain key principles that need to be considered in both private and public sector decision-making to address the barriers and implementation gaps learned from first- and second-generation responses. Each of these tenets is open for much debate and dialogue as they gain more universal appeal, and fostering that dialogue has been our intention with this book. The seven tenets perceived as critical for urban sustainability are to

1 reconcile place and space by designing 'with' rather than 'over' nature with an emphasis on regeneration;
2 design and redesign human space equally for social capital needs as well as the built environment;
3 develop robust and continuing community engagement processes and systems of governance actively engaged in regenerating the public sphere;
4 integrate scale, limits, and diversity considerations and recognize that individual communities are nested as part of larger complex and interconnected systems into decision-making, both in terms of strategic interventions and government leadership and as a means to address gaps in implementation;
5 develop strong municipal (local) leadership that takes stock and equally values the various forms of capital extant in their communities – natural and social as well as commercial and economic – and how they vary in dynamic balance over time;
6 pursue spatial justice (for example, sustainability for all) across multiple levels and scales; and
7 understand the need for fundamental institutional transformation and new governance models, to address asymmetries of access to resources, as well as for changes in our knowledge systems and policies.

Note that these tenets share a dynamic balance of process and outcome consistent with our earlier description of third-generation responses. Let us now examine them in more detail.

Designing 'With' Rather Than 'Over'

Third-generation responses are rooted in the idea of place – places that ultimately sustain us, ecologically, socially, economically, and spiritually. This requires reconciliation of these imperatives through integrated decision-making in all sectors. There is now general agreement among researchers and practitioners that the space represented by the biosphere has finite limits, and that spatiality within urban centres and how it is organized and designed within the context of place is also critical to the full realization of sustainable development. For example, we need to design places for those features we wish to sustain and that are central to our identity, such as biodiversity, through restorative and regenerative approaches. As with previous generational responses, there will be lags in the progress towards each of the imperatives – notably, it will be difficult to reconcile the human scale of activities with the dynamics of natural and ecological processes. This is due primarily to the fact that so little attention has been paid to the underlying natural processes that ultimately sustain the city.

Urban sustainability, therefore, is about designing 'with' rather than 'over' nature. Hanna and Slocombe (Chapter 2) note that the most promising aspect of the integrative dynamic in regional planning is the attention paid to the importance of natural systems and the sustainability of ecosystems. Place is more than just space with human involvement; it has intrinsic meaning in and of itself, and both informs and influences us, as we transform place through the built environment. As McDonald argues in Chapter 10, it is about reconciliation between the built and the non-built environment, but it is even deeper than that. Contemporary urbanism 'requires a multifocal perspective, one that encompasses the notions of form, function, field, and flows across and between its dynamic layers. In this sense, aspects of "culture" and "nature" are neither separate nor confused, but woven together throughout the metropolitan landscape' (Lister 2010, 2; see also Dushenko, Chapter 9; and Weigeldt, Chapter 7 in this volume).

Place and Space

The design of our space goes far beyond just the built environment; it determines our cultural, social, and, some would argue, spiritual life. Social capital is highly dependent upon the design of human place and the space we allow for connection. Without creating opportunities to connect with one another and to meet in common spaces – for example, walkable neighbourhoods, as exemplified by Newman and Waldron in Chapter 5; and community connectivity, as described by McDonald in Chapter 10 – we lose the capacity to engage in community (Etzionni 2000a,b) with one another. Connection involves being in relationship with place and with one another. One must 'know' a place, as illustrated in both the rural and the urban context by Dushenko (Chapter 9) and Lister (Chapter 3), respectively, in order to sustain it.

In third-generation responses, regaining the culture of place-making (Kunstler 1993) means designing physical places that sustain their intrinsic life-supporting systems, as well as their aesthetics. This is illustrated in integrated approaches to the regenerative built form by McDonald (Chapter 10). Thus, as all the case study communities illustrate, a key element of the third-generation response is its place specificity. The Canadian federal government has been exploring options for developing a place-based public policy framework, four key elements of which are tapping local knowledge, finding the right policy mix, governing through collaboration, and recognizing local government (Bradford 2005).

Third-generation responses, as noted by many authors in this volume, are dependent upon robust community engagement processes and enlarging the public sphere for sustained dialogue. Dialogue creates 'space' for the social interactions and the building of networks that lead to trust, social norms, and a common sense of purpose, as well as an informed civic literacy, which are central to building social capital, and effective governance. This also increases our capacity for agency – the will or intent to act (Newman and Dale 2007; see also Dale, Chapter 6) – that contributes to community resilience and our ability to adapt and change (Dale et al. 2010).

Regenerating the Public Sphere

The reconciliation of ecological, social, and economic imperatives central to sustainable development will not be achieved without active and continuing community engagement, as exemplified by Dushenko (Chapter 9), Dale (Chapter 6), and Lister (Chapter 3). It requires dynamic engagement with multiple and diverse actors from civil society and the private sector. Unprecedented levels of collaboration and social innovation and shared visions about the collective ways forward are critical to reconciliation. Reconciliation will also depend upon robust systems of governance actively engaged in regenerating the public space (Dale and Naylor 1995), since governments are perceived as being among the most honest conveners of stakeholders. Only through community dialogue and collaboration that build robust networks of diverse actors, supported by government in its transformed role as one actor among many, will our urban and rural communities be able to move to full implementation of third-generation responses as demonstrated by Robinson (Chapter 4). Such a level of public consensus is necessary to repair the disconnectivity between small, medium, and large urban centres, especially as it relates to transportation and work patterns and sprawl, that is so much a part of our existing unsustainable urban form. Kuntsler (1993, 273), for example, observes 'the culture of place-making [that] America [has] thrown away in its eagerness to become a drive-in civilization.' More critically, he notes that 'there is a direct connection between urban sprawl and the spiraling cost of government . . . likewise, there is a connection between disregard for the public realm – for public life in general – and the breakdown of public safety' (246).

Communities as Interconnected Systems

Attention to scale is important in terms of addressing implementation gaps and strategic policy interventions. The scale of intervention has changed from the macro to the meso to the micro – the community and neighbourhood level. Communities are essentially the basic building blocks of cities, towns, or any settlement for that matter. Although each operates as a dynamic and complex nested system of people, through common ties or connections, social interactions, and a sense of place (after Hillery 1955), communities do not do so in isolation. They are nested along with other communities in an interconnected network of larger and even more complex systems at municipal, regional, and provincial levels, as Hanna and Slocombe (Chapter 2) illustrate through integrated planning. These larger systems may also operate and evolve at different (usually slower) time scales than their smaller, often more 'nimble' community constituents. By addressing issues of scale and system complexity, third-generation solutions are clearly beyond the ability of any one sector, level of government, or institution to undertake in isolation. The focus now is to encourage multi-level governance arrangements and community engagement. This can occur only when community networks are engaged, believe they can make a difference with the capacity to evolve over time, and driven by the decisions of their component members (Watts 2003). Novel and diverse network formation is key to bridging the implementation gap, particularly with respect to critical asymmetries of access to resources, as observed in the interplay of rural communities and regional governance issues discussed by Dushenko (Chapter 9) and Dale (Chapter 6).

Mobilizing Community Capitals through Strong Local Leadership

Callaghan and Colton (2008) differentiate the following types of capital found in communities: environmental, human, social, cultural, public structural, and commercial. Communities require various types of expertise and social capital to bring about change, and this depends on both people's ability and willingness to lend support (Volker and Flap 2001). They also vary greatly in their access to capital and natural resources, as well as to intellectual and social capital, one of the most critical types of capital for innovation and community diversity. Natural capital is particularly important for adapting to and meeting global exogenous forces while retaining local diversity on a number of levels and building community resiliency (Callaghan and Colton 2008). Social capital is key to speeding the adoption of innovation and adaptive responses through the formation of agency within communities and linking social capital between them, such as the United We Can community case Dale presents in Chapter 6. This is particularly true in a country as large and as pluralistic as Canada.

All these forms of capital are dynamically interconnected, and what happens globally impacts locally. Dushenko (Chapter 9) argues that it is incumbent upon community leaders, including government, in urban as well as rural contexts, to recognize and take stock of the various forms of community capital and of how they vary over time, and to strengthen their dynamic interrelationships to ensure continued community flexibility and resiliency. Callaghan and Colton (2008) further note that this will require strong leadership, vision, and effective communication between municipalities and communities to facilitate a shift from the current and more common paradigm of crisis management and revenue growth to taking stock of community capital.

Spatial Justice for All

Third-generation sustainability responses will not be achieved without realizing spatial justice. Sustainability for some, but not for all, is clearly contrary to the implementation of sustainable development (Dale and Newman 2009). Third-generation responses recognize how critical it is to integrate the social imperative, and that its full realization involves the reconciliation of multiple human objectives and tensions – especially the tensions between poverty and inequitable access to resources. This tension has been demonstrated in this volume at various scales, from the resistance to rural annexation in southern Vancouver Island illustrated by Dushenko (Chapter 9) to cottage country quality issues among Greater Toronto Area residents discussed by Luka (Chapter 8) to the challenges faced in the urban setting of the Vancouver Downtown Eastside illuminated by Dale (Chapter 6).

This is another argument for the need to reconcile the three imperatives on multiple levels and at multiple scales, and for a reconnection of place and people and ecological systems. One solution is somewhat clear: sustainable community development depends on reconnecting the less 'fortunate' islands that disconnect us and on reconnecting and ultimately redesigning for greater connectivity among small-, mid- and large-scale communities. Governance leadership that understands and reconciles these differences is vital. This volume shows these elements evolving on multiple scales and at multiple levels, illustrated by approaches at the planning level by Hanna and Slocombe (Chapter 2) and Robinson (Chapter 4), and at the governance level by Dushenko (Chapter 9) and Dale (Chapter 6).

Reconciliation cannot happen, however, without appropriate forums for deliberately designed dialogue to re-engage communities in developing new shared understanding around the meaning of community (Etzionni 2000a) and to speed the building of novel network formation and social innovation. As shown symbolically by Lister (Chapter 3) and practically by Dale (Chapter 6), community engagement and network formation is a key strategy for speeding the exploitation of knowledge and learning, both formally and informally Networks can bridge asymmetries of access, scale, and implementation gaps, as well as critical divides between practitioners, sectors, levels of government, and even nations. Distributed networks accelerate both the generation and the transfer of knowledge (Seymoar, Mullard, and Winstanley 2009); however, new governance models are essential to democratizing community engagement and more integrated decision-making (Dale and Newman 2010; see also Dushenko, Chapter 9).

New Governance Models

A key principle for the implementation of third-generation responses, and probably the most controversial and challenging, is fundamental institutional transformation leading to new governance models. In addition to asymmetries of access to resources between communities, the realization of sustainable community development continues to be impeded by geographical solitudes and governmental silos and stovepipes (Dale 2001). Weigeldt (Chapter 7) illuminates the importance of 'changing the rules of the game' through decision-making processes and urban policies and bylaws for cities as they respond with place-based solutions to urban food production. This approach attempts to meet the challenges posed by third-generation sustainability head on. Possible new models for governance and integrated decision-making are also being explored in some rural communities, as illustrated by Dushenko (Chapter 9), and may also provide possibilities for local urban communities. The 'United We Can' case study (Dale, Chapter 6) is a living laboratory for the potential of government policies – in this case, integrated waste management and social policies – to help, at least indirectly, alleviate chronic issues of poverty and homelessness in large urban centres, beyond social assistance programs. This can be further advanced through progressive government policies involving integrated decision-making planning, as discussed by Hanna and Slocombe (Chapter 2) and integration of the social imperative with economic and ecological imperatives.

The level of requisite transformation requires governments that are adaptive and flexible and integrated planning processes that can respond dynamically to complex, messy, and wicked public policy problems and their inherent unpredictability. Flexibility, adaptability, and long-term planning increases the ability of diverse communities to adapt to change and still maintain an inherent, yet dynamic resiliency. For instance, Duit and Galaz (2008) observe that multi-level governance arrangements, where different governance systems (based on different forms of authority) coexist and interact over a variety of societal, geographic, and organizational scales involving multiple and diverse actors, contribute to adaptive governance capabilities. Integrated planning processes create community sustainability outcomes that are longer term, regenerative (McDonald, Chapter 10), and include considerations of what constitutes essential boundary conditions for adjacent communities (Dushenko, Chapter 9). As Hanna and Slocombe (Chapter 2) argue, the processes required to implement long-term integrated planning include the following elements:

- multiple means and multiple purpose outcomes of policy;
- multi-sectoral blending of fragmented agencies and responsibilities;
- incorporation of multiple professions and perspectives;
- active public participation processes; and,
- accommodation and compromise of interests.

If the 'rules of the game' are to change, as many of the authors in this compilation argue, other critical steps must be taken (Dale and Hamilton 2007). For example, policies, codes, and standards for the built environment vary enormously across, and between, governments, and are often simply inconsistent, as illustrated for buildings by McDonald (Chapter 10) and urban agricultural opportunities by Weigeldt (Chapter 7). In addition, initiatives at the community level are often stymied by a lack of congruence at regional, provincial, or even national levels, which can also operate on different (usually longer) temporal scales. Too often, the result is planning that is disconnected from the actual implementation and undertaken without regard for higher-level consequences. Policy inconsistencies have to be identified in order to begin efforts at comprehensive policy congruence and realignment among municipal, provincial, and federal levels. McDonald (Chapter 10), as an example, notes, '[t]he ability to break, or at least bend, institutional path dependence by different levels of government is key to advancing sustainable initiatives in building design and operation.'

Concluding Thoughts

Many critical socio-political questions remain to be answered by third-generation responses. Can a city be 'too big'? What are the ramifications of scale for community identity and place-based connections, as well as peace, law, and good order? Conversely, can a community be 'too small,' subject to criticism that it is no longer viable and that it is vulnerable to annexation by larger centres (as explored by Dushenko, Chapter 9)? Is there a way to connect the large and the small, so that a dynamic equilibrium is achieved to sustain and support the identity of both? The rural context provides parallels for community sustainability and identity in our large urban centres (Luka, Chapter 8), and there is a mutual relationship between the two: each depends upon the other and on the reconnection of place and space that is critical to third-generation responses.

Is there an optimal density – identified as a key benefit of large urban centres? What forms of density and at what cost? The problematic issue of rising poverty and homelessness in the face of plenty must be addressed if the reconciliation of the three imperatives, especially the social, is to be accomplished in municipal integrated decision-making, as discussed in the Downtown Eastside case study by Dale (Chapter 6). Is there an operational definition for integrated decision-making? Much remains to be done and operationalized as we move towards third-generation responses.

One of the most effective ways communities can respond and move to concrete 'operationalization' is through innovation, as touched upon by Robinson and Dale (Chapter 1). Innovation, particularly social innovation (Westley, Zimmerman, and Patton 2006; Biggs, Westley, and Carpenter 2010), is critical to third-generation responses as its implementation involves more than just new technology. While technical ingenuity creates new technology, it is social ingenuity that reforms old institutions and social arrangements and regenerates them into new ones (Homer-Dixon 2000). Such forms of social ingenuity are suggested by integrated planning approaches, as Hanna and Slocombe (Chapter 2) explain: 'The model of integration created by the [Fraser River Estuary Management Program] illustrates a setting where power is not necessarily exercised individually by agencies, but more within a collaborative setting. Although agencies may not always explicitly acknowledge this, their support for the program, their deference to it as an avenue for problem-solving, and their support for program enhancement all suggest an undeclared and unrecognized exercise of power through the program.'

There is also a dynamic relationship between a community's ability to innovate and the robustness of its social capital, especially linking social capital (bridging and vertical). The nature of social capital in a community, through the density and centrality of its networks and its ability to increase connections among and between its members, can inhibit or enhance the community's ability to innovate. The number of connections within a community alone, however, is not likely to be a good indicator. How well communities – and governments, for that matter – will be able to engage with sustainable development issues may be more a question of how open they are to new ideas and how diverse their network ties are (Newman and Dale 2007). Diversity, just as we observe in natural ecosystems and processes, is the keystone for community resilience in terms of the various forms of capital, the common ties or connections among people, and social interactions, as captured by the seven principles proposed above. It is, therefore, one of the most critical imperatives for third-generation sustainability responses in the next two decades, as is the realization of spatial justice extending from the local to the global scale. As Kingwell (2008, 64) notes, '[m]odern distributive models of justice rightly place emphasis on the fate of the least well off: in a non-distributive idea of justice, we can update and expand this idea: a city, like a people, shall be judged by how it treats its most valuable (and vulnerable) members.'

As third-generation responses continue to evolve in Canada, and elsewhere to varying degrees, renewed thinking, social innovation, and action around the way we live and respond to one another, the way we do business, and the way we govern will lead to more sustainable urban centres. These will be centres that are healthy, productive, and regenerative, and that contribute to restorative economies and enhanced resilience in communities everywhere, regardless of size.

NOTE

1 Lucas (in the foreword to Dawson 2006, 9) notes that '[t]he ecovillage movement was born when the ancient idea of intentional communal living met the burgeoning international green movement of the 1960s and 70s.' She defines an ecovillage as a 'human-scale settlement, harmlessly integrated into the natural world in a way that is supportive of healthy human development and can be successfully continued into the indefinite future,' including being a 'socially just . . . community.' Dawson notes, however, that such communities have operated largely independent from local government and the 'mainstream.'

REFERENCES

Biggs, R., F. Westley, and S. Carpenter. 2010. 'Navigating the Back Loop: Fostering Social Innovation and Transformation in Ecosystem Management.' *Ecology and Society* 15, no. 2: 9 [online]. http://www.ecologyandsociety.org/ol5/iss2/art9/.

Bradford, N. 2005. 'Place-based Public Policy? Towards a New Urban and Community Agenda for Canada.' Research Report F/51. Ottawa: Canadian Policy Research Networks.

Callaghan, E.G., and J. Colton. 2008. 'Building Sustainable and Resilient Communities: A Balancing of Community Capital.' *Environment, Development and Sustainability* 10: 931–42.

Cote, R., J. Tansey, and A. Dale, eds. 2006. *Industrial Ecology: A Question of Design?* Vancouver: UBC Press.

Dale, A. 2001. *At the Edge: Sustainable Development in the 21st Century.* Vancouver: UBC Press.

Dale, A., and J. Hamilton. 2007. *Sustainable Infrastructure: Implications for Canada's Future*. Victoria, BC: Royal Roads University, Community Research Connections.

Dale, A., C. Ling, and L. Newman. 2008. 'Does Place Matter? Sustainable Community Development in Three Canadian Communities.' *Ethics, Place, and Environment* 11, no. 3: 267–81.

–. 2010. 'Community Vitality: The Role of Community-level Resilience Adaptation and Innovation in Sustainable Development.' *Sustainability* 2, no. 1: 215–31.

Dale, A., and T. Naylor. 1995. 'Dialogue and Public Space: An Exploration of Radio and Information Communications Technologies.' In *Canadian Journal of Political Science* 31 (1): 203–25.

Dale, A., and L. Newman. 2009. 'Sustainable Development for Some: "Green" Urban Development and Affordability.' *Local Environment* 14, no. 7: 669–83.

–. 2010. 'Social Capital: A Necessary and Sufficient Condition for Sustainable Community Development.' *Community Development Journal* 45, no. 1: 5–21.

Dale, A., and J. Onyx. 2005. *A Dynamic Balance: Social Capital and Sustainable Community Development*. Vancouver: UBC Press.

Dawson, J. 2006. *Ecovillages: New Frontiers for Sustainability*. Foxhole, UK: Green Books.

Duit, A., and V. Galaz. 2008. 'Governance and Complexity: Emerging Issues for Governance Theory.' *Governance: An International Journal of Policy, Administration and Institutions* 21, no. 3: 311–35.

Etzionni, A. 2000a. 'Creating Good Communities and Good Societies.' *Contemporary Sociology* 29, no. 1: 188–95.

–. 2000b. 'Moral Dialogues in Public Debates.' *Public Perspective* 11, no. 2: 27–30.

Hanna, K., C. Ling, and A. Dale. 2009. 'A Template for Integrated Community Sustainability Planning.' *Journal of Environmental Management* 44, no. 2: 228–42.

Hillery, G. 1955. 'Definitions of Community: Areas of Agreement.' *Rural Sociology* 20, no. 1: 111–23.

Homer-Dixon, T. 2000. *The Ingenuity Gap*. New York: Alfred A. Knopf

Hough, M. 1984. *Cities and Natural Process: A Basis for Sustainability*. London: Routledge.

Kastenhofer, K., and C. Rammel. 2006. 'Obstacles to and Potentials of the Societal Implementation of Sustainable Development.' *Sustainability: Science, Practice, and Policy* 1, no. 2: 5–13.

Kingwell, M. 2008. 'Justice Denied: Is Toronto Being Overtaken by Buskers, Fauxhemians, and the "Knowledge Economy"?' *Walrus Magazine*, January–

February. http://www.walrusmagazine.com/articles/2008.02-urban-affairs-toronto-culture-mark-kingwell/.

Kunstler, J. 1993. *The Geography of Nowhere: The Rise and Decline of America's Man-Made Landscape*. New York: Simon and Schuster

Lister, N.-M. 2010. 'Insurgent Ecologies: (Re)Claiming Ground in Landscape and Urbanism.' In *Ecological Urbanism*, ed. M. Mostafavi with G. Doherty. Zurich: Lars Müller Publishers.

Newman, L., and A. Dale. 2005. 'The Role of Agency in Sustainable Local Community Development.' *Local Environment* 10, no. 5: 477–86.

–. 2007. 'Homophily and Agency: Creating Effective Sustainable Development Networks.' *Environment, Development and Sustainability* 9, no. 1: 79–90.

–. 2008. 'Limits to Growth Rates in an Ethereal Economy.' *Futures* 40, no. 3: 261–7.

–. 2009. 'Large Footprints in a Small World: Toward a Macroeonomics of Scale.' *Sustainability: Science, Practice, and Policy* 5, no. 1: 1–11.

Seamon, D. 1993. *Dwelling, Seeing, and Designing: Towards a Phenomenological Ecology*. Albany: State University of New York Press.

Seymoar, N.-K., Z. Mullard, and M. Winstanley. 2009. *City to City Learning*. Vancouver: International Centre for Sustainable Communities.

Soja, E. 2003. 'Writing the City Spatially.' *City* 7, no. 3: 269–80.

–. 2010. *Seeking Spatial Justice*. Minneapolis: University of Minnesota Press.

Tuan, Y. 1997. *Place and Space: The Perspective of Experience*. Minneapolis: University of Minnesota Press.

Volker, B., and H. Flap. 2001. 'Weak Ties as a Liability: The Case of East Germany.' *Rationality and Society* 13, no. 4: 397–428.

Watts, D. 2003. *Six Degrees: The Science of a Connected Age*. New York: W.W. Norton.

WCED (World Commission on Environment and Development). 1987. *Our Common Future: Report of the World Commission on Environment and Development*, chaired by Gro Harlem Brundtland. Oxford: Oxford University Press.

Westley, F., B. Zimmerman, and M. Patton. 2006. *Getting to Maybe: How the World Is Changed*. Toronto: Random House.

Contributors

Ann Dale holds a Canada Research Chair in Sustainable Community Development at Royal Roads University. She is a Fellow of the World Academy of Arts and Science, and a Trudeau Fellow Alumna (2004). A widely published author, her research focuses on virtual and place-based sustainable community development and social media research and dissemination.

William T. Dushenko is Vice-President, Academic, Yukon College. He has authored and co-authored more than forty-five scientific papers and technical reports and more than thirty papers delivered at conferences and seminars in the areas of environmental science and sustainability.

Kevin Hanna is an Associate Professor, Department of Geography & Environmental Studies at Wilfrid Laurier University. His research centres on integrated approaches to natural resources management, forest sector policy in Canada, and environmental impact assessment, including the analysis of environmental policy and the measurement of policy effectiveness.

Nina-Marie Lister, MCIP RPP, is Associate Professor of Urban + Regional Planning at Ryerson University and Visiting Associate Professor at Harvard University, Graduate School of Design. Her research, teaching, and practice focus on the confluence of landscape infrastructure and ecological processes within contemporary metropolitan regions.

Nik Luka is jointly appointed to the Schools of Architecture and Urban Planning at McGill University. His main interest is in urban design as an interdisciplinary approach to better understanding the form, processes, uses, and meanings of space in everyday settings, and how this can enable us to develop sustainable yet strategic design and policy interventions.

Rodney C. McDonald is President of McDonald Sustainability Group Inc. He develops strategy with and advises senior decision-makers in the public and private sectors, with a focus on co-creating innovative and transformative solutions that naturally result in sustainable outcomes, boosting the performance of people, organizations, and communities.

Lenore Newman is a Canada Research Chair, Food Security and Environment, Department of Geography, University of the Fraser Valley. She is a writer and an urban geographer, specializing in urban food security, community environmental efforts, and how urban form shapes our relation to nature and to each other.

Pamela Robinson, MCIP RPP, is an Associate Professor in the School of Urban and Regional Planning at Ryerson University. Her research explores the role of design, governance, and civic engagement in advancing urban sustainability, with a longstanding focus on Canadian municipal response to climate change.

D. Scott Slocombe is a Professor in the Department of Geography and Environmental Studies and holds the Dr. John McMurry Research Chair in Environmental Geography at Wilfrid Laurier University. The focus of his research is the challenge of managing diverse human activities in large regions while maintaining environmental integrity and sustainability.

Levi Waldron is a Research Fellow in the Department of Biostatistics, Harvard University. He is interested in the use of meta-analysis to improve the robustness of high-dimensional genomic analyses. He is currently collaborating on a project to discover molecular subtypes of colorectal cancer.

Nick Weigeldt holds a Masters of Urban Development from Ryerson University's School of Urban and Regional Planning. He is a researcher at the Clean Air Partnership in Toronto.